COLERIDGE, THE SUBLIME SOMNAMBULIST

COLERIDGE

THE SUBLIME SOMNAMBULIST

By

JOHN CHARPENTIER

Translated by
M. V. NUGENT

DODD, MEAD & COMPANY
NEW YORK   MCMXXIX

PRINTED IN THE UNITED STATES OF AMERICA
BY THE VAIL-BALLOU PRESS, INC., BINGHAMTON, N. Y.

To *the Great Novelist*
EDITH WHARTON
From Whom No Secrets
in English or French Literature
Are Hid

THIS ESSAY IN BRIDGE-BUILDING
IS DEDICATED

He was a mighty poet—and
A subtle-soul'd psychologist;
All things he seem'd to understand
Of old or new—of sea or land—
But his own mind—which was a mist.
This was a man who might have turn'd
Hell into Heaven—and so in gladness
A heaven unto himself have larn'd;
But he in shadows undiscern'd
Trusted,—and damn'd himself to madness.

Percy Bysshe Shelley

All that he did excellently might
be bound up in twenty pages, but it
should be bound in pure gold.

Stopford Brooke

CONTENTS

PART I

THE INSPIRED CHARITY-BOY

PAGE
I Ottery St. Mary 3
II Christ's Hospital 13

PART II

LOVE AND UTOPIA

I Cambridge 39
II The Dawn of Pantisocracy 52
III The Decline and Fall of Pantisocracy 71

PART III

POETRY COMES TO FLOWER

I From Clevedon to Nether Stowey 95
II The Years of Gold 116

PART IV

THE SORROWFUL LIFE OF THE WANDERER

I In Germany 157
II Keswick and Malta 188
III The Damaged Archangel 224

CONTENTS

PART V

THE SEER OF HIGHGATE

		PAGE
I	CREATIVE CRITICISM	257
II	VOLUNTARY PRISONING	278
III	RELIGION AND PHILOSOPHY	291
IV	SPIRITUAL HEIGHTS	314
	BIBLIOGRAPHY	330

PART I

"THE INSPIRED CHARITY-BOY"

OTTERY ST. MARY

ONE winter's evening of the year 1780, on his way home from a farm a mile or so away, with Samuel, the thirteenth and last born of his children, the Reverend John Coleridge, Vicar of Ottery St. Mary in Devon, pointed out the planet Jupiter riding between Pallas and Saturn, and explained to the small boy at some length such particulars as he knew of that star of the first magnitude.

Fontenelle's *Entretiens sur la Pluralité des Mondes* contain most of the reflections in which the good man engaged as to the marvel of creation and its boundless extent, with such conception as he had fashioned of the infinite, for in telling his son that the volume of our earth is no more than the thousandth part of Jupiter he still fell far short of the truth. Yet even had his father been in a position to quote the staggering figures we are familiar with today, it is doubtful whether Samuel, his face all rapture, would have shown greater astonishment or greater incredulity. He had a precocious way, remarkable thus early, of thinking of things, not in relation to immediate reality, but, as it were, untrammelled by the control of his senses. Nor was this the first time his father had talked to him on subjects as unlikely in the

general way to interest a child of eight. Mr. Coleridge
would often give him a ride upon his knee in his leisure
moments, and take him off with him on his steed on
a voyage of discovery through the universe, down paths
leading away from the well-beaten tracks of rational or
practical education.

John Coleridge was in charge not only of the parish,
but of the Grammar School as well. His son's religious
and secular instruction thus being committed to his care,
the good man, whose faith in theological learning and
classical lore had never faltered, considered that there was
no hope of salvation outside the pale of reverence for
Holy Writ and respect for the classics. But his teaching,
though it may have been orthodox enough in the pulpit,
was entirely lacking in method and a sense of propor-
tion in private life. Samuel, who compared him later with
Parson Adams, used to reap a great deal of enjoyment
out of these impromptu lessons given him, as an addi-
tion to his work in school, by his father, who looked
upon him, with a heart swelling with pride, as the bright-
est of all his pupils.

The child had turned his father into his blindly obe-
dient henchman, always ready to satisfy his boundless
curiosity. Mr. Coleridge never denied this voracious intellect the fuel it needed. He had from the first turned over
to the insatiable appetite for books of his five-year-old
son the *Story of St. George,* and the *Seven Champions
of Christendom,* as well as the *Arabian Nights,* and it

was already too late when he decided to destroy them all, on finding that the small boy, whom his reading had sadly over-excited, was haunted by the fear of ghosts every time he went into the dark. I do not believe that any other teacher would have been able to discipline Samuel's imagination, a prey as he was to dreams rather than mere day-dreams, or to give a sounder basis to his passionately unbridled and capricious nature. It is certain, nevertheless, that his father's influence did nothing towards steadying his feelings or his thoughts.

"I had all the simplicity, all the docility of the little child but none of the child's habits. I never thought as a child, never had the language of a child," wrote Samuel at the age of twenty-four. What he most enjoyed was to listen to his father explaining the reforms he had introduced into the teaching of the Latin declensions, or even in his guilelessness expounding the Book of Job for his benefit. He would consult the boy about the sermons he was preparing and which he was given to embellishing with Hebrew texts the better to edify his flock. The simple-minded egotism of the good parson, who was, indeed, a bit of a pedant, blinded him to the dangers to which he was exposing his son, by thus letting him share his labours so early, and he rejoiced to find so heedful a listener in Samuel, whose skill in plying him with questions stimulated both his zest as a teacher and his zeal as a Christian.

Having lost his first wife Mary Landon, by whom

he had had three daughters, John Coleridge had taken as his second wife a certain Miss Anne Bowden, and she bore him ten children. That the union was blest of the Lord was manifest in its fruitful issue, and also in the wisdom with which the reverend gentleman's second wife proved to be endowed. When John Coleridge published his *Critical Latin Grammar* in 1772, the very year Samuel was born (he had come into the world on Oct. 21st.), it was his wife who had the inspiration to append a notice informing the public that the learned cleric took in pupils *at sixteen guineas a year for boarding and teaching.* She would never have been able to frame such a notice by her own efforts, for she was barely able to read or write. But she prided herself, and, indeed, with reason, on enjoying the superiority of the careful housewife over more cultivated women, *your harpsichord ladies,* as she used to call them (though she can hardly have found many of these at Ottery St. Mary)! I picture her to myself very much as Goldsmith has described Mrs. Primrose, that is to say, as an accomplished cook, excelling in the art of making jams and jellies, and given to praising up the excellence of her own dishes at table.

Afflicted with a husband whose books, apart from his sermons, were as little read as the Vicar of Wakefield's, Mrs. Coleridge was wholly bent on making up for his unpractical ways, and keeping her humble home orderly and cheerful. It was, no doubt, owing to this watchful woman's incessant care that John Coleridge, whose means did not often permit him to replenish his wardrobe, was able to appear suitably arrayed on religious high days. But it was no use merely to put aside a pair of well-starched bands for use on great occasions, or even to keep him a wig in reserve on a homemade block. Left to his own devices, the absent-minded man would have been the last to notice the most glaring stain or gaping rent in his coat, and needed to be constantly reminded what he was to put on or leave off. Unless someone were by to see, moreover, he would end by only half doing as he had been told, or doing it in some topsy-turvy fashion, as, for example, upon that occasion when he returned from a journey with half-a-dozen shirts upon his back, because his wife, in telling him to be sure to wear a clean one every day, had forgotten to tell him to take off first the one he already had on.

Mrs. Coleridge loved Samuel as dearly as a mother may love her youngest, but she admired his nimble wits far less than her husband, and was, on the other hand, more deeply disturbed by his dislike of every form of physical exercise.

This woman, wrapped up as she was in the material things of life, could, in her rather narrow matter-of-factness, scarcely contemplate without foreboding the future that lay before an imaginative and withal idle lad, who seemed to set but little store by the trial-and-error methods adopted by the young, and already "regu-

lated all his creeds by conceptions, not by this sight."
She would rather have had him a bully, like the boister-
ous sons of the "stout yeomen," who were wont to make
of him their butt, and whose games he shunned with aversion, in order that he might go down to watch the Otter
fleeting amidst the pines, a stone's throw away from his
father's door—the "wild streamlet," as he called it, hastening to the call of the not far distant sea.

Did she, seeing him set on seeking out all lonely places,
fancy him shyer than he was, gloomy, or perhaps unhappy? It is certain that in his refusal to share in his
schoolfellows', or even his brothers' games, he would
sometimes appear pig-headed to the verge of insanity. It
chanced that once, after quarrelling with one of his elder
brothers, he ran away from home, and stayed out the
whole of one stormy night "very devoutly repeating . . .
morning and evening prayers," and thinking from time
to time "in gloomy satisfaction how miserable his mother
must be." He was found soaked to the skin, and brought
home quaking with ague. But nothing could be farther
from the truth than to fancy him sinking under a load
of melancholy; profound joys were his for the asking,
and he would be plunged in a kind of intoxication or delicious maze as he roamed the countryside, amid the
woods and fields of one of the most bewitching parts of
all England, a Normandy as lush and rich, but warmer
than the one over the water. He had a way of gazing at
things with an almost fearful fixity, so spellbound did

he seem, which stamped a lasting impression on his memory, and engraved their image on his mind for ever. Later, he would have but to close his eyes to the sun's rays to see the "bright transparence" of the Otter gleaming, as he used to watch it from a "crossing plank," when he sailed paper boats upon the river, "along whose breast he skimmed the smooth thin stone."

The Vicarage, a pleasant, two-storied stucco dwelling, was situated at the foot of rolling hills which stretch along the coast as far as Lyme Bay, and shelter Ottery St. Mary from cold winds. From the top of these hills, which he used to climb by a sheep track, Samuel used to see his village lying in a "green and silent dell," looking from far above "like a verdant cornfield." All round him in the dewy grass where he stood knee deep, the sheep were grazing and those small-bred kine peculiar to Devon, which give a rich creamy milk. Mingling with the scent of myrtles, geraniums, and heliotrope, the sound of church bells, drifting upwards over the tops of fruit and apple-trees in the valley below, came to the child's ears but little the thinner for the distance, "like a fair promise of better things." High overhead, the clouds went scurrying by, swiftly as is their wont when drawing nigh to the sea, and maybe one seagull, flying afar off, that shore-loving sister of the albatross. . . . He might walk on for an hour or two with loitering steps, like the little truant he was, when there, of a sudden, at the foot of cliffs dropping sheer down to the water's edge lay outspread the liquid sheet as far as eye could see. Over the red sand which crops out here from the soil of England, and covers the sloping foreshore to a fairly considerable depth, the waves take on a delicate, shell-like, rosy tinge, beneath their onward creeping fringe of foam.

Samuel would then wander off into contemplation, only to be overtaken by the first shades of evening, thus finding a kind of spiritual appeasement of that desire for escape, for flight into space and time, which was to haunt him all his life. Freed for the nonce from himself, and from all the music he never could attune to his friends' and brothers' chatter, he would go down again to the village where, at other times, he would air his fancies through the silent streets.

Amid the four walls of the market place, which seemed small enough, indeed, on fair days, when it was swarming with people, but looked the very picture of emptiness on ordinary occasions, the tiniest noises echoed and swelled, and even the rusty old inn sign might be heard groaning from its iron gibbet, whence it flaunted the arms of Ottery St. Mary. Samuel would creep under the arched doorway of this building, flanked with wings either side, and with a pent-house in front, formed by the posts supporting the projecting upper story. Half-timbered walls rose midway between these posts on ground level, intersecting the space in between them into so many boxes, where people might sit by themselves, drinking their golden cider or nut-brown ale. Some ruddy-faced country-

man, with his long whip propped up beside him, might
be having a bite and a sup of clotted cream out of a
bowl, whilst he waited for his horse to be shod. From
the smithy hard by would come the keen sound of the
hammer on the anvil, and further off, the dry pitter-
patter of a woman's clogs as she went down to fill her
bucket at the well. Samuel would wait until the rustic
clambered back again into his cart, then he would watch
him making off southwards, trundling in the direction
of his home round behind the square church tower, so
like those at Exeter Cathedral.

"Whence comes he? Whither goes he?" mused the
child. Questions like these seldom rise to the mind at his
age, when the picturesque side of things alone affords interest. But for this child, for whom no border-line fenced
off dreams from reality, everything was food for marvellous speculations, and for answers to conundrums more
marvellous still. Though he may have lacked that clear-
sightedness, which enables other people to distinguish
truth from error even in their most enthralling amusements, he enjoyed one advantage they had not, that of
being able to cross the barrier with which outward circumstance, or nature herself, hems in the imagination.
He could wield the wand of a magician. He may, indeed, have picked it up in that hollow under the wooded
part of the hill beneath which the Otter flows, and which
was known as the Pixies' Parlour, its roof consisting of
roots, and its walls carved with figures, amongst which

Samuel once made out his own and his brothers' initials. But with or without the enchanted wand, he could play at will upon every kind of fantasy, and more than once, as he stood in front of the parish church which had been robbed of the image of its patron saint at some time of Puritan iconoclasm, he piously returned the Virgin to her proper place, and restored limbs and heads to its mutilated saints.

CHAPTER II

CHRIST'S HOSPITAL

WHEN once the strength of the tie which bound Samuel to his native soil is realized, it is not difficult to imagine what must have been his dismay at learning, after Mr. Coleridge's death, which took place in October 1781, that he was to go into exile. One of his father's former pupils, Sir Francis Buller by name, had, indeed, written of his own accord offering to intervene with the authorities, in the hopes of procuring him a scholarship at Christ's Hospital. But the boy, who would, like his brothers, have gone into the Church had his clergyman father remained alive, had formed no other ambition at the age of nine, than to continue living more or less as he had done up till that time. Though he wanted to relieve his mother of his keep, he could not bear the thought that he might never again roam the countryside round Ottery St. Mary of a Sunday, nor sit beneath some tree in the fields, reading one of those books filled with fairies and genii, which he could only pluck up courage to remove from the library shelf "when the sun lay upon them." It is only your future men of action who long in their youth to scour the world. Imaginative folk—even though they may be destined, as was Samuel, to endure the ravages of a kind of morbid restlessness—find enough in what lies around them to satisfy their appetite for the marvellous. Such craving for change as they may know is not, moreover, of the same objective quality as with these others. It springs from a nervous cause, lying wholly outside their will. And while it is not uncommon to find that the boy who once longed to set forth upon his travels in order to appease his curiosity, is able as a grown man to find scope enough for his organizing powers in a more circumscribed circle, yet, on the other hand, the man of imagination will passively submit to follow the peregrinations of his body, which thus no doubt cherishes the delusion that it is fostering the interests of the mind's active life.

The sorrow into which Samuel was plunged by the death of the father who had been his religion—"an Israelite . . . without guile conscientiously indifferent to the good and the evil of the world," did not make him hold those places less dear where he had been wont to receive his teaching, morning, noon, and night. So when, at the end of a year occupied in Sir Francis Buller's negotiations, the day dawned on which the poor child had, for economy's sake, to climb on to the box-seat of the coach, whose horn was sounding in the courtyard of the inn where he had so often musingly stood, his heart was terribly torn. He might almost have been aware that he was not going to see his mother nor Ottery again for the space of eight whole years. . . .

Upon his arrival in London, he stayed with an uncle who had agreed to take care of him until he should enter Christ's Hospital as a boarder. Grim was the impression made upon Samuel, who came from a land of light, by his first contact with London. The town lay wreathed in fog, seemingly decked in mourning for the sun, its sooty houses lined up in sullen uniformity, as though for a funeral procession. But no character was ever more prone than Samuel's to sudden changes of mood. Bitter as his reflections may well have been, under the sway of the loneliness which was stealing upon him, (he acknowledged himself to be "a detached individual, a *terrae filius* who was to ask love or service of no one on any more specific relation than that of being a man"), the novelty of the things he was seeing must soon have served to take his mind off his grief. He admitted that he was vain, and extremely susceptible, to say the very least, to the pleasure of rousing enthusiasm, and the compliments showered upon him by his uncle were soon able to bring him solace.

He roused in this good man's mind an admiration to which he gave full vent, and imparted to a band of his friends at the chophouse to which he took the boy for his meals. There was at that period nothing dingy in the least about these London eating-houses, which comprised a large hall on the ground floor, cut up into several smaller rooms furnished with tables and benches seating four, or sometimes more, at a time. No alcoholic liquor was served, however, and there would be nothing but a little water wherewith to wash down the roasts and grills, the boiled or fried fish, the sauceless, unseasoned vegetables, unless drinks were fetched from outside, light beer or ale, perhaps, or more likely, porter at threepence a pint. A waiter from a neighbouring ale-house would make the round of the various houses to provide customers with drinks, with a strap strung round him like a bandolier, and girt back and front with a garland of empty mugs, exchanging full pint-pots as he went along for those he had left behind the day before.

Samuel found himself treated as a marvel by these stolid Londoners, who were astounded by his lively memory, and would talk things over with him as man to man. Some of his nephew's glory naturally redounding to his own credit, his uncle encouraged Samuel to show off his cleverness to these cronies of his, and the boy, with cheeks aflame, would come out with a jumble of things he had seen for himself in books, or been told by his father, talking just as exaltedly of the problem of gravitation as of some miraculous story from the *Arabian Nights*. But these exciting days were quickly over. All too soon, after a six weeks' stay at the preparatory school at Hertford, Samuel came back to London, clad in the blue gown and yellow stockings of Christ's Hospital, and was admitted to the *Head Grammar School* of the main part of the college, where Latin and Greek were imparted to boys destined for either university.

The dreary school buildings, rising on the site of an ancient Franciscan friary at the entrance to Newgate Street, and close to the celebrated prison where executions were held, were pulled down at the beginning of this century. Dim cloisters surrounded the square courtyard, in which, bareheaded according to the rules, the little prisoners of Christ's Hospital used to play in their spare time. For what else than prisoners, indeed, might the boarders of that institution be called? Despite the exalted patronage extended to it by His Majesty himself, and the system of voluntary contributions, it suffered from a shortage of funds, and combined the hardships of a poverty-stricken diet with the horrors of an iron-handed discipline.

In no other country in the world has the science—one hardly dare give it the name of art—of torturing children by keeping them on short commons, been carried to such lengths as in England. But we should hardly be able to guess today at the refinements of cruelty—and this in a country, too, where youthful appetites are most sharp set —in which, as late as the early part of the nineteenth century, private and religious philanthropy could indulge in all serenity of mind, and with every prospect of qualifying for admission to Heaven, had Dickens never written the epic story of these martyred innocents.

Samuel, who had been accustomed at his mother's table to bountiful and wholesome fare, became in literal fact acquainted with the gnawing agony of hunger while he was at school at Christ's Hospital. There was no more than one solid meal a day, at which meat, absurdly small in quantity, and in the invariable guise of a tasteless beef-stew, was only served three times a week. "I was in a continual low fever" wrote Samuel, when recalling those times of stress. Sickened to nausea by this hash, which was often so unpalatable that tradition among the boys had it that all fat must depart to the kitchen untasted, the unhappy lad used to experience the torments of hallucinations, in which, his eyes half-closing over a book he was letting his mind feast upon in some corner, he would fancy himself eating an apple-pie of Brobdingnagian proportions, quaffing gooseberry wine under the honeysuckle of the garden at home, or think himself on Robinson Crusoe's island, scooping out a room with his teeth, like a rat in a cheese, from the flanks of a huge mountain of plum cake.

Lamb, who passed several years at Christ's Hospital on the same benches as Coleridge, whose junior he was by a couple of years, has described in an essay and some memories, though not, truth to tell, in any tragical vein, what was the life led from day to day by the pupils of this antique foundation. But it is just those places which the gentle humourist skims over most lightly with a jest, which show that life up in the most lamentable colours. For it was not deemed sufficient to ration the boys most severely, corporal punishment as well was inflicted upon them, and they might, upon occasion, be cast into dungeons. The Head Master, accompanied by an usher, sent for the pupil destined for the rod to come to the appointed place. The boy took down his breeches and knelt upon a bench, his chest propped up by a desk in order to proffer his stern at a suitable height to serve as a human target. The usher then grasped the rod of pickled birch which he had taken from a small cupboard. He handed it solemnly to the Head Master, who, with arm lifted shoulder-high, administered to the culprit the number of strokes to which he had been condemned. This ceremonial did not invariably take place, being reserved for grave misdemeanours, and it did at least afford the interested party some protection. But canings might be inflicted on the spot, and not by the teaching staff alone, but also by the monitors, to whom the supervision of the younger boys was entrusted.

These "young brutes" as Lamb called them, thought nothing, for instance, of rousing twelve of their schoolmates from the sweetness of early sleep, in order to thrash them with a leather strap, upon the pretext that they had been heard talking after they had got into bed.

Profiting by the freedom allowed them, for, oddly enough, they were occasionally permitted to go out for the whole day, with no questions asked as to whether they had friends or kinsfolk, nor how they intended to spend the time, boys who had reached the limit of their endurance would sometimes try to run away. They were invariably retrieved a mile or two away from London, partly because their quaint costume brought them into undue prominence, and partly because they would soon fall exhausted by the roadside, or into some ditch. Brought back again to Christ's Hospital they were kept chained up, after being thrashed within an inch of their lives like dogs. If they tried to run away again, they were imprisoned, between two bouts of flogging, in a cell so narrow that there was only just room in it to lie at full length. On the occasion of a third attempt (and is it not in itself significant that any such were made?), the culprit, who was now doomed to be expelled, was made to run the gauntlet in a garb of shame, then scourged so cruelly in the presence of two governors of the school that, towards the latter half of the nineteenth century, a boy is known to have hanged himself, to avoid having his sentence served upon him.

The Rev. Mr. Field, who was Lamb's master, proved to be an honourable exception to the rule at Christ's Hospital. This cleric, indeed, had a horror of corporal punishment, and in his hand the cane became less an instrument of authority than an emblem "he was ashamed of." The Rev. James Boyer, on the other hand, beneath whose rod Samuel was soon to pass, was a dry-as-dust fanatic, who for any and every reason, and even for no reason whatever, would strike until he drew blood, overmastered by regular storms of hysteria. The lust to strike used to come in gusts upon this half-possessed creature. He was the owner of two wigs, the one trim and powdered for calmer times, the other tumbled and greasy for angry moments, and, according to Lamb, nothing was more common than to see him charge, head foremost, and eyes bulging from their sockets, out of his study, and into the classroom, there to clutch hold of one of the boys, bellowing as he did so: "Odds' my life, Sirrah" (his favourite expression), "I have a great mind to whip you." He did not always satisfy this sadistic desire on the spot, and would sometimes repair to his den as tempestuously as he had sallied forth, merely to bear down upon his victim later, roaring "And I *will* too" as he acted upon the half-uttered threat he had left hanging over the boy's head.

Coleridge's appearance at the age of ten, with his bushy black hair falling across his forehead, his fine eyes half veiled beneath a dreamy haze, his full lips, and sloping shoulders, must have conveyed an impression of vague sensuality, as well as somewhat drooping delicacy. But it is hard to see why Mr. Boyer should have thought him so ugly that he gave him an extra cut on that account, whenever he chastised him. But perhaps this strange man's severity sprang from special consideration rather than dislike. For, from the start, Coleridge showed such an appetite for Greek and Latin as must have enchanted his hard taskmaster. Boyer, indeed, belonged to a not uncommon class of pedagogue—men who set their faces on principle dead against any flattery, or even encouragement whatever, to the choicer spirits in their charge. These hide-bound individuals would sooner be flayed alive than give their best pupils the smallest meed of approval. They show, on the contrary, a kind of fierce determination in trying to catch them out, as though fearing lest they might take advantage of any relaxation of discipline to slip out of fulfilling the obligations imposed upon them by their exceptional gifts. Coleridge seems to have interpreted his taskmaster's strictness towards himself in this way. In fact, he congratulated himself in later life upon his escape from being treated as a prodigy, or "emasculated and ruined by fond and idle bewilderment," much in the same way as a poor soul who has been the butt of his regiment may proclaim himself glad to have "been through the mill." And surely it may be considered an overwhelming proof of the terror Boyer inspired in him, that until late in life, his dreams were still haunted by the image at once grotesque and diabolic of this inquisitor? Though Coleridge may, on account of that want of steadfastness in his make-up, to which I have already referred, have been incapable of bearing a grudge, still less of nursing hatred, his highly sensitive nature never forgot any of the impressions it had once received. Amongst those he was storing up in his innermost mind there were none which did not answer the call of secret affinities, or rise from the depths of his being to share in, and enrich, his emotional life.

Had it not been for the violence Boyer showed whenever one of his ungovernable fits of rage was upon him, the boy might have grown to love him, for in some ways he reminded him of his father; but he always paid tribute to his zeal, and praised his methods, admiring at least his zeal as a purist, if not the purity of his taste. "He sent us into the University excellent Latin and Greek scholars and tolerable Hebraists," he wrote. "I learnt from him that poetry, even that of the loftiest and seemingly that of the wildest odes had a logic of its own as severe as that of science, and more difficult, because more subtle, more complex, and dependent on more, and more fugitive causes." No doubt, like Edgar Allan Poe later on, Coleridge, who as we shall see, wrote the greater part of his best poems in a state bordering on the trance, was not sorry to give the impression that his will played a preponderating part in his creations. . . . It is none the less true that Boyer's discipline imprinted habits on his mind by which he profited, even though unconsciously. It was because of the schooling of this master, who took particular pains to correct his pupils' literary exercises, and despised all conventional turns of speech and frenzy of the imagination, that Coleridge became so profoundly steeped in respect for form and composition that, far from these detracting from the mystery of poems like the *Ancient Mariner* or *Christabel* they do, on the contrary, help to suggest it.

Boyer, so Coleridge noted again, "showed no mercy to phrase, metaphor, or image, unsupported by a sound sense." He took exception to passages "where the same sense might have been conveyed with equal force and dignity in plainer words. Lute, harp, and lyre, muse, muses and inspirations . . . were all an abomination to him. In fancy I can almost hear him exclaiming '*Harp? Harp? Lyre?* Pen and ink, boy, you mean, Muse, boy, Muse? your Nurse's daughter, you mean! Pierian spring? Oh aye! the cloister pump, I suppose!" Sound criticism enough, but as usual it did not bear fruit until much later, for youth never realizes how valuable are its fetters. Everything that hampers its flights seems fatal, and in imitating the masters of the past, it is inclined to take over their faults, and carry them to exaggerated lengths.

The verses Coleridge composed at the age of twelve or thirteen are merely exercises in style. It would be a mistake to suppose that inspiration was fretting him thus early. It seems to me that children are never precocious in this way unless they have a certain gift of language or a plastic sense, but are lacking in inner life. This child was already harbouring a world so richly intricate in the secrecy of his soul, that he felt not the faintest desire to seek expression for it through the vocabulary he had at his command, shorn as it was of all deeper reality or sensuous significance. Nay more, what relation could he possibly have established between the ineffable things stirring within him, and the phrases he was obliged to show up in school for Mr. Boyer to harangue upon? He found an outlet in books and at the same time, even from them the excitement, the intoxicating clarity he needed, for lack of which he was cast down again into dull despondency, and through which he was lifted up on to that super-earthly plane, to which he later tried to find access through opium when clogged by illness.

For he went on reading prodigiously and at random, and not school-books alone, such as Vergil, which his friend and ally Middleton, future Bishop of Calcutta, one day surprised him conning "for his pleasure," but anything and everything he could lay his hands upon. He was more averse than ever to the amusements suited to his age, nor had he any skill in them, and reading enabled him to escape the horrors of his captivity in Christ's Hospital, where he "saw naught lovely save sky and stars." Nowadays, as at Ottery, nothing which interested his schoolfellows had any hold over him. Did the "playless day-dreamer" as he called himself, ever show a fancy to share the games with which the boys whiled away their free time, he was sure to begin by breaking the rules. Not, indeed, that he was a spoilsport, but absent-minded, and unable to shake off his mental isolation, save by fits and starts. He was fond of laughing and joking, had a ready wit when he chose, and what is more, a most taking appearance. It proved impossible, however, to interest him in anything which had not first roused his curiosity, or stirred up his imagination of its own accord. Apart from school hours, he never enjoyed himself so much as when, profiting by the outing the Blue Coat School freely allowed its boarders, he loitered through the London streets, finding his way round St. Paul's massive bulk, down towards the water-logged banks of the Thames. He was especially fond of haunting the Old Bailey, no more than a step or two from the criminal prison of that name, a legacy from a bygone century, with its booths, and its leprous overhanging roofs nearly meeting over the pavement. In this part of the town he made the acquaintance of an honest shoemaker whose friend he soon became, and he even went so far as to suggest entering into an apprenticeship with him. What, indeed, can he have found to talk about to this humble craftsman, as he sat stitching with waxed thread in the stifling atmosphere of his shed, heavy with the sour reek of leather? Of anything that entered his head no doubt, for he had a habit of jumping with disconcerting swiftness from one subject to another, as soon as he met with an attentive listener, to whom he could let himself go. Anyone with a mind to argue would find him ready to bandy words with him. Whenever a new light broke in upon him, he would stop the first Tom, Dick, or Harry he might meet, to tell him about the fresh truth that had dazzled his mind. His brain would whirl like a kaleidoscope, and he would set out in high glee to describe, one after the other as they fell into shape, the patterns that went ceaselessly trooping past his mind's eye, jostling each other upon their way.

An almost inexhaustible fund of reading material suddenly came his way one day, in the street of all places, in such a portentous fashion that it might have served to convince him, had he needed any such proof, that miracles were the rule, rather than the exception, in the fictitious world in which he dwelt. As he was strolling down the Strand, striking out to right and left with his arms as he went, under the impression that he was Leander swimming the Hellespont to meet Hero, one of his hands brushed against a gentleman's coat-pocket. London has ever been a nursery of pickpockets. The gentleman never for a moment doubted that Samuel, in spite of the uniform he wore, had impudently tried to rob him, and, seizing him by the wrist, "What," he exclaimed, "so young and so wicked?"

But Samuel soon sobbingly convinced him of his innocence. He explained that he had been imagining himself to be Leander, and the gentleman, who, like any good Briton, knew an eccentric character when he saw one, was so struck by this out of the way adventure, and so soon won over by the boy's intelligence and ingenuousness, that he at once enrolled him among the subscribers to a lending library.

At about the same time that he thus began to "run all risks in skulking out to get the two volumes" which were his daily allowance, and which he picked out, almost with his eyes shut, from the catalogue, his brother Luke came up to study medicine in London. Samuel dogged his footsteps, and followed him every Saturday on his hospital rounds, becoming so enthusiastic over his profession that he begged him to take him on as his assistant. Luke found it impossible to abate zeal such as this. Weary of the struggle, he allowed his younger brother to apply plasters and to dress wounds. Textbooks of anatomy and pathology were at this time as meat and drink to Samuel. He had nearly the whole of Blanchard's *Latin Dictionary of Medicine* by heart, and so surprising did his newly-acquired knowledge appear, that his brother was more than half-inclined to grant him his wish to throw up everything else, and to apprentice him to a surgeon. But philosophy soon claimed him for its own, and turned his thoughts in another direction. A translation from Plotinus, *Concerning the Beautiful,* by Thomas Taylor, published in 1787, which he got to know by some means at about this time, suddenly threw open to his gaze so marvellous a field for speculation, that diseases and their cures were in a moment forgotten. He was filled with rejoicing, and felt that he must impart his raptures to all the world.

"Come back into memory, like as thou wert in the dayspring of thy fancies, with hope like a fiery column before thee—the dark pillar not yet turned—Samuel Taylor Coleridge—Logician—Metaphysician, Bard!" cried Lamb, recalling the days at Christ's Hospital when his friend, "the young Mirandola" as he called him, astonished all comers as much by the vastness of his knowledge as by the liveliness of his mind. "How have I seen," the delightful humourist goes on to say, "the casual passer through the Cloisters stand still, entranced with admiration . . . to hear thee unfold, in deep sweet intonations, the mysteries of Jamblichus or Plotinus, (for even in those years thou waxedest not pale at such philosophic draughts) or reciting Homer in his Greek, or Pindar— while the walls of the old Grey Friars re-echoed to the accents of the *inspired Charity-boy!"*

Coleridge, whose mind had become prepared for scepticism through his studies in physiology, had lately gone through a phase of doubt, and, indeed, of almost out-and-out atheism, following upon his reading of Voltaire. But it did not stir him to the depths. "With my heart I never did abandon the name of Christ," he was able truthfully to say. Moreover, Mr. Boyer helped him, by a master stroke from his cane, to rid himself of all such foul bedevilments—"the only just flogging" so Samuel saw fit to point out, that he ever received from him.

He became absorbed in Plato, and the fusion the Neo-Platonists attempted to make of all the systems of the ancient world. Matter and the "seminal principles" which give it its form; pure Being; the two souls of man, the one he receives from the universe of whose nature it partakes, and the one which constitutes his essential self, enabling him to rise by its means to the Good and the Beautiful. Fine subjects for meditation, these, for a schoolboy! How unsettling, too, for his mind, which the first onslaught of puberty was making more impressionable than usual! Thenceforth he spurned everything, as he

said, that was neither metaphysics nor theological controversy. History and individual facts lost all interest for
him. Novels seemed insipid and so also did even poetry
—or, at any rate, the rhetorical or stylistic exercises which
he took for that divine art. He fared, or rather, floated
through the world of ideas like "an archangel" as Lamb
put it, and from those heights whence the shams of appearance fade away, and the Invisible stands forth as the
only true reality, humanity showed as no more than a
drifting cloud of dust. . . .

This boy, however, who was so unaffectedly astonished
at the strength of his own powers, and dizzy with the
exaltation of the spirit, showed no overweening haughtiness in his pride. I have already described how impatient
he felt to impart to others the truths he had discovered,
or thought to have discovered. His mind was on terms
of hail-fellow-well-met equality with all other minds, in
a way that no other intellect of like quality has ever been
before or since. When he withdrew into himself, it was
but to come up like a diver, with his hands full of treasures from the depths to which he had plunged. Methodical or carefully calculating individuals, who deduce ideas
rigidly from premises, or act according to fixed plans,
build up a wall between themselves and all other men.
Not so dreamers such as Coleridge. They do not collect
and concentrate their thoughts, they scatter them rather.
Nor do they, at any rate, ever do anything which might
tend to break off communications between themselves and

their fellow men. All unwittingly, they are borne along upon some current, and when they find themselves far out from shore, they are filled with dismay, and seek to make excuse for their absence of mind.

Coleridge had a generous, even a prodigal nature. He was sensitive, and in spite of the inconstancy, or instability, of his mind, remained strongly attached to the people he was fond of. Hence they held by him, in spite of his weak points. Lamb, who was his best friend at Christ's Hospital, remained so all through, and even when they were parted by circumstances, he never lost sight of him. It may be wondered, in fact, whether he were not the only person who ever really understood his genius. And yet that genius never held itself aloof. A spiritual pleasure was increased two-fold, five-fold even, in Coleridge's eyes whenever he could make the people round about him share in it. The day he was given William Lisle Bowles's sonnets, as a present, fourteen of them in all, and their limpid harmony revealed to him what lyric poetry might be, he at once made forty pen-and-ink copies to distribute among his school friends. He could not imagine that the happiness he himself felt might not touch them. A new life came flooding in upon him, and he had to pour it forth for the benefit of others. . . .

It is hard to restrain a smile at the thought that it was through Bowles's agency that Coleridge first recognized the poet within himself. That writer of sonnets, delicate enough in their way, but in nowise exceptional, did, in fact, achieve the miracle that neither Homer nor Vergil, Shakspere nor Milton, had been able to accomplish. This, as Coleridge has explained to us, was because "the great works of past ages seem to a young man things of another race, in respect to which his faculties must remain passive, and submiss, even as to the stars and mountains. But the writings of a contemporary, perhaps not many years older than himself, surrounded by the same circumstances, and disciplined by the same manners, possess a *reality* for him, and inspire an actual friendship as of a man for man."

Bowles's sincere and pensive tenderness went straight to Coleridge's heart, and he later defined the kind of emotion he had received from him, when he thus expressed his thanks to the man who had initiated him into the charm of poetry:

My heart has thanked thee, Bowles! for those soft strains
Whose sadness soothes me, like the murmuring
Of wild-bees in the sunny showers of spring!

The first time that inspired human utterance ever went straight to his heart with the fresh note as of a confidence imparted, he heard it with his own ears, not through the dry-as-dust medium of a classical education; and its melancholy character echoed his own most secret aspirations.

He was by now going on for eighteen. Since leaving Ottery, he had only once been back there, upon the death of his sister Ann which took place in 1789, and was shortly followed by that of his brother Luke. And the infrequent letters he had received from home had done nothing to diminish his longing to return to his own West country but had, rather, increased it. He had just been seriously ill as the result of a rash action on his own part. He swam fully clad across New River, and then allowed his garments to dry upon his back, with the result that, with the low powers of resistance to disease he had inherited, decreased by that childish escapade I have mentioned, he contracted violent rheumatic fever, which was soon further complicated by jaundice. He was tended in the school infirmary, where he fell in love with the nurse's daughter, "Sweet Genevieve." It was for her he wrote the verses beginning:

> "I've seen your breast with pity heave
> And therefore love I you sweet Genevieve!"

It was because he saw her breast "with pity heave" that his own breast was in its turn softened towards her. Nothing could be more elegiacally expressed, nor come closer to his dear Bowles's own sentiments. But whilst he listened to the voice, sweet "as seraph's song," of the compassionate damsel, to fall in love with whom was prescribed by all the rules of good form at the Blue Coat School, and as he gazed into her bright eyes, he would often, surely, weave around these sensations of the moment wavering impressions full of a vaguely delicious charm. It is difficult to know how much this singular being used to borrow dreams from reality, or vice versa. It is doubtful if he knew himself. As Genevieve smilingly stood over him, with a cup of beef-tea in her hand, he may have substituted for her another girl, the mere imagined presence of whom by his sick-bed would serve to clothe her proxy in borrowed grace.

This girl was Mary Evans, the sister of a friend he had taken under his wing at school, giving him a helping hand with his usual kindness of heart, and thus rescuing him from many an imposition, or even an occasional flogging. He made the acquaintance, and then the conquest of Mrs. Evans, a widow who had two younger daughters besides this son, and Mary, the eldest of the family. This kindly woman, of whom he became deeply fond, "I loved her," he wrote, "as a mother," welcomed him to her house with the open-hearted hospitality traditional amongst the English, which is one of the chief, if not, in fact, the chief of their virtues. He was asked to spend every week-end with this friendly family, and then he savoured the illusion of being home once more.

"What hours of Paradise," he cried, "had Allan and I in escorting the Miss Evanses home on a Saturday, who were at a milliner's whom we used to think, and who I really believe was, such a nice lady; and the pillage of the flower gardens within six miles of town, with Sonnet or Love Rhyme wrapped round the nose-gay." It was to Mary he dedicated poems and flowers, but maybe the charm of her younger sisters had power upon him too. . . .

With a temperament such as his, I suspect him of yielding himself up unthinkingly to the spells woven round him by the three maidens, without concerning himself as to which contributed most to the pleasure he was aware he felt, though he could scarcely have given it a name. A serious flirtation with three girls at the same time is not smiled upon in England, still less where sisters are concerned, and he had, no doubt, fallen into a habit of speaking into Mary's ear alone, the words of bashful and almost brotherly love that rose to his lips, when, towards the close of some sultry afternoon, he and his girlish friends strolled homewards in the direction of Mrs. Evans's house, through the green lanes that then lay about the outskirts of London. If he never told Mary of his love, nor hardly ever paid her marked attention, this was because he was far from feeling any passion for her. Just as Bowles had revealed to him the existence of poetry, so did she reveal the existence of love. Both of them had helped to turn him aside from the study of metaphysics, and had ushered him, as he said, into "the era of poetry and love," where he could live on the surface of his being, instead of clambering down below in the "unwholesome quicksilver mines of metaphysic depths." It was with his whole heart, indeed, that when, in later life, he fell ill once more of what he called the "mental disease" he had suffered from at fifteen, by which is to be understood his curious researches into abstruse problems, he sighed for the "long and blessed interval, during which my natural faculties were allowed to expand," and his "sense of beauty in forms and sounds" developed.

Mary profited by the mood he was in, which made his heart rather ready to blossom and unfold than to give itself outright. The happiness he enjoyed was passive and carefree, like the pleasure a man may know during convalescence. And so, when he came to describe it, he was reminded of the "gentle south-west wind" as it blew across the willow-fringed meadows at Ottery St. Mary. . . . He allowed "poetry and love" to lap him round, if not to steep him in their seduction. But he barely attempted to translate them into action. When, at long intervals, he wrote down a few lines of verse, he drew mainly upon the impressions the country had made upon him during his recent journey to his home, (*Inside the Coach, Life, Devonshire Roads,* etc.). The joys of seeing, hearing, and drawing breath, a pleasure almost entirely physical, these are what chiefly emerge from his songs, even when philosophical accents mingle with them too. It was not until about his twentieth year, when he had already left London for Cambridge, that he threw himself into the writing of "Effusions," a name it was usual to give at that time in England to those poems written in a confidential strain which were the first expressions of romanticism, but might as suitably be applied, in his case, to the intimate movements of his heart.

PART II
LOVE AND UTOPIA

CHAPTER I

CAMBRIDGE

COLERIDGE left Christ's Hospital on the 7th September, 1790, with a scholarship of forty pounds to his credit. On the 5th February 1791, he obtained a sizarship at Cambridge, all his expenses as an undergraduate thus being met. He went into residence in the following October at Jesus College, one of the sixteen children of the theological Alma Mater, and finally matriculated as pensioner on the 5th November in the same year. Such was the temper of his soul, and so strong his attachment to the people he knew, and to the places where he had lived, whatever these might be, that he wept almost as much as upon leaving Devon when he emerged from the gaol-like fastness of the Blue Coat School, though later on he was to liken the Head Master, the Reverend Mr. Boyer, to "a grim idol whose altars reeked with children's blood."

Did this betoken mere dislike of change, or some mysterious foreboding of the future? Maybe the agony that tugged at his heartstrings, when he thought of leaving the dark night of the old cloister archway behind him for ever meant something of the kind, though Hope gladly murmured of "future joys," as she hovered around on "the brilliant wings of Fantasy." All that he was forsaking seemed to glow and glimmer to his sight now that absence was to veil it from view. On the other hand his brooding, unquiet spirit, that seemed to possess some subtle power of reading the future, peopled the unknown of which he was about to cross the threshold with fearsome shadows. We have already noted how ready he was to make the most abrupt changes in his existence. But nothing could be more unlike the fate he had mapped out for himself in daydreams, when some caprice of the moment was upon him, than the life he was destined to lead, which governed him by its own immutable law. Thus do those who put on the boldest face to meet some adventure which they imagine likely to bring them happy chances, flinch at the daily round. . . .

He could no doubt have found no real cause for alarm in the prospects opened up by his entry into Jesus College. He had no need to read the official report which accompanied him, and in which the good chances he stood of Church preferment were enlarged upon, in order to realize that his pathway lay smooth before his feet. But he was less stimulated by the rewards and hopes held out to his zeal, than lowered by them in his own estimation. And behind the security which seemed to offer, masking its awesome dullness, what pitfalls might not be lurking in ambush for the dreams which of all things lay nearest his heart?

His immediate aim was to make certain of one of the seventeen Rustat scholarships, (founded by Tobias Rustat at Cambridge for sons of the clergy), and he at once settled down to this task, and to the kind of life led by his fellow undergraduates, with the careless adaptability that was second nature to him, and derived in his case, side by side with a nobler kind of resignation, from his imitativeness and intellectual plasticity.

There was no kind of life he was not ready to throw himself into, in order to fashion for himself in its image a certain type of manners, a way of feeling, in fact, one might say, a kind of soul. But at first, at all events, he was not much attracted by the varied architecture of the ancient college buildings, for, in a high-spirited letter written to Mary Evans' sister soon after he went up, he compared them to workhouses. The rugged masonry showed mean and unaspiring beside the Oriental sumptuousness of his dream towers, whose luxuriant tracery was one day to blossom forth into stone in the palace of Kubla Khan. Jesus College, especially, looked "thin," in spite of its famous battlemented tower, and he had to force himself to overcome an indefinable feeling of dismay when he sat down to table in its echoing hall. He preferred Christ's Hospital, wrapped in mystery by the inextricable maze of the London streets.

The town which lies huddled together in the midst of flat scenery on the edge of the lower fens, is a dismal one, with houses built at sixes and sevens alongside narrow streets, and for eight months out of the twelve it is lapped in mist or lashed by rain. It is the very type of the small

English provincial town, exuding boredom from every brick in its walls, and setting a body sighing after the sprightly uniformity of large industrial centres such as Birmingham and Manchester. There is no open country for five miles around. The only bright spots are the Backs, and the lawns and gardens through which the Cam flows upon its way. But college feeling is picked up fast enough, and Coleridge soon felt proud of belonging to Cambridge, the Whig university, rather than Tory Oxford, which, moreover, he soon learnt to call "a childish university."

Though tutors did not keep their pupils as haughtily in their place as at Oxford, it must not be thought, nevertheless, that cordiality reigned throughout this kind of lay monastery. To begin with, there was no intellectual intercourse between the various colleges. Each had its own statutes, and boasted of teaching all that a student was required to know. Nor was there any division of labour among the tutors in any one college. Each man was responsible for the work of all pupils under his charge. And finally, at Cambridge, as at Oxford, young men of the nobility enjoyed special privileges, or were not bound by the same rules as other undergraduates. The gold braid borders to their caps marked them out from the sizars, who were obliged to remain standing whilst they ate their meals, if not, indeed, to wait upon them at table. Whilst discrepancies in income, in a place where the richest undergraduates might get through as much as two or three hundred pounds during the seven months of the academic year, were bound to make life more painful for penniless young men.

It is amusing to find our young neophyte confiding the following tale of an orgy to the Evanses very soon after his arrival at Cambridge. "A party of us had been drinking wine together, and three or four freshmen were most deplorably intoxicated. (I have too great a delicacy to say drunk.) As we were returning homewards, two of them fell into the gutter (or kennel). We ran to assist one of them, who very generously stuttered out, as he lay sprawling in the mud: 'N-n-n-no! save my f-fr-fr-friend there; n-never mind me, I can swim!' "

What a chance to give the dear girls in London something to open their eyes at! There is no doubt that he soon settled down at Cambridge and adopted the tone of the place. This was hardly exemplary— "To those who remember the state of our public schools and universities some twenty years past," Coleridge wrote in his *Biographia Literaria* "it will appear no ordinary praise in any man" (he is talking of Southey), "to have passed from innocence into virtue, not only free from all vicious habit, but unstained by one act of intemperance."

Sport was brutal, betting madly rife, and intemperance was the rule in all its forms, including that of language, which drew largely on sailor slang. On coming out of one of the parties I have mentioned, during which port and sherry were freely partaken of, it was no unusual thing to go and see the night out at a brothel at Barnwell, a village lying half-a-mile out of the town, and the haunt of all the street-walkers attracted thither by the male population of the colleges, and forbidden by law to enter the town. In spite of the supervision exercised by the Proctors, it was not only at Barnwell that scandalous proceedings took place. Gownsmen used to molest townsmen, keeping up a hurly-burly under their windows by night, and sometimes maltreating the representatives of authority who had the misfortune to interfere, just as in the Middle Ages the clerks would fall foul of the nightwatch on its rounds.

It was not with the meagre pocket-money allowed him from time to time by his brother George, now a clergyman, that Samuel could hope to play his part in his friends' entertainments. But just as there were sirens at Barnwell, so were there sharks at Cambridge—for where either of these are gathered together, there will the others be also—and Shylock was willing to give unlimited credit to young men hard pressed for cash. The tailors, the furniture dealers, the livery stablemen, the confectioners, the proprietors of eating houses, would all gladly open accounts with the undergraduates, well knowing when the day of reckoning arrived, and those inordinately lengthened bills came in, they could always find their trembling fledglings in the nest.

Samuel, ashamed of always accepting other men's hospitality, now began to run up bills on his own account. He turned his rooms over to the upholsterer, and upon being asked how he wanted them furnished replied, "Just as you please, Sir," with a lofty unconcern that would not have sat ill upon a dandy. This munificence alone cost him a hundred pounds. He had his own little court, an ever attentive audience, whom his conversation enthralled, and he gave some memorable supper-parties. He bought a fiddle, and used to scrape away upon it to goad some of his neighbours to frenzy. And I make no doubt that his conduct was even wilder than his biographers seem to suggest. It would indeed have been unlikely that, amid the unbridled licence of his companions, Coleridge alone should have remained unscathed.

His activity at this time was truly prodigious, and bore some of the signs of over-excitement. His dissolute way of life did not prevent him pursuing his studies with the utmost brilliance, winning, in particular, the Browne Medal in 1792, for a Greek ode on the Slave Trade. He obtained a Foundation Scholarship on the 5th June of the following year, and was elected with three other men to sit for a Craven Scholarship which, however, he failed to obtain. He declaimed in public a speech in the manner of Cicero on *Posthumous Fame,* wrote songs, occasional and elegiac verse in English, set to work again upon the *Monody on the Death of Chatterton,* which he had begun in 1790, and thought of bringing out a volume of selections from the Latin poets, with verse translations alongside.

He continued, nevertheless, to keep up his epistolary

relations with the Evans family, and wrote as much to
Mary as to her mother or sisters. She answered whenever
he wrote. He corrected her faults in spelling, took her to
task generally—he was a born preacher—and was careful
to adjure her not to grow vain of her beauty. Doubtless
he appreciated this beauty the better now he was far away,
than when he could feast his eyes on its sight. He dreamed
about it. Dreamed about it, even when the complaisant
hussies of Barnwell so brazenly flaunted theirs, his imagination flaming the more with longing for the past, because of the kind of shock that waking to reality was
bound to occasion. . . . But the fire raging within cast
no reflection on his correspondence. He avoided any
mention of his feelings which might stir up Mary's. This
is what he later called having endeavoured to smother a
very ardent attachment. But what was there to hinder
him from writing to tell her he loved her? No sound
nor solid reason whatever. In England, where people
sometimes enter upon an engagement as much as ten
years before marriage, mere uncertainty as to the future
would not of itself have daunted a young man in love.
So when we hear Coleridge invoking this pretext later
on, and in circumstances which so patently give it the lie,
we shall know how to take it at its real value. Truth to
tell, if he kept the tender longing she inspired in him
from Mary's ken, it was because he took an egoist's delight in seeing the happiness she stood for continually
shaping and reshaping itself before him. There was noth-

ing he wished for less than that the wraith he sported with so joyously in his daydreaming moods should ever, by any rash decision of his, be brought to a stay, or even frozen to stone altogether. A curious attitude, this, for a young man to adopt. But it goes to prove that this young man took refuge from the demands of instinct by throwing himself with a kind of unconscious intuition into that frame of mind of fearing all things, yet hoping all things, in which love's deepest and divinest pangs are most acutely felt. Yet at the very time in our lives when we are most in bondage to love, we find it easiest to fling ourselves into other occupations.

Coleridge, at all events, contrived to pursue his studies and to dabble in politics as well, during the time when his passion for Mary was growing up in his heart. It was no doubt expected of young men at Cambridge to take an interest in current events, and the principles upon which they rested, for these were never so hotly discussed as at the end of the eighteenth century, in the full blast of the French Revolution. Coleridge took a leading part in all debates, as much on account of his mental alertness, as of the weight of his intellect and learning. He enthusiastically sang the praises of democratic ideals, as he had formerly celebrated the *Fall of The Bastille,* and glorified the revolt of genius from the "dread dependence on the low born mind" in *Chatterton.*

Any society which would tolerate the sight of people of superior gifts being ground down, and would not rather do what it could to develop their exceptional powers, must, so he believed, be defective. He soon went further than merely retailing Fox's pamphlets, which, with his astonishing memory he was able to read through in the morning, and then reel off verbatim for whole pages at a time, for the benefit of his acquaintance. He boldly began to oppose the opinions of the University authorities, which were also professed by Pitt, then Member for Cambridge. Not that he ever showed himself favourable to the cause of France. Indeed, scarcely a single example can be cited of any Englishman who sympathized with France in 1793. And Coleridge only knew her by repute, as an aggressive and war-loving nation. Apart from Rousseau, for we have seen how early he threw off Voltaire's influence, it was not from French thinkers that he learned to love liberty.

The word has, in fact, quite a different meaning on either side of the Channel, and the English do not, as do the French, associate it with the idea of the emancipation of the individual. The Englishman looks at liberty realistically, in its practical aspect, and hence from an utterly different standpoint from that of the Frenchman, who sees it with the eye of the idealist, following it out into its remotest bearings, to the absolute, to absurdity even. The Englishman confines it within bounds. He keeps it strictly to laws he has himself laid down, never, for instance, allowing it to impinge on the field reserved for morality or faith.

It was under the influence of Frend, Priestley's disciple at Cambridge, that Coleridge became a social reformer, though he did no more than urge an extension to the franchise. In a pamphlet called *Peace and Union,* he tried to justify the execution of Louis XVI, and denounced the war with France. But what he yearned for in the main, was the return of mankind to a state of innocence, and to a kind of primitive life. Moreover, I suspect that he showed more enthusiasm for Frend, who was sent down from the University, and Priestley, who was turned out of the kingdom—for the men representing Liberal ideas, in fact, that is—than for those ideas themselves. These were too vague and inconsistent, of too mirage-like and distant a beauty, to charm him as anything else than ideas divorced from all reality, and they had no stronger hold over him than he over them. It is only necessary to read *France, an Ode,* a poem not written until 1797, but full of recollections of his Cambridge days, to see how metaphysical was the conception of liberty he had adopted. It stood to him for life itself, setting forth with Love and Joy, its two inseparable companions, to summon man to the conquest of the earth, in the wake of the straying winds and shifting waves.

These visions, however, and the sight of the persecutions Frend and Priestley had to endure, sufficed to keep him at a white heat of excitement. This rebellious mood was, moreover, not unmixed with the bitterness he felt upon failing to obtain a prize with an ode on astronomy, which he thought the finest poem he had written. About this time, his ignorance of mathematics disqualified him from sitting for the Chancellor's Medal. A longing, which soon became irresistible, grew up within him, to find what psychologists call an "imaginative compensation" for his disappointment. He felt compelled to cut loose from his moorings, to escape from college, and go forth, whither he could not tell, but somewhere where there would be no clerics nor proctors, nor tutors, "owls and other two-legged cattle," not to speak of creditors, who had begun to dun him persistently for the mad sums he had disbursed.

Fresh circumstances had arisen too, in regard to Mary Evans. Women, whose minds are more practical than men's, or who, at any rate, are less likely to be deterred by the opening out of some imaginary vista, from pursuing the goal which destiny assigns them, can see no reason, once their choice is fixed, to delay answering the tender yet imperious summons their whole nature tells them to obey. The greater patience they possess under trial by love, the more anxious they are to make trial of it. Mary, who had guessed what were Coleridge's feelings towards herself, and did not fail to return them, was beginning to wonder why this singular suitor did not speak out. She did not, however, dare to "violate the rules of female delicacy," for she felt that Coleridge was unlike any other young man she had ever met, and that coldness or prudence could not entirely account for his silence. She hinted that marriage was being urged upon her, and spoke of the wooers to whom she had so far turned an indifferent ear, but for whom, for aught she could tell, she might some day. . . .

Besides the pangs of jealousy, Coleridge was now forced to endure the torments, which to a nature like his were even more unendurable, of having to make up his mind. He did not know where to turn, for fear. "Love," he told the friend in whom he confided the secret of his love for Mary, "is a local anguish." The only thing that might assuage his grief would be to go elsewhere, amid fresh scenes and faces, and so find a fresh outlet for his activity. By the end of 1793 he had surreptitiously left Cambridge, and found his way to London with a handful of coppers in his pocket.

CHAPTER II

THE DAWN OF PANTISOCRACY

THE counterblast of the French victories in Belgium could still be felt in London when Coleridge arrived in it. It was filled with the clash of arms, whetting to martial ardour the hatred borne by City merchants and the middle classes for the *sans-culottes,* who not only seemed unwilling to leave Dunkirk in the hands of the Empire, but were even pursuing the struggle for its possession to the very mouth of the Scheldt. Coleridge, whose love for peace was only equalled by his horror of things military, must have felt at sea when he stepped forth from the intellectual life of Cambridge into the truculent atmosphere of London. But since the best publishers and most of the great newspapers had their offices there, where else would he have found such a chance to use his talents? And luck seemed to be with him, at any rate at first. He sold a poem for the sum of one guinea to the *Morning Chronicle,* which also published, towards the end of 1794, his sonnet sequence *On Eminent Characters.*

This paper, which was owned by James Perry, was a Whig organ, and it may perhaps be wondered why Coleridge did not choose to send it prose rather than verse. Though political journalism, that is to say, defending party policy in current events, may not have been his bent, he was not at all unfitted, as, indeed, he gave proof later, to succeed in criticism and essay writing, that eminently English form of art. But the detached Liberalism and abstract vagueness of his ideas must have equally alarmed the editor of this famous radical paper. At all events, Coleridge soon perceived that he could not hope to make a living by his pen, even at the rate of one poem a month, and that once his guinea was exhausted, he would literally be on the streets.

He decided to resort to the last hope held out by His Majesty, through a recruiting sergeant, to such of his needy subjects, under the age of twenty-five as might be sound in sight and limb. On the 4th December he enlisted in the army for a period of eight years. I have just said that he felt the liveliest antipathy towards the military, a phenomenon by no means rare among his fellow-countrymen, but, what is much more uncommon, he also hated animals, more particularly horses. He enrolled in the cavalry "to cure myself of these absurd prejudices," as he alleged. More likely, he simply accepted the first offer, without thinking of the consequences, and attracted by the comparatively large bounty. He kept to his own initials, S. T. C., in the fantastic, punning name by which he signed, Silas, Titus, or Tomkyn Comberback; this done, donned the uniform of the 15th Light Dragoons, then stationed at Reading—red tunic with gilt buttons, and dark blue breeches with yellow braid.

"Verily my habits were so little equestrian," he used to say jestingly later on, "that my horse, I doubt not, was of that opinion." But he soon wearied of being tossed, and drawing the jibes of his squad down on his head, every time he appeared on the tan of the riding-school. However philosophical a man may be, he will find it hard to avoid a bitter thought or two at finding his clumsiness mocked by a set of rough louts, when his talents have been the admiration and envy of the elect. Luckily remembering that he had learnt, under his brother Luke, to apply dressings, our far from brilliant recruit gained permission to work mainly in the infirmary, and was soon sent to Henley to nurse a fellow soldier.

Set free from most military duties, and shorn of the attributes which lend glory to "Bellona's darling," as the couplets of the day were wont to have it, Coleridge won back something of his old ascendancy. The moment he left off playing soldiers, and slipped back into his accustomed civilian shell, his superiority was bound to strike even those who least had eyes to see. Though his pretensions to horsemanship had been howled down, he could now make himself heard, and was listened to with interest. Ridiculous though they had thought him at first, the men began to find out his charm for themselves. They asked his opinion on subjects that cropped up, and consulted him about the letters they meant to write. They even made him write for them, when they wanted a particularly well turned phrase, and he became the unofficial regimental scribe. Love letters, however, he would only tackle very charily, like the cat in the fable flicking chestnuts out of the fire. They reminded him of Mary Evans, who knew nothing of this mad escapade of his, and must surely be perplexed, or even alarmed, at receiving no answer to the last note she had sent him at Cambridge.

He was living with the sick man in his charge in a solitary summerhouse in a garden, where the only face vouchsafed to his view was that of a beautiful girl. Did she, perhaps, take a fancy to either of the two dragoons to whom she came to bear company? I should imagine she preferred the invalid, not only because of his helpless condition, but because he doubtless looked the part of a soldier better than his companion. She did but furnish Coleridge with a peg on which to hang melancholy meditations upon his love, and when he used to leave her by his comrade's bedside to take the road to Reading barracks nearly every day upon a "horse as young and untrained as himself" we can well imagine what gloomy and disillusioned reflections must have passed through his mind as he followed the Thames upstream.

We must try for an instant to put ourselves into the position of this poet of two-and-twenty, and think of him trotting along the slippery road, burnished by frost, or greasy from thaw, if we are to form some idea of what his mental anguish must have been. There was no way out of this blind alley down which he had turned, and none but his own family to come to the rescue. But he could not bring himself to seek their help. . . . He had only himself to blame, and felt he could curse himself for his uncontrolled thoughts and feelings. His nervous system was out of joint, "images of horror" haunted his days and fevered his nights. Then, in a despondent moment, acting as though swayed by some power outside himself, he took a piece of charcoal, and wrote this sentence in Latin—an echo of Boethius—on the white-washed stable wall at Reading. *"Eheu! quam infortunii miserrimum est fuisse felicem!"* In sooth, he cannot have thought what he was doing, for he might as well have signed his name in full, as write a Latin sentence in any place as remote from intellectual contact as a spick and span English barracks stable. Captain Nathanial Ogle, who may not have known the language of Cæsar, but had education enough to know it from English when he saw it, guessed whose hand had indited the unusual phrase—a hand that was, indeed, better skilled at holding a pen, than polishing jackboots, or currying horses.

This captain was, fortunately, a gentleman, and he could not rest until he had obtained Coleridge's release. A chance meeting of the latter with his Cambridge friend G. L. Tuckett coinciding with his own discovery of his identity, he spent his time in hastening the procedure that was to ensure the prodigal's release from bondage. Tuckett sent George Coleridge, now a clergyman, news of his brother's escapade. What must Coleridge's relief have been, at being able to disburden himself of the cares and regrets which oppressed him, by framing his own indictment in his letter to his elder brother! His gladness can be measured by the over-emphasis of the terms in which he admitted himself wholly in the wrong, and expressed the depth of his humiliation and despair at the weakness of his will, and the excessive subtlety of his soul. Its complexities were beyond him. He had erred and strayed in the inextricable maze of his heart. He had brought shame and disgrace on all who loved him, he had been idiotic to the point of madness, and all he could now hope was to be forgotten, or rather that things might go on as though he had never been. . . .

This violent crisis, in which he thought his better self would founder, was bound to come, ere Coleridge could plumb the depths of his own deceptive personality, and settle down, as it were, with a resignation not unmixed with pride, into the very heart of his restlessness. Twenty times or so, in verse or prose, written before this date, the words *dream* and *dreaming* occur, and in a poem called *Happiness,* written in 1794, he spoke of his "fat vacuity of face." But after the extravagant language he had uttered, the feeling he had hitherto vaguely entertained as to the ease with which he could shake off all contact with practical life, and neglect the real for an imaginary world, began to grow apace. He was under no illusion as to his inability to adapt himself to outward necessity, and admitted that, although he might be a man "whose energies were vigourous" by fits and starts, yet he found carrying a plan through to the finish the hardest thing of all. He meant that, with all his intense power of decision, of straining every faculty to attain one particular object, and of concentrating upon the right means to make use of that object, he was yet equally lacking in perseverance and in coherence in his ideas.

But he could guess what intellectual wealth his feeble struggles might imply. Knowing his own speculative genius, he felt some pride in the spiritual loneliness to which this vexatious temper condemned him. He no doubt foresaw that in the innermost depths where he was fated to keep a constant watch over his own being with its eddying currents, he would get closer to reality than other men more able to meet the claims made upon them by the world outside. We shall be able to see, in the following pages, whether this intuition was at fault. But let us not forbear to notice here and now, that, while he strove "to feel what he ought to feel," and reproached himself in all good faith with being unable to do this thing which the rest of the world found so easy, he yet had been learning, at an age when most people are living on the surface of life, a precious lesson as to the discord sown between life and his own nature, and the ensuing trouble, directly he ceased to withdraw into his cloud-cuckoo universe, and tried to step into the world of action.

"Wisdom may be gathered from the maddest flights of

imagination," was the conclusion he came to in one of the letters he wrote to his brother George, during the time which he spent in negotiating for his release, with the further help of his brother Captain James Coleridge. Since he knew this to be now merely a matter of weeks or of days, his despair had vanished. His brother George having forgiven him, he sent his brother James a letter full of practical good sense, pointing out the best way to get the contract cancelled.

He was now wholly absorbed in self-analysis, and in examining his attitude towards the religious beliefs of his earlier days. In the inn where he was lodging, he met a "man of the greatest information and most original genius," who claimed to be divinely inspired. With him he carried on transcendental conversations of such interest that the vexations of yesterday vanished to the limbo of worn out moons. Right on until midnight, or sometimes into the small hours, would this extraordinary roommate keep him awake, as he expounded ideas which struck chill to the marrow of his bones "from their daring impiety," or astounded him "with their sublimity." It may possibly have been in this interchange of thought with a partner so worthy of his metal that Coleridge laid the foundations of that essentially platonic philosophy, whose elements he was finally to gather and garner in Germany, but which corresponded to his own predilections.

Ontology, to which Wolff had not as yet given its

special meaning as the study of being in itself, but in the more general sense of metaphysics, was the subject of the speculations into which he plunged so feverishly, by the light of one guttering candle, which I seem to see darting its shadow athwart the bare walls of this lodging-house, whose echoes had assuredly never before been wakened by debates like these. "My memory tenacious and systematizing would enable me to write an octavo from his conversation," he affirmed, and I am persuaded that he was telling no more than the truth. But, with Coleridge, whenever there was no link connecting thought with deed, nor fulfilment of one in the other, a gulf yawned between his plans and their achievement which time could only widen; and in point of fact, nothing has ever reached us of these high soaring flights of his on the eve of his departure from Reading.

He went up again to Jesus College at the beginning of April, unenthusiastically, but not unwillingly, and as casually as though he were just returning from a stroll through the streets of Cambridge. And on the twelfth of that month, having assumed a fitting air of contrition, he was admonished by the Master, in accordance with the statutes, in the presence of the assembled fellows.

It was springtime. Daisies were starring the green lawns of the Backs, and the Cam flowed in renewed vigour between the rushes growing along its banks, and the bridges which bestride it with varied look and gesture, like so many page-boys at play. Coleridge found no great difficulty in tackling the task given him as a kind of punishment, which consisted in translating Demetrius Phalereus, and in keeping within certain bounds. He was even given a hint that his translation might be published, if he were to add a preface, and "to exert erudition in some notes," and however slight this hope of glory may have seemed to a young man who felt the divine spark within him, it did serve to induce in him a proper state of mind.

During his time in the army, Coleridge had formed a habit of early rising, and was up by four o'clock. How life-giving the sweetness and joy of dawn in those first days of spring! How good the damp earth smelt after four months in barracks. He felt a blessed relief at plunging into books once more, and even into "antique Granta's" daily routine, after the experiences he had gone through. He had not, however, given up his liberal ideas entirely, and while he composed Latin speeches and Greek odes, and topical verses for visiting actresses, he had time to follow the course of Frend's trial, and to meditate upon the most effectual means of securing the happiness of mankind.

In June, the ban on his movements being now lifted, he set out for Oxford, where Robert Allen, an old friend, had invited him to stay. There is no doubt that Allen, at that time an undergraduate at Oxford, had meant to spring a surprise on him by this invitation. This young man knew of Coleridge's opinions. He admired him, and

wished him to make the acquaintance of a fellow undergraduate, Robert Southey by name, for he had every hope
that they would find much in common.

The meeting took place in Southey's room in Balliol,
whither Coleridge made his way, upon the first morning
after his arrival. It would be impossible to find a more
strikingly contrasted pair than these two young men,
whom Allen introduced to each other with all the self-
assurance of his twenty years. Their ages might be similar, in all else they were poles apart. Take their personal
appearance, to begin with. Coleridge has left a description of himself at about this period, and there is a portrait of him painted by P. Vandyke in 1795—only a few
months later, therefore, than the momentous encounter
at Balliol—to be seen at the National Portrait Gallery.

We shall have occasion to refer again to this picture
of Coleridge by himself; let it suffice for the moment to
say that he was quite right in insisting upon the irresolution to be shown in his face. With a fine brow, beneath
a shock of black hair parted into ringlets falling to the
shoulders, with a pair of especially magnificent grey eyes,
he yet had the flabby, puffy face and blunt nose of the
man whose mind is eternally waiting to be made up. His
lips were thick, and gapingly revealed his upper front
teeth, for he found it difficult to breathe through his nose,
an affliction he never lost. Whenever his face was not lit
up by eloquence, his expression was glum, and "expressive
chiefly of inexpression" as he humorously put it. He was

of fair height, but awkward in his movements, and shambling in his gait. There was something about his appearance reminiscent, though why I cannot tell, of the Celt, or even of the Oriental, at any rate almost entirely un-English.

Southey, on the other hand, was the complete Englishman: a long angular face with clear cut features, large pale eyes with beetling eyebrows, tufted and rather shaggy, fair hair straggled across the top of his brow, which seemed, as it receded, to pull into line with itself the hooked nose, whose bridge gave further proof of an enterprising spirit. Resolution, in default of genius was marked on those cold features, lit by no flame of enthusiasm but frozen by conviction. At the spark which flew from its first contact with this flint, the tinder of Coleridge's heart burst into flame.

The orphan son of a Bristol draper who had died leaving his affairs in a pitiable condition, Southey had been brought up at Bath by a spinster half-sister of his mother's, Elizabeth Taylor, a woman of masterful character, a typical English blue-stocking, and a great theatre-goer. His childhood was in some ways not unlike Coleridge's, owing to the harsh treatment he had met with at an Anabaptist School. But he had revolted against corporal punishment at the hands of the masters, instead of resignedly making the best of it like the charity-boy of Christ's Hospital. Some time later he was sent to Westminster, but was expelled for his share in the secret production of a paper called *The Flagellant,* wherein he had lashed with the whip of satire those who had chastised him with a quite unmetaphorical rod.

He was sent up to Oxford through the generosity of an uncle, the Rev. Herbert Hill, who vainly urged upon him an ecclesiastical or medical career. Here he distinguished himself at swimming and rowing, but read nothing beyond epic poetry and mythology, apart from Spenser, whose exquisite suavity he had discovered for himself at the age of fourteen. The Goethe of *Werther,* Rousseau, and Epictetus, these were his favourite authors at the time when he made Coleridge's acquaintance. The democratic ideal attracted him as much as it did his friend, but being of a far more practical than speculative turn of mind, he was trying to carry out this ideal in real life.

These two, utterly different in temperament and mind, complemented and charmed each other in the most astonishing way. They were to clash in the course of time. But Southey's uncompromising republicanism, his fanatical love of virtue, inspired by Rousseau, and reinforced by the Stoics, his way of underpinning his opinions with fixed principles, impressed Coleridge from the very first by their virility. As he listened to Southey laying down the law, his own diffuse ideas seemed to acquire a certain body. Through the gaps which Southey neatly cut in the tangle of ideas Coleridge brought him, Coleridge in his turn revealed to Southey horizons stretching to infinity. He lifted him out of himself, and, as a letter

Southey wrote to James Montgomery goes to prove, Coleridge gave him a feeling for the sublime, by converting him to his philosophy, and by initiating him into his own religious understanding of the world.

They were soon of one mind as to the best way to set about abolishing individual property, and to bring about the return to nature which they both had at heart, for which, indeed, Southey had already drawn up a plan. But, as M. Joseph Aynard has well said, "What was to Southey's mind only a limited project which was to aim at allowing a few just persons to live apart from the wickedness of society, Coleridge turned into a complete system to regenerate society." The kind of community or smallholding (phalanstery Fourier would have termed it), that the new friends proposed to found, calling it by the name of Pantisocracy, was to serve as a model to future generations, and to be the signal perhaps even in this one, for a general movement to free the oppressed. The second generation was to combine "the innocence of the patriarchal age with the knowledge and genuine refinements of European culture."

"Twelve gentlemen," wrote Coleridge, "of good education and liberal principles are to embark with twelve ladies in April next. . . . Their opinion was that they should fix themselves at—I do not know the place but somewhere in a delightful part of the new back settlements." If each individual did two hours manual work a day, it should prove possible to assure food supplies for the colony, to provide means to improve conditions, and to found a fine library from the start. For, as there would be time for leisure, it was to be spent in study, in discussion, and in educating the children according to a rational system, founded, no doubt, on the lines advocated by the author of *Émile*. The women were not only to help, of course, in this education but they were to share the men's intellectual relaxations. Free love was not under consideration, since the couples were to be joined in matrimony before they left their native land, but it was still a moot point whether divorce was to be obtained by mutual consent, or upon the wish of one only of the parties.

There was thus, on the whole, nothing very subversive about the constitution of this society, in which, as I have said, Southey saw no more than the possibility of realizing an earthly Paradise in keeping with his literal and matter-of-fact ambitions. But Coleridge at once began to declaim in Sibylline accents, "Pantisocracy! Oh, I shall have such a scheme of it! My head, my heart, are all alive. I have drawn up my arguments in battle array: they shall have the tactician excellence of the mathematician with the enthusiasm of the poet. The head shall be the mass, the heart the fiery spirit that fills, informs, and agitates the whole."

His calculations were founded upon the remotest of probabilities, and he grew impatient to make a start. Indeed, of the one hundred and twenty-five pounds it had been reckoned that each disciple would have to subscribe towards the cost of the fares and the fitting out of the expedition, not a single one was as yet forthcoming. He decided to set out on a tramp through Wales, in order to solve this one knotty problem, the gravity of which he could not but see. A friend of his named Hucks accompanied him, and he would hold forth for hours in endless monologue to this voluntary listener—on one occasion until the tide overtook them unawares—and became more firmly convinced than ever of the extraordinary persuasive and reasoning powers with which he had been gifted. He was able to put them to the test at Llanfyllin. One day, during their stay at that place, "two great huge fellows of butcher-like appearance danced about the room in enthusiastic agitation," at hearing him set forth his ideas. One of them, calling for a large glass of brandy "drank it off to this his own toast, 'God save the King! And may he be the last.' "

Coleridge now made up his mind to go down from Cambridge with no further delay, and to give a course of lectures on the subject nearest his heart, with a view to raising the sum he needed himself as well as a like amount for Southey, and perhaps one or two other future settlers besides.

At Wrexham, he very nearly ran into Mary Evans, who, by a rather curious coincidence, happened to be there at the same time as himself, and though he pretended not to see her, he could not catch a glimpse of her beloved features without feeling a sharp pang. Coleridge, in his

role of true knight of the ideal, looked upon this journey
—which he had undertaken in order to instil some order
into his ideas—in the light of a vigil. "I had been wander-
ing," he wrote, "among the wild wood scenery and terrible graces of the Welsh mountains, to wear away, not
to revive the images of the past." He knew Mary had,
as they say, a head on her shoulders, and that she would
never consent to follow him into exile. When Southey had
spoken of the necessity for every emigrant to take a wife
with him, it would never have occurred to him to put
forward her name. And it was to purge his heart of
dross, to cast out a memory too deeply rooted there, and
so to fit himself to do all that a good Pantisocratist should,
that Coleridge had set out along with Hucks, stick in hand
and pack on shoulder.

Mary undoubtedly recognized him, in spite of these
accoutrements, but she fortunately never realized he was
pretending not to see her, or her courage might have
failed her. He was in full space of ideas and feelings, already seeing himself, as in a trance, pitching his tent in
the Far West. Roused by some stray inquirer's questioning, his face shone like a seer's. "Up I arose, terrible
in reasoning," he said of himself on one occasion, nor
could he have more happily described the appearance he
must have presented to all and sundry, whenever they
gave him the chance to plead the cause of Pantisocracy.
To hold an opponent at bay, and gradually bring him
round to his own opinions, seemed to him the same thing

as putting his theories into action, or better still, being let off taking any action whatever. The wonderful prologue in which he told his audience one by one, with a dazzling wealth of detail, all the beauties of the masterpiece he meant to act, was surely as good as any play, however exciting. Even his most prosaic listeners, the least likely to be blinded by his rare merits to his lack of the inferior qualities which might have brought him to practical success, could not help admiring him, if their hearts were at all in the right place. Later on, he revealed a depth and subtlety in his impromptu conversations which delighted the best minds of his time; but he never made such an appeal to all men as at this time of his life, when, armed with his own brand of logic, he challenged their spirits at every turn.

And so, when he pushed on down into Somerset, so as to parley with one of Southey's recruits, he roused as great an enthusiasm as in the hearts of the "butcher-like men," but it was destined to last longer, and to influence his fate for good. He did, in fact, convince Thomas Poole of his genius, though he could not win him over to his ideas. This man of determined character and enlightened mind, the son of a tanner at Nether Stowey, had taught himself everything he knew, including reading and writing, and had then gone as an ordinary hand into some London works, in order to improve his knowledge of his father's business. Being now come to the age of twenty-nine, he knew too much of the world to encourage Coleridge in his schemes, and doubtless stifled his first impulse to hand over to the Utopian young man whatever he wanted to take him to America. The worthy fellow made up his mind to follow Coleridge's career, giving him help whenever need should arise. For he could see by certain signs unmistakable to anyone as observant as himself, that Coleridge was far more likely to take to poetry or philosophy as a career, than to lead the simple life according to Jean-Jacques Rousseau, as a colonist in a far country.

One month later, Coleridge returned to Bristol as penniless as he had left it, but more eager than ever to overcome the difficulties that kept him still bound to English soil.

CHAPTER III

THE DECLINE AND FALL OF PANTISOCRACY

THOUGH, for his part, Southey had not collected any money either, during the month Coleridge had spent in scouring Wales, he had been making ready for the expedition in another way. He had, that is, become engaged to be married to a young lady from Bath named Edith Fricker.

There were five Miss Frickers of whom four were of a marriageable age. They all earned their own living, and supported their mother, who was the widow of a bankrupt hardware manufacturer in Westbury. Edith was the second of the family. Mary the eldest was shortly about to marry Robert Lovell, Southey's ablest lieutenant, and this fact hastened on his decision to secure her younger sister for himself. Nothing, he thought, was more likely to cement union among the Pantisocratists than marriages such as these, upon which the Frickers looked so kindly, all except Martha the fourth girl, who had spurned the suit of Burnett, another member of their band. So, when he introduced Coleridge to Sarah, the third daughter, he was delighted to observe that the young man seemed to find her attractive. Sarah, who was fairly tall and well set up, with brown curly hair, thick eyelashes and languishing black eyes, though her nose seemed to have been given an odd upward tweak, was the more likely to appeal to Coleridge in the state of excitement he was then in, because, being his senior by about a year, she at once grasped that all she had to do to find the way to his heart, was to appear to take an interest in his liberal ideas and his communal plan of society.

Coleridge, with his usual impulsiveness, lost not a moment's time in conjuring up for Sarah the picture of the idyllic existence in store for every married couple in his colony, nor in pointing out to her the happiness she might enjoy as one half of any such couple. From this to hint that he hoped to be the other half himself was but a step, and I am convinced that it was a step he took. . . . Whilst he was dreaming of an ideal state of life, surely he must have made it seem more alluring still, by including amongst its ingredients the friendly damsel who listened to him with such flattering attention. As he was preparing to leave for Cambridge, however, to inform the authorities he intended to go down, the incorruptible Southey, who had led him on into compromising himself, informed him in a tone admitting of no reply, that he had gone too far with Sarah to escape unscathed. He assured him that he had given the third Miss Fricker cause to fall in love with him, and was bound in honour to ask her hand in marriage.

Coleridge could scarcely credit his ears. What sort of

a man, then, was he, to have led Sarah on, whilst his heart was still full of Mary's image? How could he have found such a perverse amusement in the game, that he had carried it on against his own conscience? He confided his ill-starred love affairs to Southey, who convinced him of the levity of his conduct. Nor had Southey any need to rely on that "impartial observer" who was one day to impress upon De Quincey that he had never seen any man so fascinated by a woman, as was Coleridge when he described the delights and advantages of Pantisocracy to Sarah. Southey moreover recalled to his friend that there must be no celibates in their colony. And pointing out his error in remaining faithful to Mary's memory, whom he knew to be opposed to his political opinions, he finally forced him into promising marriage to Sarah. The promise was sealed by a kiss, "breathed on Sara's lovelier lips," as a poem called *Kisses* bears witness. It is dated July 1793, but had been written a year earlier at Plymouth, for someone who was not Miss Fricker.

Once on the road again for Cambridge, Coleridge began to rouse himself a little. Perhaps he did, after all, feel for Sarah, or Sara as he liked to write her name, all that she felt for him, if Southey said true? He thought her, at any rate, a suitable helpmeet for himself—this girl who understood him so well and who so heartily approved of the picture he drew of a better state of society. And as to Mary, had he ever done aught but worship her in secret, knowing his cause was hopeless? Absence making his heart grow less fond, his platonic vision now saw in her no earthly being. She was the undying symbol of his noblest aspirations, and her image remained in "the sanctuary of his heart whence it could never be torn away but with the strings that grapple it to life." How could any wife whom he might take unto himself to carry out his plan, whether Sara or another, have the right to feel jealous of her? And this plan, on the other hand, excused his conduct towards his poetic lady. His duty, since he believed in Pantisocracy, lay in being a Pantisocratist, and since he could never become a full fledged Pantisocratist unless he were to marry, then marry he must and would.

He wrote in partial delirium to Southey "America! Southey! Miss Fricker! Yes, Southey, you are right. Even love is the creature of a strong motive. I certainly love her. I think of her incessantly and with unspeakable tenderness—with that inward melting away of soul that symptomatizes it"— A strange error of judgment, indeed! Sara symbolized his own idealistic madness, and it was this that he clasped to his bosom, with the gentle glow of an almost sensual excitement. It is not often that flesh and spirit are so neatly caught in red-handed complicity.

Coleridge returned to Jesus College having entirely made up his mind to join his life to this woman's, whom Fate had apparently destined for him, by making her sister to the future wives of the most steadfast followers of Pantisocracy, namely Southey and Lovell. He had, too, recently collaborated with his two friends in writing a three-act tragedy, the *Fall of Robespierre,* the lately fallen tyrant, a work that betrays the influence of Godwin. He wrote the first act of this tragedy after the style of *Julius Cæsar,* Southey writing the second act, and then the third, which had first been entrusted to Lovell, but not been considered worthy of the rest. Coleridge was to bring out this work under his own name, and surely no two authors have ever shown a rarer proof than this of generosity towards a third? The play is a second rate, and even tedious one, and its rhetoric is, in places, closely allied to ranting. No matter. As de Musset has it:

> "La muse est toujours belle
> Même pour l'insensé, même pour l'impuissant,
> Car sa beauté pour nous, c'est notre amour pour elle"

Coleridge would have been mortally vexed with himself had he betrayed his friends' trust. Such open-handed confidence as this encouraged him to realize his dream, whose beauty he never felt more clearly than when he could enjoy it in his own way, away from the objections raised by other Pantisocratists, or their too pressing reminders of reality.

On his way through London he met a former schoolfellow, now engaged in land speculation in the New World, who prevailed upon him to persuade his friends into buying the three hundred acres needed for their scheme, for the sum of two thousand pounds. They could find no spot more suitable for farming, this land-broker averred, than the banks of the Susquehannah, a river flowing into Lake Ontario from the south-east, through a magnificent part of the country, less molested than most by Indians and bison. But Redskins and buffaloes were no more than a myth to Coleridge, who was particularly taken with the euphony and picturesqueness of the name Susquehannah, which he now heard for the first time. He was filled with rejoicing, and sent Southey one letter after the other in which his imagination ran riot.

They must commission a ship. . . . With twelve of them to put their shoulders to the wheel the land could be cleared in four or five months. It was easy to make a living by writing over there. Mosquitoes? They could be no more troublesome than the gnats which breed in stagnant pools at home. Southey announced that Shadrack, his aunt's factotum, had decided to throw in his lot with theirs, and Coleridge wrote in capital letters:— SHAD GOES WITH US: HE IS MY BROTHER! He never opened his mouth save to talk of the settlement, which he knew down to the last detail as well as his own home, and in which he lived so intensely, that everything else seemed dull beside it. He was in an even worse state than on his journey through Wales, and the last weeks of his stay at Cambridge were beset by continual hallucinations. His personal magnetism was so strong, that a fellow undergraduate whom he sought to imbue with his doctrines, said that he "would not answer for his sanity, sitting so near a madman of genius."

Mary's influence was again invading his peace of mind, and in the hopes of keeping it at bay, he may have been stimulating his fever by artificial means, trying to outdo himself in his enthusiasm for Pantisocracy in order to escape this obsession. Mary received a hint as to Coleridge's intentions from some unknown source, and now broke through "the rules of female delicacy" to tell him, without mincing matters, that they revolted her common sense. She wrote hinting as before at other offers, "I have heard that you mean to leave England and on a plan so absurd and extravagant that were I for a moment to imagine it true, I should be obliged to listen with a more patient ear to suggestions, which I have rejected a thousand times with scorn and anger. Yes! Whatever pain I might suffer I should be forced to exclaim

'O what a noble mind is here o'erthrown
Blasted with ecstasy!'"

Coleridge at that time made the acquaintance of Miss Brunton, an actress as lovely as she was witty, and as he danced attendance upon her he found out for himself how fickle are men's desires, and proved to his own satisfaction that, just as it had been possible for him to become engaged to Sarah Fricker whilst still adoring Mary Evans, so he could keep troth with Sarah while his thoughts went roving after Miss Brunton. The letter from Mary, whom he had loved since the age of seventeen, left him prostrate. She gave him clearly to understand that he had only to speak the word, and she would send the suitor her mother favoured about his business. After that, it was no use her writing "I shall always feel that I have been your *Sister,*" for he realized that she loved him still, and this discovery "rent his heart in twain," as the poem he wrote beneath the brunt of his emotion, *On a Discovery Made Too Late* bears witness.

"In a few months I shall enter at the Temple," he wrote "and there seek forgetful calmness where it only can be found, in incessant and useful activity." He was insane at the idea that Mary, whom he had given up all thought of marrying, could become another man's wife. According to Marcel Proust, jealousy is nearly, if not quite, the whole of love. In this instance it worked like a strong leaven. Coleridge wished to make certain whether Mary were engaged or no. He was careful, however, not to give away the fact that he was on the point of getting married himself, and that he had lightly entered into a decision as regards Sarah, for which he could produce the best excuses for never having made as regards herself. "The man of dependent fortunes, while he fosters an attachment, commits an act of suicide on his happiness. I possessed no establishment" (But did he have one now?) "what expectations could I form?" "I formed no expectations—I was even resolving to subdue the disquieting passion, still some inexplicable suggestion palsied my efforts, and I clung with desperate fondness to this phantom of love, its mysterious attractions and hopeless prospects. It was a faint and rayless hope! Yet I nursed it in my bosom with an agony of affection, even as a mother her sickly infant."

Unless Southey had been in the background, we cannot tell to what lengths he might not have gone, in order to prevent Mary Evans marrying, so unbearable did he find the idea of marriage in connection with this girl, whom he thought of as a sort of Laura or Beatrice. But the young Cato from Bristol, who well knew his friend's moodiness and weakness of character, was careful not to leave him to his own devices. He posed as a victim who had endured everything that the pure souled Pantisocratist must know how to suffer for the cause, for his aunt Miss Tyler had just turned him out of her house, on being informed of his plans, forbidding him ever to set foot in it again. He sent Coleridge sententious epistles, ceaselessly exhorting him to do his duty. He claimed the right not only to exercise a strict control over his feelings for Sarah, but to see that he kept up a regular correspondence with her as well.

With the shade of Southey peering over his shoulder, Coleridge wound up his letter to Mary, by telling her that the tortures of jealousy he had been describing to her were diminishing. In fact, he had stifled them altogether, and was ready to take a second place in favour of his rival. Let her make no mistake, he meant his *rival*. What Mary had merely glanced at as a possibility, he was determined to see as an actual fact. He declared himself ready to give a warm welcome to the man whom his beloved had honoured with her affection. "I shall love him for your sake," he wrote, "the time may perhaps come when I shall be philosopher enough not to envy him for his *own*."

It seems to me that all this smacks of the machiavellianism common to all lovers, those most unscrupulous of created beings, which makes one party throw the initiative for breaking off relations on to the other, or the responsibility for the step which will, for some reason, force him to abandon the fray. The idea of Mary's approaching marriage sent Coleridge's thoughts bounding down like a stone into the abyss. And had he never known what it was to plumb this feeling, he would hardly have been so ready to turn the vague admirer into the accredited lover, nor to harp upon the idea of honouring the man he had reason to hate.

Mary Evans, who seems to have been a sensible girl, with plenty of dignity of her own, did not persist in trying to extort a proposal of marriage out of Coleridge, which she would have been glad to accept if he had made it of his own accord. She answered him kindly but firmly, thus putting an end to their adventure, and the letter she received from Coleridge in return, dated the 24th December 1794, was a final farewell.

Yielding to the whim which came upon him whenever gales blew fiercely round his head, our fantastic friend was now again on the move. He had hastened on his departure from Cambridge, in spite of the protests of Dr. Pearce, the Master, who wished him to take his degree, and returned to London with none of the qualifications for the ecclesiastical career for which he had been destined. In vain did Dr. Pearce put forward the best of arguments to prove that no wise man can be a democrat, still less a republican. Coleridge cut him short, and left him no leg to stand upon, by declaring he was neither the one nor the other, but a Pantisocratist.

Coleridge had succeeded in getting the *Fall of Robespierre* published, by appending to it an essay on the revival of literature, and some translations from the Latin poets. He now resumed his ephemeral contributions of the preceding year to the *Morning Post* with the sonnet sequence on *Eminent Characters* mentioned above. He had a few guineas in hand, and was not sorry to try his wings alone in London for a little while. The evenings he would spend with Charles Lamb his former schoolfellow at Christ's Hospital at the *Salutation and Cat* in New Street where he would talk poetry, and lay bare his heart, still full of his love for Mary. He wanted to shake off the hold his future brother-in-law exerted over him, which was becoming irksome; and, strange to relate, he barely mentioned the word Pantisocracy. It may have sounded less attractive, now that Southey's masterful countenance loomed like a shadow between him and it, whenever he called its radiant image to mind. Like most people of strong intuitions, whom the world never credits with seeing much of the game, because they do not pose as keen observers of life, Coleridge could see very clearly, and he was able to gaze right into Southey's puritanical soul, and discover that charity and broadmindedness were what he most conspicuously lacked. Southey had annoyed him by again urging him to Bristol. "Precipitance is wrong," he wrote to him, "there may be too high a state of health, perhaps even virtue is liable to a *plethora.* Your undeviating simplicity of rectitude has made you rapid in decision. Having never *erred,* you feel more indignation at error than *pity* for it."

The tender-hearted but mischievous Lamb moreover, lent a sceptical ear to Coleridge when he talked of his schemes for leading the communal life, and he hurried him off the battlefield of ideas to a happier hunting-ground. That rare spirit, clairvoyant and sensitive, cared less for Coleridge the Utopian, than Coleridge the erudite and passionate lover of literature. He had already held for some three years now a minor position under the India Company, and on his meagre pay supported an invalid mother, and a sister whom he adored, but who later went out of her mind. It was for this sister that Lamb was to sacrifice his own hopes of happiness. In 1796 in fact, Mary Lamb, who was a mantua-maker, and overworked to the point of mental breakdown, ran round

the room knife in hand after one of her workgirls, and
mortally wounded her mother when she tried to interpose.

If Lamb listened with so much interest whilst Coleridge told of his unhappy love-affairs—though he smiled
at his plans for settling in America—it was because he
was himself at the time, as he said, "sore galled with disappointed Hope," and his own frame of mind made him
pay more serious attention than it deserved to Coleridge's
disappointment. Coleridge, with his usual intellectual elas-
ticity, found it easy to take his cue from Lamb and his
valediction to the Reverend James Boyer, the master who
had given him many a flogging, is almost an echo of that
delightful stammer: "Poor J. B.!—may all his faults be
forgiven; and may he be wafted to bliss by little cherub
boys, all head and wings, with no *bottoms* to reproach
his sublunary infirmities."

But what one might not have suspected, was the depth
of sympathy that overflowed from out Coleridge's generous heart when Lamb told him the lamentable circumstances of his life. Some time later Lamb wrote to him:
"You had 'many an holy lay that mourning soothed the
mourner on his way' . . . they yet vibrate pleasant on the
sense."

Coleridge, though he was, as yet, a rather inferior
craftsman in verse, whose work was still clogged by reminiscences of other people's, was already a poet in virtue
of his imaginative wealth. The torrent of ideas and
images surging up within him sprang from the fountain

head of all lyric feeling. The contradictions and uneven-
ness of his work are themselves a proof of his sincerity.
In spite of the pedantic claptrap of the *Religious Musings*
of 1794, his prophetic declamations strike a sublime note,
and the most hardened sceptic is carried away in spite of
himself. His outpourings of soul do, indeed, as he told
the Master of Jesus College, spring from a faith that was
neither republican nor democratic, but simply and solely
Christian. The love of all created things, as for instance
in the poem *To a Young Ass,* increased its ardour, and
nowhere did he see the glory of God as in the face of the
Crucified.

There must surely have been elements of the simple
beauty that even the humblest may grasp, in the language
used by this young man, who was so precociously learned
in all philosophies, and who punctuated his remarks with
quotations from Plato, Plotinus, and Berkeley, since people of every class would listen to him with interest and
even enthusiasm. And in "the little smoky room" at the
Salutation and Cat, where Lamb and he would sit
"through the winter nights beguiling the cares of life with
poetry," his eloquence achieved the wonted miracle. Fascinated by the two young men, who used to sit hour by
hour holding forth in loftiest strains upon the state of
their feelings, and all the great problems of eternity, the
landlord of the inn would stand hovering over them,
whilst the Welsh rarebits he had just brought them, (*o
noctes cœnœque Deum!*) grew momentarily colder,

singeing his wings like any moth at this two-fold flame of heart and mind. Everything he could overhear of the conversation, or that Coleridge imparted to him on his own account, surprised and delighted him to such a degree that he offered his customer board and lodging free of all expense to himself.

But Southey, unfortunately, had his eye upon him. From the tone of Coleridge's letters, which had fallen off in number, he guessed that his zeal for Pantisocracy was waning, and his love for Sarah no doubt passing under an eclipse. So in January 1795, he journeyed up to London, in order to dislodge him from his place of shelter, and take him down with him to the lodgings at 48 College Street, Bristol, where he himself was at that time living upon credit.

Coleridge's fainting heart began to revive under the stimulus of the thought that the whole Headquarters Staff of Pantisocracy relied upon him, that is to say, Robert Allen, Edmund Seaward, the two members who were betrothed to the two Miss Frickers, and also poor George Burnett, whom Martha, the youngest Fricker, had slighted. He had some thoughts of starting a review, but, with an eye to more immediate wants, decided to give a course of lectures.

He was aided and abetted in this design by a young publisher, Joseph Cottle by name, a friend of Lovell's. This young man of four and twenty was the oddest mixture of frankness and fatuous pedantry, of good nature and spiteful fondness for showing off. Coleridge had only to inform him that a London publisher had offered him six guineas for his book of poems, for Cottle to promise him thirty on the spot. Being himself something of a scribbler, and own brother to that Amos whom Byron slyly prodded as one of "Bristol's sons" in *English Bards and Scotch Reviewers,* Joseph Cottle took upon himself to act the part of Providence towards the Pantisocratists, secretly hoping that they would never set sail for the banks of the Susquehannah. He made them a loan of five pounds to pay the landlord at College Street, and gave Southey the same amount as he had given Coleridge for the MS. of his poems, promising him a further sum of fifty pounds for *Joan of Arc.* He undertook moreover, to pay Coleridge at the rate of a guinea for every hundred lines, whether "rhyme or blank verse" which he sent him. This works out at about sixpence a line, a surprisingly large sum for those times, and one upon which even today some of our poets would not look askance.

This could hardly lead to a fortune, nor even to sufficient capital to purchase land in the New World, but it meant that the future was assured, provided they got straightway into harness. And as far as Sara and Edith were concerned, it meant the possibility of an early marriage. Joy and confidence reigned supreme among the Pantisocratists, and Coleridge set about preparing his first two lectures. He gave them in Wine Street, in the Assembly Room of the *Plume of Feathers,* which had, of course, been taken for the occasion by Cottle, who had also attended to all the advertising, and sent out the necessary invitations.

These first lectures, of a mainly historical character, were followed less than a month later by a couple of others. In these Coleridge brought the comparison he had been making between the English Revolution of the seventeenth century, and the French Revolution of the eighteenth, to a conclusion. This first course of lectures, at least, did not encounter the lack of enthusiasm, or downright hostility, which the public displayed towards those he gave some weeks later, under the catchpenny title of *The Plot Discovered,* with the avowed intention of showing up Pitt's intrigues. "Truth," declared Coleridge, "should be spoken at all times, but more especially at those times when to speak truth is dangerous." He was, indeed, taking no small risk in thus attacking that inscrutable statesman, who allowed no feeling of compunction to stand in his way, when he found it convenient to get rid of people who hampered his machinations, and spread a network of spies all over England and the continent.

Coleridge, moreover, had been rash enough to denounce the Slave Trade, upon which many a mighty fortune in Bristol had been founded, and he found the benches more sparsely occupied each time he gave his lecture. He began by sketching in the sociological and theological background to his subject, but soon gave this up, although it seemed to him of primary importance, and he had been hoping that it might bring in subscriptions towards his communistic experiment. The lectures came to an end in June, with the eleventh of the series, and only three out of them all have survived to this day, under their published title of *Conciones ad Populum.* They show undeniable signs of logical ability, as well as of closely-reasoned fervent and vivid eloquence. Even the over ambitiousness of which he may be accused, in that he approaches the problem of reform from too vast an angle, seems to me to prove the depth of his ideas. The question whether Coleridge's political application of revealed religion could ever be put into practice is, however, beside the mark. But it would, to my mind, be impossible to re-state the case for the equality and brotherhood of man better than by taking it, as he does, on the grounds of Christianity. It may be Utopian to suppose that only in so far as the individual approaches towards intellectual perfection does the outlook for humanity improve, for that involves the assumption that mankind is constantly evolving in the direction of better things. But, on the other hand, it implies a clear understanding of the truth, that no revolution can be a lasting one, nor can it finally suppress injustice, unless it proceed from "a general illumination of minds."

The disappointment which the comparative failure of his lectures and sermons occasioned Coleridge, was heightened by a difference of opinion between Southey and himself as to the proper way Pantisocratists should live. Coleridge wanted to have no servants in their society. It seemed to him a heresy to subject some men, and not others, to certain forms of manual labour. Southey, on the other hand, though he was quite willing that Shadrack and his children should be treated as equals, and in particular should eat at the common table, was yet determined that this old servant of his aunt's should continue to carry out the menial tasks to which he was accustomed.

No day now passed without one side or the other raising some fresh objection to the project which had seemed but yesterday so easy of realization. They were astonished to find how many obstacles had first to be overcome, and mutual fears arose as to the difficulties which would have to be smoothed over as soon as it was put into effect. The outlook was indeed black. "The more perfect our system is, supposing the necessary premises, the more eager in anxiety am I that the necessary premises exist," Coleridge explained to Southey. "O for that Lyncean eye that can discover in the acorn Error the rooted and widely spreading oak of Misery! *Quaere:* Should not all who mean to become members of our community be incessantly meliorating their temper and elevating their understandings? Qu: Whether a very respectable quantity of acquired knowledge (History, Politics, above all Metaphysics) without which no man can reason but with women and children?"

As for women, someone at Cambridge had prophesied to Coleridge that they would set the whole community by the ears, and ruin everything. This someone would no doubt have turned out a true prophet, if Pantisocracy had ever come into existence. Southey even wondered what would happen if "the greater part of our female companions should have the task of maternal exhaustion at the same time," thus leaving all housework to the rest. "This," answered Coleridge in all solemnity, "is very improbable. And," he continued, "though this were to happen, an infant is almost always sleeping and during its slumbers the mother may in the same room perform the little offices of ironing clothes or making shirts."

In *English Bards and Scotch Reviewers* Byron has left a picture of the Pantisocrats at Bristol, sitting and whiling away the time, thanks to their publisher's generosity, over great bowls of punch, in an atmosphere thick with tobacco-smoke. It is true that, having been unable to sail for America on the appointed date, owing to the shortage of funds, they did fritter away a good deal of time in grubbing up the last roots of what Coleridge had called the tree of Pantisocracy, and in scattering the sapless remains abroad in pointless discussions. Coleridge, who found this way of passing his life amid the dreams rather than the reality of things very much to his liking, contrived to put a fairly good face upon the matter, and appeared to be still living in hopes. But Southey, who had expressed the fear in February that it might not prove

possible to leave for several years, declared himself, by
the time May came round, to be "worn and wasted with
anxiety," throwing out a hint that they might do worse
than settle in Wales. . . . In vain did Coleridge apply
the "medicine of argument." He could not be revived,
and it became patent to all that Southey had lost heart.
His uncle, the Rev. Herbert Hill, had recently offered to
take him to Lisbon, and to make him an allowance until
he could take orders, when a living worth three hundred a year would be ready for him; and this, no doubt,
had something to do with his turning his back on schemes
of which he had laid the first foundations.

After he had prevailed upon Coleridge to follow Lovell's example, who had just fixed the date of his marriage
to Mary Fricker, and to plight his troth with Sarah at
St. Mary Redcliff, "poor Chatterton's church," on the
4th October 1795, Southey himself was married to Edith
six weeks later on the 14th November. Having thus done
all that his scrupulous conscience could suggest, he set
sail for Portugal the very day after his wedding, returning his disconcerted bride back into her sisters' keeping.
And her status seemed to her to have altered so little,
that for the time being she could see no good reason to
exchange her maiden name for the one that was now
legally hers to use.

PART III
POETRY COMES TO FLOWER

FROM CLEVEDON TO NETHER STOWEY

It was at a place some fifteen miles south-west of Bristol, upon the wide estuary of the Severn, and looking out over the Irish Sea, that Coleridge made his home immediately after his marriage. Thanks to sums advanced by his publisher, Cottle, he was able to rent for the modest sum of five pounds a year, a cottage at Clevedon, standing in its own garden, and comprising a ground floor with an attic above. The rusty tints of autumn creeping over the trees already foretold the approaching slumber of the countryside, when he entered into possession of his rustic retreat, but there was a promise of happiness in these last waking hours of all things.

Coleridge, who had seen the humble little place decked in all the fullness of summer, knew how charming it could look, with tamarisks screening it from view, myrtles surrounding it, and bushy jasmine rioting over the porch. At the slightest breath of air, the topmost rose on his briar would tap softly at his casement, or peer curiously within whenever he opened his window. Nothing there could offend its gaze—white-washed walls, a tiled floor, a dressing table which lacked a looking-glass, the bed. With the impetuosity of his years, Coleridge drank deep of a delight such as no mere clandestine pleasure had ever allowed him to guess at. After his engagement he had sung, rather foppishly perhaps, of triumphing over a maiden's fears, of the "Sweet Falsehood than endears Consent" so that the "Whispered 'No' is little meant." Now he unresistingly let "the gentle violence of joy" have its own way with him, amidst scenes reminding him of his childhood, and in much the same conditions, manual labour apart, as the Pantisocratists might have had to face. He was happy, although material comfort was almost entirely lacking. Most of the necessities of housekeeping were absent, and on the second day of his stay at Clevedon he was obliged to write to ask Cottle to obtain a number of articles in common use, from "one small tin tea-kettle" and "one flower dredge" (sic), to pairs of candle-sticks and of slippers, and a "keg of porter, raisins, currants and catsup," not to mention a Bible, as indispensable as the tea-kettle to an Englishman of Coleridge's faith.

Coleridge who, from the age of eight, had been torn from the sweetness of family life to lead a parasitic or vagabond existence elsewhere, could hardly fail to feel a sort of enraptured bewilderment on finding himself with a home of his own. The sensuousness which was in him, and in no way incompatible with his tendency to dream, could now be satisfied in a thousand ways. Abstract natures can take an entirely detached pleasure in their sensations. Coleridge, whose intuition was never so subtle

as when working in unison with the physical and spiritual
forces of his being, could perceive a deep and essentially
divine reality beneath the shows of earthly things. And
living as he did, thanks to his sensitive contemplation,
at the very heart of that harmony in diversity where it
no longer seems impossible to find some way through, or
round, the tangle of the universe, this is the way in which
this young man of twenty-three was the first to express
that law of inter-correspondences which was taken to
form the basis of a fruitful system of æsthetics:

> O! the one Life within us and abroad,
> Which meets all motion and becomes its soul,
> A light in sound, a sound-like power in light,
> Rhythm in all thought and joyance everywhere.

He discovered, as he put it, "dark similitudes" in the
most widely divergent objects and feelings, and even in
the way that sad thoughts and voluptuous impressions
seem to be linked together.

When, during the last days of the autumn of 1795, he
listened to the "stilly murmur of the distant sea," with
Sara's "soft cheek reclined" upon his shoulder, he was
storing up impressions which were to instil fresh elements
of beauty into his poetry. This had hitherto been sincere
and generous enough, but remarkable chiefly for its eloquence and faintly suggestive of the sermon. Now his
heart leaped in answer to each change in the face of

sky or sea, with a sympathy which was a proof of his originality, and lent his verses that personal note that is of the essence of lyrical feeling and, indeed, conditions it. Even in his best days he never sketched in a landscape with a surer hand or more vivid colours than at this time, when the impressions of his early manhood over-laid the woodland memories of his childhood or revived their freshness.

"the bleak mount
The bare bleak mountain speckled thin with sheep,
Grey clouds, that shadowing spot the sunny fields;
And river, now with bushy rocks o'er-brow'd. . . .
. . . Dim coasts, and cloud, like hills and shoreless Ocean.
(Reflection on Having Left a Place of
Retirement)

The true Coleridge, with his flashes of arresting expression, and an exactness in description which enriched his dream fancies with an amazing unfolding of reality, made his appearance in the poems he wrote at Clevedon, or immediately after leaving it, for, through one of those curious accidents which fate seemed to delight in putting in his way, he was only to enjoy its calm and solitude a bare three months. It almost seemed as though he were doomed never to taste any pleasure to the full, nor to carry out the plans his eager mind was apt to imagine as already accomplished. When his choice had lit one summer's day upon the little cottage which was to make a home for his wife and himself, he foresaw, as usual, a time of future happiness ahead, which was cut short by his departure before the return of spring.

Cares of all kinds were, indeed, thronging upon him. He realized afresh as he had done when serving with the Dragoons at Reading, how quickly difficulties increase and multiply, directly life is lived to the full, and not merely dreamed away. Because of that inability to conform to circumstances which we have already had occasion to note, he began to accuse himself of lacking in a sense of duty. Actually, until his heart stopped beating, he was continually to seek out human beings round whom his hopes might centre, a condition of things and a society that might seem the very image of his own design.

He could not bring himself to write the verses for which Cottle had promised to pay him at the rate of a guinea a hundred, and was in despair over his powerlessness to overcome the horror which the thought of writing to order inspired in him. The future seemed blotted out by a wall of darkness, and wherever he turned thorns seemed to enter his flesh. He would, so he told Cottle, have been more grateful to God "if he had made me a journeyman shoemaker, instead of an author by trade." He was shocked and distressed at the thought of having to beg bread for himself and his wife, yet her sighs and moans prevented him from committing the "flights of inspiration" to paper. He had to make an honest living in some way, and, failing poetry, which cannot, it is true be produced with clockwork regularity, he would seek to earn a livelihood by means of a review, such as he had contemplated starting some while back.

The year was barely out when he left Clevedon for Bristol, and set out at once upon an advertising campaign in the Midlands. He was still deeply imbued with the ideas which he had been thrashing out for the past year with Southey and the Pantisocratists; and the defection of his friend, to whom he had written that he considered him lost to himself, since he was lost to virtue, did not make him go back upon his principles.

Southey, whom he had worshipped so blindly had disappointed him by dallying "with that low, dirty, gutter-grubbing trull, worldly prudence"; but Pantisocracy was "not the question." Were it no more than "a miraculous milennium," he would never cease to look towards its light. He could, moreover, still remain faithful to its principles by founding the periodical to be called *The Watchman*,[1] and would even further the cause, for by it he would clear the sky of the lies and errors which obscure Truth.

The influence of Thomas Poole, whom he had visited at Nether Stowey a month before his marriage, doubtless contributed to the formation of his plans, and probably the statement of his aim "to proclaim the State of

---

[1] He had chosen this epigraph for *The Watchman:* "That all might know the Truth, and the Truth might make them free."

the Political Atmosphere, and to preserve Freedom and her Friends from Robbers and Assassins" is due to him as well. But it was, of course, Cottle who provided most of the funds needed to launch the review, and enrolled the first subscribers in Bristol itself. *The Watchman,* which was heralded by a prospectus called *Knowledge is Power,* was to see the light on the first of March. It was to cost no more than fourpence, and to be closely printed on thirty-two large octavo sheets. In order to avoid paying the stamp duty on weekly papers it was to appear one day later in each succeeding week. This was a plan not wanting in ingenuity, but it estranged people in practice, by giving them an uneasy feeling that their habits were being tampered with. But Coleridge never made the mistake of looking on the dark side, and he turned his face towards Birmingham where he first intended to preach, armed with impenetrable faith in his own success. He set out on this tour to the North, from Bristol to Sheffield, for the purpose of procuring customers, preaching by the way in most of the great towns as "an hireless volunteer, in a blue coat and white waistcoat, that not a rag of the woman of Babylon might be seen on me."

Robert Hancock has left a pencil drawing of him, now in the National Portrait Gallery, showing him in the costume he wore upon this missionary campaign. It is a pleasing likeness enough of this youthful champion of democracy and unitarianism, though its charm is marked by a certain effeminacy. What matter, since not by might was he to triumph? His ardour in no way damped by his failure in David Jardine's Chapel at Bath, where, by the end of his trial speech upon the corn laws, the whole of his audience—all very small fry, it is true, and no more than a handful in number—had dwindled away. He merely exchanged his blue coat for a black one when he went to speak at Birmingham, there recruiting a large band of subscribers, though not without a hard tussle for it.

A tallow-chandler, in particular, put up such a stiff fight, that, after "beginning with the captivity of nations," he thought to bring him to terms by announcing "the near approach of the millennium," though the man held out until he had quite finished dazzling him with "some of my own verses describing that glorious state out of *Religious Musings.*"

"And what, Sir, might the cost be?" asked the good man, his great round eyes staring out of a face as red as a sirloin, recovering himself after a succession of apparently knockout blows. Slightly taken aback, in his turn, by the question, which was far from what he had been expecting after such a spate of eloquence: "Only fourpence, Sir, each number to be published on every eighth day."

"That comes to a deal of money at the end of a year," observed the simple soul, who had, nevertheless, a head for figures.

Coleridge thereupon plied him up hill and down dale with proofs—that however large it might look at first sight, this sum was a mere nothing when put beside the quantity of goods he would receive in exchange: thirty-two pages at each delivery. But he felt slightly crestfallen when he saw that this huge figure, far from overthrowing his would-be subscriber's scruples, made him instead decline the honour of placing an order for *The Watchman.*

"Thirty-two pages," exclaimed the "taperman of lights"—"That's more than I ever reads, Sir, all the year round. I am as great a one, as any man in Brummagem, Sir! for liberty and truth and all them sort of things, but as to this, (no offence, I hope, Sir!) I must beg to be excused." Coleridge had imagination or guile enough to suggest that his reluctant customer might be supplied with the review cut down by a half, or even two-thirds, of its proper length, but this true man of business had so strong a dislike of everything that seemed to savour of overtime, and above all of intellectual overtime, that he declared that even this remnant would be too tiring to read. . . . The subject was then dropped.

Coleridge was to meet with many another a rebuff, and one he describes in *Biographia Literaria* as happening at Manchester, may serve as a sample of the rest, since it combines their features into a characteristic whole. A rich cotton-broker, whom he had been advised to approach, received him with contemptuous condescension.

He stuffed the prospectus Coleridge handed him into his pocket, without so much as a glance at it, and, completely turning his back on his unfortunate interlocutor, muttered that he was *"over-run* with these articles."

Coleridge was, no doubt, less able than the friends he made in every town he passed through, to judge of his own unfitness to make a success of the piece of work he had put in hand. The shrewd tradesmen of Birmingham, in particular, who had taken his cause to heart, insisted that he should turn his task over to others. A certain incident had finally convinced them that, like Tiresias, he could only stumble in the common ways of men, although his far-ranging vision could take in a wider sweep than theirs.

Invited to dinner with the liberal-minded shopkeeper who had given him the introduction to the tallow-chandler, Coleridge made ready, towards the close of the meal, to go and spend the rest of the evening with a dissenting minister of his acquaintance, but his host played him to smoke a pipe with him first over a glass of beer, in the company of a small group of "illuminati of the same rank." He was at length constrained to accept, though he at first begged to be excused, on the score that he had only smoked three or four times or so in his life, and nothing but medicinal herbs at that. Hardly, however, had he taken more than one or two puffs at his pipe, whose bowl for some unexplained reason he had filled half with tobacco and half with salt, than his eyes began to stream, and the glass of ale he had drunk made him feel squeamish. He walked on to the minister's house, on the plea that he needed fresh air and exercise, when he was once more overcome, and sank into an arm-chair, looking as white as a sheet, and oblivious to all that was going on in the room, where about fifteen to twenty people who had been specially invited to meet him were now collected. He slowly came to, and gazed all around him with eyes half-blinded by the glaring lights.

In order to give him time to recover from the embarrassment he must feel on coming to his senses again, someone inquired of him: "Have you seen a newspaper today, Mr. Coleridge?" Whereupon he answered, rubbing his eyes with his knuckles, "I am far from convinced that a Christian is permitted to read either newspapers or any other works of merely political and temporary interest." It may well be imagined what peals of laughter rang out on hearing such an answer on the lips of a man touring the country for the cause he was known to be promoting.

After visits to Nottingham, Derby, Sheffield, as well as Manchester, as already mentioned, Coleridge returned to Bristol, with over a thousand subscribers on his list. In spite of this comparative success, however, he was far less enthusiastic than before setting out, and seemed to have a secret foreboding that *The Watchman*'s days were numbered. It did, in fact, expire two and a half months after birth, with the tenth issue. The first came out slightly after its due time, but it might have been better had it never appeared. No one liked it. With the exception of one poem by the chief contributor, and a criticism of *Burke's Letter to the Duke of Bedford,* it contained nothing that could not be found elsewhere. What was more, it made no special appeal either to the Whigs or the Tories, nor yet to genuine republicans, and like all independent concerns, it was bound to meet with indifference from the public, which was only capable of being roused by party politics.

Far from toning down the impression made by the first number, the second only made matters worse. It contained an essay against fast days, with a motto from Isaiah, "Wherefore my bowels shall sound like an harp," and this satirical application of the text, by alienating the religiously-minded, lost it over five hundred subscribers at one blow. And Coleridge finally estranged the democratic element among his readers by declaring himself in the third and fourth numbers, in favour of the "Gagging Bills," for, he said, "Whatever might have been the motive for their introduction, they would at least have the advantage of preventing politicians from taking the floor upon subjects the principles of which they had never bottomed," and of hindering them from trying to plead to the poor and ignorant, instead of pleading for them.

Soon after its seventh appearance, *The Watchman* was to be found put up for sale in bundles as so much waste paper "in sundry old iron-shops at a penny a piece."

Coleridge had soon been forced to realize that the difficulty of founding a review is as nothing to the difficulty of filling its pages when once started. To that end he tossed pell-mell into his own all or nearly all he knew, served with a sufficient seasoning of rhetoric. An historical sketch of German manners, religion, and politics was followed by a study of the sugar question in the West Indies, and the whole wound up by an appeal to France to evacuate Holland. The encouragement which might have spurred him on was lacking, although there were some interesting ideas enough in his lucubrations, and above all, some fine images here and there, in which the poet was revealed. But he was quite ignorant of the art of feeling the pulse of the public, still less of flattering its tastes. On the 13th May, he was compelled to bid farewell to those few who had remained true to the end.

This he did half humorously. "Henceforward," he declared, "I shall cease to cry the state of the public atmosphere. The reason is short and satisfactory. The work does not pay its expenses." Part of my subscribers," he went on to add, "have relinquished it because it did not contain sufficient original composition, and a still larger because it contained too much."

And he recommended the first to transfer to the *Cambridge Intelligence,* the second to the *New Monthly* magazine—

Underneath this flippant tone, the poor day-dreamer

concealed a deep disappointment, and still deeper dismay. He wrote to Mr. Edwards, the Birmingham minister in whose house he had passed such a miserable evening under the baneful effects of tobacco flavoured with salt: "Since I last wrote you, I have been tottering on the verge of madness—Such has been my situation for the last fortnight—I have been obliged to take laudanum almost every night."

Thus the first time, it may here fitly be remarked, that the fatal drug appears in his life, it was under the influence of the despondency ensuing upon the most earnest effort he ever made to provide by his own exertions for his material wants. Later on, by a natural downhill slope he was to take to opium to deaden physical pain, yet the first time he resorted to it, he had hoped to soothe his mental distress. His young wife had already been pregnant for three months when he saw the edifice he had reared to shelter his whole household come tumbling about their ears. He had neither pluck nor presence of mind enough to stand up against adversity, and as it was a simple matter at that time to obtain any drug without prescription from a chemist, (only two thousand of whom from among a nominal ten thousand in the kingdom were qualified practitioners), he made no struggle against the temptation which lay ready to his hand, and which someone or other had recommended him to try as a means of escape from his miseries.

Fortunately Poole, who, it will be remembered, had

held his hand when Coleridge asked him to espouse Pantisocracy, now took it upon himself to suggest raising a subscription in favour of the unfortunate editor of *The Watchman,* putting his own name down for forty pounds. Numbers of subscribers had never paid their dues, and the business was being wound up with a deficit large enough to have sent Coleridge straight into a debtors' prison, had Cottle not taken upon himself to settle with the creditors.

Anxiety thus being over for the moment, Coleridge at once recovered his spirits. Besides, his book of poems had lately come out, and had been fairly well received. Coleridge was enjoying a minor triumph. He had friends and admirers with whom he corresponded voluminously. John Thelwall, in particular, had been exchanging letters with him, as a sequel to an article on Godwin, in *The Watchman,* and Coleridge now sent him a moral and physical portrait of himself.

I have already alluded to this portrait. Beginning by describing his face and appearance generally, Coleridge goes on to define his character and tastes, insisting, a little complacently perhaps, on their originality, but keeping, on the whole, fairly close to the truth: "I am and ever have been, a great reader, and have read almost everything—a library cormorant. I am deep in all out of the way books, whether of the monkish times, or of the puritanical era. I have read and digested most of the historical writers; but I do not *like* history. Metaphysics and poetry and 'facts of mind' that is, accounts of all the strange phantasms that ever possessed 'your philosophy,' dreamers, from Thoth the Egyptian to Taylor the English pagan are my darling studies. In short, I seldom read except to arouse myself, and I am almost always reading. . . ." He completes this sketch elsewhere: "I feel strongly and I think strongly. Hence, though my poetry has in general a hue of tenderness or passion over it, yet it seldom exhibits unmixed and simple tenderness or passion. My philosophical opinions are blended with or deduced from my feelings, and this, I think, peculiarises my style of writing, and like everything else, it is sometimes a beauty and sometimes a fault."

He wanted to convince Thelwall, whose atheism grieved him, that his faith was not due to sheer ignorance and that he had made the round of every philosophy in turn, and yet could see things from the spiritual or Christian standpoint. Nothing could be more curious than the ease with which he could slip from one style into another according to his correspondent, and his deftness in adapting himself to their respective habits of mind and temper. He is not the same man when writing to Poole as to Thelwall, and with Lamb he would shake off all solemnity, and talk as man to man. He was not merely making himself agreeable, still less was he being hypocritical. It was an effect of sympathy. The longing to understand naturally led him to take on the colour of those in whom he felt an interest. And now, all unmindful of the theories he had thrashed out with Godwin's disciple, or of the consolations he had lavished upon his ancient companion in misery at Christ's Hospital in the tragic grief that had befallen him, he poured out his heart in page after page not unworthy of Rousseau, for the benefit of a young man three years his junior whose mentor he had lately become, and who looked up to him with enthusiastic devotion.

This was Charles Lloyd, whom he had met at Birmingham, during his advertising campaign. He wrote, and even published, a certain amount of verse, in itself a sign of eccentricity in a wealthy banker's son. But he was a typically romantic young Englishman, to whom art, philosophy, and social idealism were a religion. He was a disciple of the author of the *Vicaire Savoyard, Émile* and the *Contrat Social,* and Coleridge seemed to him to reincarnate his deity. No sooner did he see him, than he was seized with an urgent desire to enjoy the close intimacy of such a man as this, whose conversation seemed, as he said to be a "revelation from heaven," and his parents must perforce allow him to throw in his lot with his. Coleridge, however, quite won their hearts, and Mr. Lloyd, a pious old Quaker, thanked the Lord for granting him the opportunity to hand his son over to the care of so remarkable a poet, "a very sensible religious man, who was educated for a clergyman, but for conscience sake declaimed that offer."

A bargain was soon struck as to the conditions upon

which Coleridge was to put the finishing touches to Charles's education, whose positive knowledge was by no means his strong point. He was to be paid eighty pounds a year, for which sum he was to endeavour for three hours every morning to impart to his pupil, languages, the elements of chemistry, geology, mechanics, metaphysics and optics, the science of mankind and of man, and, in short, "that knowledge and those powers of intellect which are necessary as the *foundation* of excellence in all professions, rather than the immediate science of *any*."

Coleridge, who had, since the 19th September, become the father of a son, to whom he gave the name of David Hartley, after the "great master of Christian philosophy," was anxious to take up his duties, and by the same token, to draw his first salary. He went, with Charles in his wake, down to Kingsdown near Bristol, where his little family was already established, and for the next two months he tasted all the delights of an existence that was almost all he had ever imagined. Charles seemed to him to have the makings of a genius. He discovered that his charge had a heart of rare goodness, and was charmed by the delicate affection and lively goodwill he showed towards himself.

"Charles Lloyd wins upon me hourly," he wrote to Poole, "his joy and gratitude to Heaven for the circumstance of his domestication with me I can scarcely describe to you." He began to toy once more with his Pantisocratic fancies, and had a vision of himself as a patriarch, surrounded by a numerous progeny. "I am," he declared to Mr. Lloyd, "anxious that my children should be bred up from earliest infancy in the simplicity of peasants, their food, dress, and habits completely rustic."

Alas, it was not long before Charles, who had given way to an apparently "ceaseless and indolent melancholy" and had been attacked by a painful bout of conscientious scruples, now suddenly revealed the malady hitherto latent in him. He fell prone on the ground one day, before the horrified eyes of his hosts, and began to roll on the floor in convulsions, and foaming at the mouth. At first they had no idea what ailed him. But these attacks soon returned and Coleridge was forced to admit to himself that his pupil must be suffering from epileptic fits. He was thrown into a state of unutterable despair. His conscience insisted that Charles should be sent straight back to Birmingham, but this meant destroying that certainty for the future he hoped to have acquired at last. He passed many a long day in the throes of indecision, not knowing whether to do as duty bade him, or to succumb to the desire to keep on this lodger, who assured him at any rate his daily bread. He was torn by terrible anxiety, made worse by neuritic pains which kept him awake all night; and hoping to "sop the Cerberus" by finding rest for body and soul, he again resorted to opium.

He wrote to Poole: "I take twenty-five drops of laudanum every five hours." There was nothing else, he excused himself by thinking, that could lighten the tortures that racked him mercilessly, and obliged him to "run about the house naked endeavouring by every means to excite sensations in different parts of my body and so to weaken the enemy by creating diversion." Poole must at all costs find him some kind of a small house with field attached where he could farm, somewhere in the neighbourhood of the tannery he owned at Nether Stowey. Had he not talked, not so very long ago, of "earning his bread by the sweat of his brow," in conversations with his faithless friends, and Southey, that "selfish, money-loving man"? He could rear enough corn and vegetables on an acre and a half of arable land to support himself, as well as his wife and child.

Poole's objections sent him off into endless lamentations. His impulsive, uncontrolled nature, which could change swiftly from the dreariest state of depression to excitement verging on hysteria and rising at times almost to violence, could never brook contradiction. No more practical plan than this could possibly be devised and he did not intend to hear a word against it. Some friends in whom he had confided, had set the seal of their approval upon it. They had gone further, and praised his great foresight. . . . He loathed having to beg for help or patronage. Besides, his habit and feelings had undergone a radical change. He hated company, and whenever he had to mix in it would "keep silence as far as social humanity will permit." His poetical vanity and political madness were over and done with. "All he now longed for was to live with Sara, his child, his books, and nature, and with Poole too, if Poole would but realize that his hopes of happiness in this world and the next depended on his finding him a roof to put over his head. "The evil face of Frenzy looks at me," he said, and there is no doubt that, as he wrote, he saw his wife dying of sorrow, and little Hartley of hunger, if he were to be thrown on the tender mercies of the literary profession. The ultra-imaginative whirlwind spirit saw the horrors rising ahead of the destiny which would overtake him, if once he were to tread the same pathway as Otway and Chatterton.

Poole took compassion on this mighty brain, wrestling in delirium with a nervous attack of childish or almost feminine affright. And as Coleridge had made up his mind to part from Lloyd, he asked him, at the end of 1796, to move into the cottage he had taken in his name, for the sum of seven pounds a year, at Nether Stowey.

THE YEARS OF GOLD

THE first thing that Coleridge did upon going to live at Nether Stowey was to revise the book he had brought out in the preceding year, with a view to a second edition. He cut out a few pieces, and added a few more, notably an *Ode to the Departing Year,* which is, in some sort, the political testament of his youth. Strong in the knowledge that his own conscience was clear, he once more took the "boastful bloody son of Pride" to task, and bade the world good-bye, announcing his intention of earning his bread by the cultivation of his own poor little plot of land alone. Lamb, indeed, made light of this resolve. "What does your worship know about farming?" he questioned. But although Coleridge may have been guilty of some exaggeration when he declared himself to be an expert gardener after no more than a few weeks' stay in the country, informing the Rev. Mr. Estlin that both his hands could "exhibit a callous as testimonials of their industry," he spared himself no pains until he had dug over every sod in the place, with a view to sowing corn and raising potatoes and other vegetables. He kept ducks and geese, besides the two pigs he talked of to Poole, and he found it easy to fancy himself running a considerable farm, or at any rate, one large enough for a man of moderate needs such as himself.

The two-storied house he was living in stands at the foot of the well-wooded Quantocks five or six miles inland, in a pleasantly picturesque part of the country, watered by rivers which flow through dingles, heather clad for the most part, or overrun with brambles. Three steps, widening out at the top into a broad balcony, lead up to it in front, with a low wall all round, such as may often be seen in Normandy. The front part of the house is plain, with a little porch to the door, and four windows, two above and two below. Close by there ripples past a stream of pure, clear water, trilling out over and over again the three notes of the only little song it can sing. But the rear of the cottage is far the prettier, with its gushing well and kitchen garden in the shade of a bowery lime tree.

Coleridge had a single servant, Nanny, for his wife was still nursing Hartley, and housework was too much for her, more especially as Charles Lloyd, whose health had lately taken a turn for the better, had once more come to live at his tutor's. He stayed a very short while, it is true, and as soon as he had left, Coleridge soon felt his loneliness weigh heavy upon him. In spite of all he might say, he could not do without society, or at any rate, a circle of attentive friends, able to stir up his ever active mind into formulating his thoughts, or into giving substance to the dreams ever coursing through it. He did, indeed, try to induce Thelwall to come to live near him. Meanwhile he invited Cottle to stay, then Lamb, who paid him a visit in July, and he himself went over to Racedown in Dorset, to see William Wordsworth, whose acquaintance he had probably made in Bristol in 1795.

He was immediately taken captive upon meeting him, as upon that other occasion when he met Southey. But that first time, one part alone of his nature had been aroused, and that no doubt the shallower. The first flush of a young man's political ideals, particularly when these are of a generous nature, is soon overpast.

Although Wordsworth was a republican, it was no mere mental tie which drew Coleridge so closely to him. He had recovered from his enthusiasm for democratic ideals, and the fealty he still paid them was based on his religious philosophy alone. When he thought of Wordsworth merely as a man who had travelled in France and attended meetings of the Jacobins, he had done no more than share the same regrets that their country was opposing the ideals of the Revolution. No other person after Southey could have kindled his ardour for social reform. What Coleridge now delighted to find in Wordsworth was the poet who had withdrawn into the country, in order to devote himself to his art, wearied and shocked by the excesses and aggression of the demagogues of the Revolution. He had already known his *Descriptive Sketches* whilst still at Cambridge, where he had been

struck by the deep feeling and intelligent observation
which they showed.

Wordsworth's conversation, which had its springs in
what might be called a philosophy of the countryside,
rather than of nature, completed the conquest. He could
discern in Wordsworth's words that faculty of discern-
ing the poetic elements contained in the humblest things
which he himself possessed, independently of his deep
sense of the mystery of life. But it was through the contrast in their thought that Wordsworth revealed him to
himself, or awoke his as yet slumbering creative energy.
Wordsworth would, perhaps, not have made so strong an
impression upon him, had he only discovered the points
they had in common. Just as Southey's doctrinaire spirit
had furnished him with the lively antithesis to his own
Utopian genius at the age of twenty-three, so did Wordsworth's fine moral soundness weld it together and off-
set it, thus enabling him to understand, as he had dimly
guessed at the time of the Reading episode, how he might
put his sadly wavering meditations, his lack of steadfastness, and the difficulty his soul felt in adapting itself
to reality, to lyrical account. Wordsworth's grave attitude,
proclaiming that "every great poet is a teacher," gave
him no encouragement to continue in the eloquent or
discursive vein in which his imagination had first expressed itself, and turned him from the didactic purpose
for ever.

"I cannot write without a body of thought," he had written to Southey in a letter dated 1794. Wordsworth's idea of the duty devolving upon all writers, in prose as well as verse, convinced him he had been mistaken in making social injustice the theme of most of his poems. As soon as Wordsworth and he had been talking for an hour or two, Coleridge saw that he had fallen into a grievous error in devoting himself to a kind of poetry quite unsuited to his temperament, just as a man might realize how useless it is to try to imitate the nightingale's song as soon as he has heard it for himself.

Wordsworth, however, was no great talker. He was, on the other hand, silent or almost taciturn, with something of the rough hewn uncouthness of the country preacher or even the peasant about him. Coleridge had to bear most of the brunt of the conversation, whilst Wordsworth would listen with grave attention, putting in from time to time a well-considered word or two, which would reveal his original outlook and reflective habit of mind. He gave an impression of power, especially to Coleridge, who yet was unable to prevent himself feeling slightly restive under this ponderous stillness. "The Gods approve the depth and not the tumult of the soul," said Wordsworth. Nor could anyone have possessed a less bookish kind of intellect than this solitary man, who spent the better part of his time in watching men and things around him. Though Coleridge sprinkled literary and philosophical allusions through his works with a free hand, Wordsworth seemed determined, out of a kind of stolid coquetry, never to draw upon other men's stores, as though making it plain he was rich enough to do without. He talked to Coleridge about himself, in tones that were neither braggart nor unduly humble, with the self-sufficiency of the type of man who is impervious to irony, and who, moreover, forbears, or else disdains, to survey his thoughts in the round, from a little distance away, as though they were someone else's and not his own.

This conception of poetry had come to him in a moment, in a lightning flash, whilst he was strolling along an English country lane, and its certainty, founded as it was upon supporting facts, imposed itself upon him. Having lost the religious faith of his early youth, he was still uncertain as to the character he wished to give to the glorification, or exaltation, of the phenomena of nature he had studied with minute and almost scientific care. Coleridge, by celebrating the omnipresence of God, enabled him to discover spiritual life in the smallest, as well as the greatest things of creation, and convinced him that each one of them has its own way of interpreting the divine language. The idea that nature is a real being, the mouthpiece of God speaking through its agency to man, was actually Coleridge's own, having already been expressed by him in *Religious Musings*. Wordsworth, though he widened its scope considerably, nevertheless borrowed the idea from him. He felt for Coleridge nearly as great an admiration as he inspired in him. "The only wonderful man I ever knew was Coleridge," he declared, and by leaving Racedown in July to settle at Alfoxden, three miles from Nether Stowey, he proved what store he set by his new friend's acquaintance.

His sister Dorothy accompanied him thither. This girl of twenty-six, his junior by a year, was in herself an unusual person. She responded with an almost morbid delicacy, so prompt and subtle was it, to the daily sights of nature, or to the ideas and feelings expressed in her presence, and noted her impressions in her journal, a storehouse from which her brother drew forth treasures to enrich his poems. She was not unlike another Lucile de Chateaubriand, but there was something more country-bred, more of the wild creature about her passionate ardour, her very fineness— "Exquisite," so Coleridge described her, enchanted by her depth of feeling. "Her taste is a perfect electro-meter," he cried with half jesting enthusiasm. He rejoiced to see how tensely she was set quivering by the faintest and most fleeting changes in light and sound. She noted down her almost miraculously fresh sensations quite simply and directly, neither heightening them nor toning them down, and though Wordsworth, when he profited by them, clothed them in the grave symbols of his thought, Coleridge would have accused himself of profanation had he done more than test the truth of his own experience with the help they provided.

"We are three people, but only one soul," cried Coleridge, who had definitely given up delving in field or garden, and passed nearly all his time at the Wordsworths', from whose house the elms hid from view the cottage where dwelt in peace "my babe and my babe's mother." . . . For Sara had no share in these conversations among the three, Samuel, William, and Dorothy, who would often set out together for long rambles up the lower slopes of the Quantocks, or through the deeply winding combes, hotly discussing as they went the questions they had so much at heart. That unassuming soul, though she may, as Lamb averred, have written verse at one time, was never carried away by questions such as these, nor did she, indeed, feel any jealousy towards the kind of wild woman of the woods of whom her husband thought so highly, plain and swarthy though she was (a gypsy De Quincey used to call her), and afflicted with a slight impediment in her speech. She would see the three off as they set out on one of their expeditions with a faintly ironical and yet indulgent enough smile.

Coleridge, she knew, was not the man to take love lightly. All or nearly all of its pleasures which he had known, he had known through her. The marriage tie apart, he was a creature scarce compounded of flesh at all, save in so far as to heighten the images his imagination craved, and which he identified with his dreams, though only to enjoy them in an indolent and passive fashion. Those he might have known in Sara's arms were too chaste to have any part or lot in the delirium of his senses. Passion lay beyond his ken and as, for lack of it, he did not, by a kind of æsthetic perversion, associate the joys of sight, scent, and hearing with the pleasures of the flesh, he never put those pleasures on the same level as the impressions made upon him by the animate world, which appeared to him like an infinitude of other worlds, perceptible down to their minutest details. This much at least must be said: whether it were that the possession of a woman never came up to the expectations of his mind, or that it lay outside the scope of the ideal world disclosed to him in the song of a nightingale, the fragrance of a rose, or the shifting colours of the sky, it meant no more to Coleridge than a passing gratification; and he no more mingled the satisfactions of the sexual instinct with his pantheistic ecstasies, than those of eating and drinking. It was in the pure region of immaterial life that he would, as Baudelaire would have put it, carve out a niche for the disembodied soul of woman, though he adorned that niche with the splendours nature had lavished. So we may be forgiven for thinking that, without the shadow of a guilty intention in his thoughts of her, (*guilt was a thing impossible with her*), without even realizing the exceptional nature of the feelings she inspired in him, he yet loved Dorothy with the best and finest part of his nature, and re-fashioned her daily in the likeness of his musing thought.

Did she, girl as she was, care for him in any other way? For although, for the first "three minutes" of their acquaintance, she thought him very plain, describing him as pale, thin, "with a wide mouth, thick lips and not very good teeth," yet she soon went on to admire his beautiful and intelligent eyes, which spoke "every emotion of his animated mind." It is possible. But her virginal innocence kept her unaware, even when she was led by her impulsive nature into showing too lively a sympathy, and she would suddenly turn self-conscious and seem shy or awkward, remembering her sex and that she was but a girl. She played—as a child might—a glorious game with Coleridge, as well as with her brother. And, in reality, she saw no more than a brother in this friend of hers, whose lot had been cast in the same lines as her own, and who, moreover, was already provided with a wife. "His conversation teems with soul, mind, and spirit," she wrote, and rejoiced to find him so kind and merry, "noisy" and "gamesome as a boy" was how Wordsworth described him—and of such an even temper.

He had just finished a play called *Osorio,* commissioned by Sheridan for Drury Lane. Later, when the play was not accepted, he re-named it *Remorse;* for Sheridan, indeed, never so much as took the trouble to acknowledge it, and allowed it to be sent astray by some unknown person. Coleridge already revealed in it how much his mind was haunted by the supernatural, of a kind which he still confused with the fantastic which was in vogue at

the time, and quickened by the novels of Mrs. Radcliffe
and Lewis, author of *The Monk*. The feeling for the invisible world does, however, shine through his drama,
mingling with landscapes of dream, and though it is full
of the usual stock-in-trade of melodrama—as for example,
the efforts made by Alvar, one of the chief protagonists,
to kindle a spark of remorse in the breast of his brother,
who thinks he has caused his death—yet the underlying
psychological springs are often strikingly shown.

It may be seen from Coleridge's correspondence with
William Lisle Bowles, that he was already aware that
a poet or novelist must give a basis of spiritual truth to
the supernatural, if he would not disappoint the curiosity
he has aroused. "The interest," he writes, "is completely
dissolved once the adventure is finished, and the reader
when he has got to the end of his work, looks about in
vain for the spell which had bound him so strongly
to it." He is disappointed, that is, and feels a kind of
distaste because this spell was of a merely physical nature, with nothing moral nor intellectual about it.

Coleridge read *Osorio* to Wordsworth and Dorothy together. She hung upon his words, and the lightest signs
of approval or disapproval this girl gave him taught him
more about the good and weak points in his work than
all the plaudits and criticisms of the public.

It was now October. Among the rocks on "Kilve's
delightful shore," where they usually preferred to sit,
looking out across the yellow waters of Bristol Channel,

to where the coppery mass of the hills loomed darkly above them, an interchange, nay, an intermingling of soul took place, which must surely count among the events that have most strongly influenced the march of mind. The only talk, however, was of poetry. Thelwall, who had, temporarily come to stay in Coleridge's neighbourhood, was himself smitten with the same fever as the three inseparables, and, though he never, perhaps, took part in their transcendental discussions, he did, at any rate, refrain from introducing the subject of politics.

"Citizen John," said Coleridge to him one day, when he and Wordsworth were showing him a remote valley near Alfoxden, "this is a fine place to talk treason in!"

"Nay! Citizen Samuel," replied Thelwall, "it is rather a place to make a man forget that there is any necessity for treason!"

A spy whom Pitt, alarmed at hearing of "such a conjuration of extreme politicians," had dispatched to Nether Stowey, soon wearied of his watching. All he had been able to overhear of the conversations of these dangerous disturbers of the peace, as he stalked them in their walks abroad, convinced him that the only plot they were hatching was to "put Quantock and all about here in print." He sped disappointedly back to London, foiled of his mission, and feeling an increasing contempt for rhymsters who were fit only to brew sedition against the laws of syntax.

Truth to tell, it was far more than a mere revolution

in form that Coleridge and Wordsworth were contemplating. Though it may have seemed a trifling matter enough which decided them to write in collaboration— they wanted to pay the expenses of a little expedition to Linton in North Devon—yet they were obeying a far more momentous call when they decided to yoke their genius to compose the *Lyrical Ballads*. Breaking with the tradition that had reigned over English poetry since the so-called Classical Era, two writers of verse were determined for the first time to define, illustrating by examples, the two kinds of lyric poetry to which all others may be reduced, or which contain them all.

But we must refer to the *Biographia Literaria,* in which Coleridge gives a critical analysis of his work, explaining it with dazzling lucidity, laying stress on the intentions underlying it, which, as I have already stated, were manifestly the result of the impact of Wordsworth's personality upon his own.

"During the first year that Mr. Wordsworth and I were neighbours, our conversations turned frequently on the cardinal points of poetry, the power of exciting the sympathy of the reader by a faithful adherence to the truth of nature, and the power of giving the interest of novelty to the modifying colours of imagination— The thought suggested itself (to which of us I do not recollect) that a series of poems might be of two sorts. In the one, the incidents and agents were to be, in part at least, supernatural; and the excellence arrived at was to consist in the interesting of the affections by the dramatic truth of such emotions, as would naturally accompany such situations, supposing them real. And real in *this* sense they have been to every human being who, from whatever source of delusion, has at any time believed himself under supernatural agency. For the second class, subjects were to be chosen from ordinary life; the characters and incidents were to be such, as will be found in every village and its vicinity, where there is a meditative and feeling mind to seek after them, or to notice them when they present themselves.

"In this idea originated the plan of the Lyrical Ballads; in which it was agreed, that my endeavours should be directed to persons and characters supernatural, or at least romantic; yet so as to transfer from our inward nature a human interest and a semblance of truth sufficient to procure for these shadows of imagination that willing suspension of disbelief for the moment, which constitutes poetic faith."

It is of no moment to ask here whether Wordsworth fulfilled that part of the program which concerned himself, that is to say, if he always limited himself as he had proposed to giving the charm of novelty to things of every day, and to exciting in the mind feelings as intense as any the supernatural can arouse, by awaking it to the beauty of the world unfolding around it. . . . But though the author of *The Excursion* became more didactic than suggestive as he grew older, though at the end of his glorious career, he sank from familiar simplicity into childish triviality, and from the serene meditation of the philosopher into the garrulous anecdotage of the moralist, this cannot detract from the excellence of his point of departure. He and Coleridge had seized from the very first, two aspects, essentially differing, under which poetry is revealed to the artist, and appears to him in its integrity. There is no ambiguity possible. Whether it be objective (or realistic), or else subjective (or imaginative), the changes it forces a poet to wreak on life itself by the mere act of interpreting it, must be imposed either upon the neutral or affective plane, granted that the well-known saying: *Nihil est in intellectu quod non prius fuerit in sensu,* is even truer of the heart than of the mind. By taking nature as his model, and his own nature as his study, by keeping watch upon himself as he loved and suffered, and upon the lives of men and things, by diving down into consciousness, and sweeping the light of analysis over those dark and turgid depths, Wordsworth did, by adopting all or part of this program, stand at what Coleridge called one of the two cardinal points of poetry. There remained the other. Everything seemed to suggest that Coleridge should take this as his own. The inspiration which had made him choose the supernatural as his lyrical province, persuading him that its sole interest is psychological, he derived from his metaphysical genius. This by a vivid, but diffused sensuousness, led him to see the aspects of life as a visionary in a spectral light.

It must be noted in passing, that objective poetry, which is in its essence realistic, especially depends upon the character and moral personality of its author. The mania for preaching to which Wordsworth was to succumb is proof enough of this. It is quite the other way with subjective poetry. It depends upon the temperament of its creator. Indeed, by intellectualizing his sensibility, it bears it aloft into regions where it is safe from the influences of the outer world, and there is free to manifest itself in its purity, utterly indifferent to, or rather ignorant of, all that lies outside itself, and its own desires and pleasures. The apparent exclusion of all reality from the poems which Coleridge was about to write, was the result of his detachment from practical life, his perplexity at the laws, and boredom with the duties, prescribed by men. Not, as will sufficiently appear in the sequel, that he did not wish (with the ardour we bring to those tasks for which we are least fitted) to play his part honourably as a man, whilst yet, and above all other things, accomplishing his divine mission. He had a conscience, and that a clamorous one. But to do its bidding, filled him with care rather than joy. Coleridge was a speculative genius rather than a moral intelligence. And moreover the time when he was writing the *Ancient Mariner, Kubla Khan,* and the *Three Graves,* as well as the first part of *Christabel* was the period of his life when he was most stirred by reading Berkeley. He was filled with such enthusiasm for that philosopher, that he called the son who was born to him on the 30th May, 1798 by that name, just as he had called the child born in 1796 by the name of Hartley.

What then was Berkeley's teaching? That we possess no ideas apart from particular ideas, all of which, even those which seem most general, can be reduced to ideas of qualities with which our senses acquaint us. We know nothing beyond our own sensations. (Objects have no being unless they are perceived, *esse est percipi*). To explain our ideas as coming from the exterior world we do not know, is to explain what is dim by something dimmer still (*Obscur non per obscurius*). They can only reach us through a spirit, i. e. God.

Berkeley, therefore, interprets ideas through sensations, or to put this somewhat differently, he sets up the principle of the idea as sensation, and in so doing eliminates matter. To believe only in matter involves materialism. To believe in it, and in God as well, involves pantheism, since it is impossible to separate matter from God. All that lies between God and us, or the divine ideas and ourselves, are our sensations, which enable us to know these.

Until he read the *Treatise on the Principles of Human Understanding,* Coleridge had never—not even at the time when he made a study of Spinoza—found a philosopher whose teaching matched so perfectly as Berkeley's his own belief in the ideal nature of the world. In the

great Irishman's absolute spiritualism, his speculative genius found the most favourable soil of any for the growth
of the work his ardent imagination and sensitive temperament suggested to him.

Everyone knows the story of how *The Ancient Mariner*
came to be written. Whilst Coleridge was on a walking
tour with the Wordsworths near Dulverton, the idea of
this immortal poem was suggested to his mind by a
dream of a phantom ship told him by his friend Cruik-
shank, as well as by a story from Shelrocke related to
him by Wordsworth, of a voyage round Cape Horn during which an albatross was shot down by some sailors,
in the hope that its slaughter might lighten the foul
weather. But though he began to write it in the early
autumn of 1797, he only finished it, according to Dorothy
Wordsworth, some months later in November, on "a
beautiful evening, very starry," lit by the gleam of "the
horned moon." Others think that Coleridge borrowed
part of his idea from the *Epistle of St. Paulinus to Maca-*
rius. But in alluding to the sources from which *The*
Ancient Mariner may be derived, I have no wish to seem
to explain away the miracle of its composition. Coleridge
was at the time obsessed with the idea of remorse, round
which *Osorio* is written. And the spiritual truth of the
succession of psychological states set down in *The Ancient*
Mariner owes nothing to any story.

Set beneath the luminous blazon of a quotation from
Thomas Burnet, of which the following is the first sen-

tence, *"Facile credo plures esse naturas invisibiles quam visibiles in rerum universitate,* Coleridge's poem reveals a new aspect of man's spiritual activity. No artist before Coleridge's time had, by forcing his imagination on to the plane of the ideal, contrived so happily to make a world after the image of his own personality, with elements borrowed from ours. No artist had realized so fully before his desire to quicken the dreams of his religious and philosophic thought into life, or to rationalize the phenomena of life in accordance with his thought. In *The Ancient Mariner,* Coleridge achieved a miracle. He created a whole mythological world of his own, so that we accept it as ours all the time we are reading the poem, which for his purpose is quite sufficient. The poem is the most extraordinary example of sleight of hand ever seen. It is an incantation, an enchantment observant in its least details, and in the whole atmosphere which envelopes it, yet never does he seek to force his supernatural upon us.

And in the first place, where are we? in a harbour. But at what period? There is no answer. Coleridge's ballad is compact of anachronisms. Whilst everything we can gather about the rustic wedding that is being celebrated in the wings, and the character of the musical instruments playing dance tunes, might lead us to imagine ourselves in the eighteenth century, yet when the Ancient Mariner kills the albatross, he does so with a cross-bow, a weapon seldom used later than the sixteenth century. And again,

if at the entrance to the harbour stands a lighthouse,
which would therefore seem to suggest the time of the
first great voyages of discovery, how does it then come
to be haunted by a hermit, the same as those who used to
build their little oratories at the foot of some oak tree in
Celtic forests? And what had the sailors gone to seek
in those southern seas, where they seemed to be following
on no man's tracks? Were they merchant-adventurers,
pirates, or skilled navigators? asks M. Jules Douady in
La Mer et les Poètes Anglais, in an ingenious commentary which I have here reproduced in part. No man
knows. And never before, either, has any ship been the
butt of such queer and tricksy hostility from the elements.
To what capricious powers has the God of Christians—
who undoubtedly exists, since we are told of the intervention of the Virgin Mary, what time the rain began to
fall—handed these elements over, and do not these same
powers belong to some pagan cosmogony, in the mysterious laws which govern their actions, as well as in the
arbitrariness of the decrees they issue in the name of an
iniquitous morality? Infernal they cannot be, since it is
a sin to offend them, yet horrid creatures dwell within
their kingdoms, as in the caverns of the nether regions,
and their supreme officers of justice, Death, and Life-in-
Death, decide their victims' fate by the throw of the dice.
And yet, though they can do as they will with the bodies
of those who have offended them, and can even save
them from decay, they can have no hold over their

souls. Where these are concerned, the angels re-assert their rights. And finally, by slaying the albatross, the Ancient Mariner must have done more than commit an act of cruelty; he must have been guilty of some real crime, that is to say, he must have slain a man in the guise of the innocent bird, according to the Brahminic belief in the transmigration of souls, since he has to undergo so awful a penalty. Buddhism, however, denies the efficacy of prayer, and we have seen that it is in prayer that the poor luckless wight seeks salvation. There is, indeed, no single line in Coleridge's disturbing poem—wherein, as he has himself remarked, the very ship's course is described awry—which does not give rise to an objection or require a commentary. But, as M. Douady again says, "The kind of marginal gloss which accompanies it, strophe upon strophe, serves to strengthen the impression of physical and moral mystery it breathes. This gloss might almost have been penned by some monk of the Middle Ages, a contemporary of the hermit of exorcizing powers, in whose cell many a volume of forbidden lore lay hid from view."

The Ancient Mariner has been worked out with such magical skill that it reads plausibly, in spite of its unusual happenings. Its supernatural world is made convincing by the realism of the telling, whilst the mind is overpowered by the force and beauty of the images through which this realism is made manifest. The poet takes care to make no appeal to the reason, so that he

makes us his accomplices in the creation of his phantas-
magoria. He only appeals to the most primitive instincts
of our nature to approve his choice of materials for the
spiritual structure he is building. He lets high-tensioned
emotion obtain control of his imagination, and his thought
is closely bound up with pictorial and musical suggestion. Thus, although his tale is pitched in narrative form,
he achieves what is known in England as *absolute poetry,* or what M. Paul Valéry recently described as
poésie pure, thus improving upon the pleonasm invented
by the Parnassian School, who were the first to speak
of *poésie poetique pure.*

Coleridge's contemporaries, as we shall see, paid little
attention to his poem. But from the first there was an
inner ring of intellectual people whom it puzzled. They
picked faults in those very things in which its originality lies. Southey, who could see no more in *The Ancient
Mariner* than the "mystery" then in vogue, called it a
"Dutch attempt at German sublimity," the Dutch being
looked upon at the time as the country cousins of Europe. Wordsworth echoed Lamb, who said he was sorry
that Coleridge had not been aiming at the truth, and
reproached him with the vagueness of the principal figure
in the poem. He thought that the character of the Ancient Mariner himself did not stand out distinctly enough,
and that he was swept on by events without acting for
himself.

In later years Coleridge never acknowledged the faintest truth in any of these criticisms. Instead, he came to regret that his poem had any more moral at all, "than the *Arabian Nights* tale of the merchant sitting down to eat dates by the side of a well, and throwing the shells aside, and lo! a genie starts up, and says he *must* kill the aforesaid merchant, because one of the date shells had, it seems, put out the eye of the genie's son." But his conviction that he had, by metaphysically interpreting the phenomena of nature, succeeded in creating a kind of poetry that was truer than reality, was somewhat shaken by the unanimity of the opposition it met with. The second edition appeared with the sub-title *A Poet's Musings,* to show that he had not drawn his picture from life. But this was only a momentary hesitation. At bottom, Coleridge remained convinced that poetry should never be at the pains to prove anything, and should never aim at edification. It may, however, soothe the anxious soul, and through the musing mood it induces, lead to some guiding rule of conduct. He refused, therefore, to believe that poetry should obey the laws of logic, or that the literature of pedestrian utility was to serve as a model for the literature of pleasure in the fullest sense of the word. So to Coleridge, as later on to Edgar Allan Poe, the true antithesis to poetry seemed to be science. The man whose business lies with words, and the feelings and ideas these express, he placed at the opposite pole to the man whose business lies with facts. He was convinced that the poet's synthetic intuition supplies the place of the exactness required by the scientist, who can never take precautions enough in his experimental researches.

But when he went straight to Shakspere, to study the workings of lyrical creation as they were to be seen in the mind of that prolific genius towering so high above himself, he showed this intuition, as we shall see, entering into, and taking possession of the universal soul it has already dimly perceived. At the time when he wrote *The Ancient Mariner,* and was on the point of writing other poems, such as *Christabel* and *Kubla Khan,* that were yet airier and more insubstantial, he already knew that the poet can only transmute the plant, mineral, and animal life around him into an ideal world, if he can attain to that state in which dreams become the only true reality.

"O Wordsworth! We receive but what we give," he cried a little later than this, in *Dejection;* which is as much as to say, that there is, for the poet, a close bond between nature and his own nature, or that the people and things which seem to him to be thronging earth and sky are only the projections of the very forms of his own existence. We receive "the light reflected as a light bestowed," says Coleridge again, in the poem *To William Wordsworth.* Once it is possible, through the power of the intellect, to distinguish an object from the emotion it has called forth the miracle never happens at all. This eliminates the imagination, through which alone man could go back to the state of innocence he was in before he tasted the forbidden fruit, and when he still thought that the phenomena of life in general, and of his own life, were the same. The highest achievement of lyric poetry must, therefore, be to lend reality to heavenly things, or divinity to material things, through outward influences and the properties of our own selves combined. Every attempt to refer to reason, or to judge for ourselves, can only hinder its accomplishment. Macaulay has put this well: "Poetry produces an illusion on the eye of the mind, as a magic lantern produces an illusion on the eye of the body. And, as the magic lantern acts best in a dark room, poetry effects its purpose most completely in a dark age. As the light of knowledge breaks in upon its exhibitions, as the outlines of certainty become more and more definite, the hues and lineaments of the phantoms which the poet calls up grow fainter and fainter. We cannot unite the incompatible advantages of reality and deception, the clear discernment of truth and the exquisite enjoyment of fiction."

Coleridge was aware of this. He knew that unless a poet could create a world anew for himself, full of darkness as at the first, so that he might interpret life under cover of that darkness, he would be unable to secure "the willing suspension of disbelief for the moment which constitutes poetic faith," or to produce the illusion which men would ever expect of him.

Coleridge never looked upon a poem as a demonstration, or as merely illustrating some truth. On the contrary, it came to him as an indistinct impression, which would only flow into rhythm as each of its component parts was embodied in some image. There could, of course, be no more difficult task than to dive down into the ecstasy in which the mysterious necessity for the existence of a poem of this kind is borne in upon the mind. It takes an exceptional nature, in which the powers of thinking and feeling are equal, to combine the spiritual and emotional powers needed, and it is impossible simply to dismiss the miracle as chance.

Ninety-nine times out of a hundred an inspiration that seems of staggering importance at the time is no more than a jumbled shadow-show, which is seen to be devoid of any suggestive value when once its bizarre outline has faded on the screen. No such inspiration can succeed in spreading its beams abroad, unless it be lit up from within by some clearly defined principle or a pure intellectual concept. But in Coleridge's case, it is surprising to find that the part played by the will in the phenomenon of that "magic transformation," which is, according to M. Henri Brémond, pure poetry (a part which was, however, greatly exaggerated by Edgar Allan Poe), proved to be little or nothing. Traces of the art of the "literary histrio" which Poe analysed slyly in the *Rationale of Verse* are still to be found in *The Ancient Mariner*. But it was only through exceptional powers, such as fakirs employ to fall into a trance at will, that Coleridge could, as in writing *Christabel,* reach that blissful condition—

the dream condition in fact—in which the mind unfolds and develops completely, ignoring the laws governing the relations between man and man, as well as those of the universe. Except for Blake, who composed his *Milton and Jerusalem* by thirty lines at a stretch, as though writing under dictation, no other poet has done creative work so wholly free from the control of his reason as did Coleridge, by yielding himself up to that psychic automatism of which the Surrealists would like to make use as a process.

Most writers have known moments in the heat of inspiration when, having left some vague idea lying fallow in the mind, they have later found that it has clothed itself in some image. It is a process they do not seek to define, nor do they make any deductions from it of a cause lying outside themselves. Now this process, which is exceptional in the case of other writers, was habitual with Coleridge. More highly favoured than they, he was able to eschew convention and rid himself of reality. And in his "day dreams" he found it an easier matter to forget the data of experience altogether, than to pay any attention to them at all.

Hence comes the ineffable charm of *Christabel,* beyond even the fascination in which *The Ancient Mariner* is steeped. Walter Pater had *Christabel* in mind when he said that even Shakspere's ghosts seem coarse, beside the airy delicacy with which Coleridge's spiritual imaginings glide into "our inmost sense." There is no miraculous element in *Christabel,* as there is in *The Ancient Mariner.* Coleridge achieves his effect by a "daylight enchantment," of such subtle power that Shelley is said to have fainted, the first time he read the poem. But in spite of the brooding atmosphere of an impending struggle between the forces of good and evil which goes to make the organic unity of the poem, it has no structural unity of composition. It is easy to see why Coleridge never felt he could finish it unless he could return to the same state of spiritual grace in which it had first come to him. Later, Dr. Gillman declared that Coleridge had explained to him how he meant *Christabel* to end. Although he stated a year before he died, that the whole plan of the poem was still present to his mind as it had been all along, yet I should rather be inclined to believe that its idea, or substance, was too elusive to be grasped by the usual intellectual methods he could command. Clear though it may have been to his inward eye, it grew dim whenever he tried to withdraw it from his subconscious mind, to be handled and examined like any chain of circumstances or set of facts by his memory and his reason. Even so do the towers and spires we build in dreams come toppling down when we wake in the morning, the more busily we have spun our cobwebs. Only those which are made of any coarser material are likely to remain standing. *Christabel* was born of an impression which was ever shrouded by a veil of transparent unreality. It took on an outward semblance of fragile beauty, but the power was never strong enough to allow of anything further being grafted upon it. Lamb, in fact, with great good sense, advised Coleridge to leave his unfinished masterpiece alone.[1]

Further proof of the strange faculty Coleridge possessed of composing his impalpable yet coherent poems in a state of waking trance may be seen in the circumstances which led up to the writing of *Kubla Khan,* which materialized in his mind during sleep, with its rhymes and rhythms ready made.

This is the way in which he himself relates the circumstances. "In the summer of the year 1797,[2] the Author, then in ill-health, had retired to a lonely farm-house between Porlock and Linton, on the Exmoor confines of Somerset and Devonshire. In consequence of a slight indisposition, an anodyne had been prescribed from the effects of which he fell asleep in his chair at the moment that he was reading the following sentences, or words of the same substance, in 'Purchas's Pilgrimage'; " 'Here Kubla Khan commanded a palace to be built, and a stately garden thereunto. And this ten miles of fertile ground were inclosed with a wall!' The Author continued for about three hours in a profound sleep at least of the ex-

---

[1] *Christabel* which, like the *Three Graves,* was never finished, is written in two parts. The first was composed in 1797 at Nether Stowey, the second, three years later at Keswick in Cumberland on Coleridge's return from Germany.

[2] Coleridge, who wrote these lines in 1816, mistook the date when *Kubla Khan* was written, which was, in reality, 1798.

ternal senses, during which time he had the most vivid
confidence that he could not have composed less than
from two to three hundred lines; if that indeed can be
called composition in which all the images rose up before him as *things,* with a parallel production of the
correspondent expressions, without any sensation or consciousness of effort. On awaking he appeared to himself to have a distinct recollection of the whole, and
taking his pen, ink and paper, instantly and eagerly wrote
down the lines that are here preserved. At this moment
he was unfortunately called out by a person on business
from Porlock, and detained by him above an hour, and
on his return to his room found to his no small surprise
and mortification, that though he still retained some
vague and dim recollection of the general purport of the
vision, yet with the exception of some eight or ten scattered lines and images all the rest had passed away like
the images on the surface of a stream into which a stone
has been cast, but alas! without the after restoration of the
latter."

In this case, no doubt, it was partly because Coleridge
was under the influence of opium, (for the anodyne he
mentions must have been some preparation of the poppy),
that the sentence he had read laid such powerful hold
upon his imagination that the seeds of musical and pictorial suggestion it contained germinated so soon. But
it would, nevertheless, be a mistake to suppose that his
marvellous powers of poetic invention were due to the

drug.[1] It is a recognized fact that opium paralyses rather than excites the creative powers. Coleridge was not taking laudanum when he wrote *The Ancient Mariner,* the first part of *Christabel,* and *The Three Graves,* which describes a case of auto-suggestion with the neighbourhood of Nether Stowey as background. He took narcotics, as I have said, first in order to relieve physical ills, then to procure oblivion of mental distress. In consequence, all they did for him was to send him artificially, and with no personal benefit to himself, into that ultra-lucid state which was for him the supreme lyric mood. They gave him the illusion, or showed him mirages, of spiritual felicity which he enjoyed with no trouble to himself, and which took upon themselves the forms of masterpieces of ethereal beauty. But soon, after spoiling him of his wealth, and setting it where no effort of his art could grasp it, they came in the end to deny him the bare pleasure of watching it develop. A profound depression infallibly succeeds the psychical excitement which opium at first provokes. The subtle well-being which it induces is short-lived. Unless he is careful to observe the infinitely delicate and complicated conditions described by M. Nguyen-Te-Duc in the course of his recent work *Physique et Psy-*

---

[1] While speaking of *Kubla Khan,* I cannot too heartily urge my readers to peruse the article M. René Lalou has devoted to this subject in the *Revue Européenne* of 1st May, 1926, accompanying it with a very happily-worded translation. M René Lalou is of the same opinion as myself; he does not believe that the "hypnogogic hallucination" which gave rise to *Kubla Khan* was a purely passive one.

chique de L'Opium, the opium-eater falls sooner or later
into the kind of torpor De Quincey analysed, and which
Laurent Tailhade has pathetically contrasted with the
beatific state it so cruelly ransoms. Once he has passed
through the elevatory, or revelatory, period, during which
he attains, or thinks that he attains, to a complete understanding of his own being or of the universe, the drug
fiend goes step by step down a stairway ever growing
darker and darker, down into the bottomless depths of
night. "The rainbow mists," writes Tailhade,[1] "the float-
ing gases, the vapours of Nirvana draw their curtains
closer; the fog which lent existence the charm of hazy
outlines becomes an impenetrable wall, a dungeon whence
the prisoner may not escape, save at the cost of thrice
accursed pain."

To deny that opium played a part in Coleridge's life
would be to deny the evidence we have, and I shall have
but too much cause to refer to that part again, for it was
a considerable one. But far from seeing in stimulants a
cause of his inspiration, it is only fair to Coleridge to in-
sist that the use he put them to was an *effect* of his character, and of the genius whence that inspiration arose.
It was not because he took opium that he became a waking dreamer, it was because his imagination was fantastic
or speculative that he turned to this poison to stimulate
his visionary power when he felt it flagging.

It may, however, be asked whether Coleridge did not

[1] *La Noire Idole,* in the *Mercure de France,* 1st February, 1907.

try to over stimulate his magic gifts, so as to make them give him at all times and seasons what he could, after all, only hope for at fairly infrequent intervals. As rarified an atmosphere as that of *The Ancient Mariner, Christabel* or *Kubla Khan* is not always easy to breathe even for the sublimest of mortals. Coleridge ought to have been able to make his will reënforce his inspiration; to have obtained so great a knowledge of unconscious creative process, that he could have reënforced it by means of art. Will-power, however, is a modality of the character, and not a function, as Ribot thought, and Coleridge had no will-power. The elements of that modality were, in Coleridge's case, so complex, that he found it a difficult matter to enter upon any course of action, and an impossibility to make up his mind. His enthusiasm, indeed, seemed as though it should have forced him into action, but it was neutralized by his excessive emotional powers. The promptness of his imagination, which was always ready to anticipate every event, or exhaust its interest beforehand, constantly hindered him from coming to any decision whatever. And finally, his great intellectual range disturbed his judgment. He was far too easily influenced, and was incapable of coming to a decision, or of sticking to it, owing to his eclecticism, that is to say, his habit of looking at every aspect of a thing at once, as well as his inability to use certain ideas practically, by making them relative instead of absolute.

However this may have been, Coleridge who had

stopped taking opium whilst he was at Nether Stowey, was now enjoying a very satisfactory state of health, and was in a mood of great serenity. The *Stories from the World of Spirits* which express his genius at its best, date from this period. He also wrote a series of poems—which would of themselves have served to ensure his fame— under the gently intoxicating influence of living in the lap of nature, amid a revival of sweet memories and ten- der feelings. These poems are full of the brooding atmos- phere Coleridge could create, and of the minute observa- tion he revealed in such fine detail, that no one but Keats has ever equalled them. It is true that the creative power of *The Ancient Mariner,* for instance is not shown in the poem to his brother George, in the verses to *This Lime Tree Bower My Prison, Love, The Nightingale* or *Frost at Midnight.* They are familiar verses, composed for some special occasion, as Goethe says, and, indeed, they are rather a catalogue of his feelings and sensations, than an interpretation of his thought. He did not, as upon these occasions when he made use of the marvellous, harmonize them symbolically, to bring out a spiritual idea of mystery.

Though these poems may be autobiographical, in their mirroring of nature, their simple transcript of emotion, nevertheless their quality of impressionism, of brooding wisdom, makes them far superior to any mere narrative or description for its own sake. The inspiration which had begun to dawn in the poems Coleridge wrote immediately before his marriage was now at its meridian. It was not, however, at all like the hypnotic state into which Shelley used to pass. In Shelley's case, the powers of sensation would be tyrannically overmastered, so suddenly and so absolutely that he would lose all knowledge of his own consciousness, and identify himself with the universal. Coleridge, however, would experience a sort of opening out of the soul to the quickening breath of life, so that his whole heart and mind were steeped in the flowing universal tide. Coleridge never projected himself into the object of his thought. He yielded himself up to its dream-like charm, expanding beneath it as a jelly-fish uncurls its medusa-like coils to the sea it rides so gently.

I spoke of Keats just now. Though it may be true that the sensuous poet who wrote *Endymion* could have conceived *The Nightingale,* and himself evoked that bird

> "That crowds and hurries and precipitates
> With fast thick warble his delicious notes
> As he were fearful that an April night
> Would be too short for him to utter forth
> His love chant."

I doubt if he would ever have described a peaceful night, as Coleridge did in *Frost at Midnight:*

> "So calm that it disturbs
> And vexes meditation with its strange
> And extreme silentness."

The fact is that Coleridge had a wider emotional range than Keats, for his mind could react to other influences

than those of joy. The prodigious sensuous activity that
Keats,—to whom art was an end in itself—knew in his
dionysiac moments was limited to impressions of ecstasy.
The temple which he built to Beauty in the country of the
sun cast no shadow. Coleridge, on the other hand, was
morbidly sensitive. Realities affected him like visions, and
even the pleasure he felt at the sight of the world around
him could cause him mental and psychological distress.
Whenever he felt that his soul was unable to find an outlet for itself in expression, because he was unable to rise
to the heights to which he could attain in dreams, it
could not shake off the influence of mere sensation. His
consciousness was for ever being distracted by the earthly
appearances of things, and he could not help responding
to the call. His mind could never forget its heavenly origin, in the true Christian sense of the word. And everything that befell it would turn it scrupulously inwards
upon itself, longing for the serenity which it could see in
God's handiwork alone.

For Coleridge would have reproached himself had he
tinged that harmonious handiwork with the color of his
passing humours. He could not, as did most of the later
romantics, call upon the mountains, fields, and forests
to share his grief. "No sound is dissonant which tells of
Life," he cried, and it was on this theme of the moral
action of nature that he wrote *This Lime Tree Bower My
Prison,* and on that of experience that he composed *Frost
at Midnight,* in which he meditates over his child's

cradle, brooding at the same time over his own unhappy
and prison-bound childhood.

Was it that he already realized, when these two poems
were written, that his exceptional nature had set him
apart, and had determined to attune his life to the greatness of his work? There is ground for it in the effort
he made at this time to renew closer relations with his
family. He first approached his brother George, who
had stepped into his father's old living at Ottery St. Mary,
and dedicated the second edition of his book of poems
to him. The neglect of his relations, who had had nothing to say to him since his unfortunate Reading episode,
had sorely tried him, and in the lines he dedicated to
his brother, he complained of having been transplanted
from the soil where first he saw the sun, "ere yet my
soul had fixed its first domestic loves." And at times
he told him:

> My soul is sad that I have roam'd through life
> Still most a stranger, most with naked heart
> At mine own home and birthplace. Chiefly then,
> When I remember thee, my earliest friend!
> Thee who didst watch my boyhood and my youth;
> Didst trace my wanderings with a father's eye;
> And boding evil yet still hoping good,
> Rebuk'd each fault, and over all my woes
> Sorrow'd in silence!

But alas, even if George Coleridge felt touched by
the sentiments his brother Samuel expressed towards

himself, with an emotion no one could suspect of insincerity—even although he spoke of having acquired the "sad wisdom folly leaves behind"—he was chiefly conscious of the embarrassment he felt at the broadcasting of these sentiments. The poor parson felt some natural annoyance at having a book dedicated to him by this younger brother of his, who was a friend of the Republican agitator Thelwall, and had become a Unitarian, and his annoyance was the greater because he knew it to be full of the most subversive ideas. In terror for his own reputation, he repulsed his brother's advances in a letter, blaming him for his want of consideration. Convinced that he could look for no moral support from his family, Coleridge turned to "chasing chance-started friendships," a quarry he now determined to pursue because his natural sympathies had been unable to find an outlet.

Knowing that he had been able to be of some use to Lamb in his sorrow, he felt more drawn to him than to anybody else, and had, it will be remembered invited him and his sister down to Nether Stowey. Coleridge one day scalded his foot, and was obliged to send the two out for a walk by themselves, when he wrote for Lamb the poem entitled *This Lime Tree Bower My Prison,* in which his tenderness for him (*his gentle-hearted Charles*) overflows in sweet simplicity. He sets his friend's life of hard work and heroic resignation before him as an example, and his courage grows stronger at the thought that "Nature ne'er deserts the wise and pure."

A year before, on the eve of writing *The Ancient Mariner,* he had adopted a watchword: *"Awake to Love and Beauty."* This ideal still inspired him. He took a vow to make a fresh start, and to educate his child as he had, unfortunately, never been educated himself, under the salutary influence of Nature, whose "sweet voices" he said in *The Nightingale,* are "always full of love and joyance."

PART IV

THE SORROWFUL LIFE OF THE WANDERER

CHAPTER I

IN GERMANY

THE *Lyrical Ballads* which were published by Cottle in
1798, Coleridge being paid fifteen guineas for his share
in the joint production, contained nothing of his apart
from *The Ancient Mariner,* except *The Nightingale* and
two scenes from *Osorio* including Alvar's monologue at
the beginning of the fifth act. Sara Coleridge, who had
never been allowed to take part in the discussions and
debates which had given birth to the poems comprised
in this collection, which, for the most part wrongfully
usurped the title of ballads, was perhaps not sorry to find
they "were not liked at all by any." This they could hardly
be, nor could their originality be appreciated at a time
when men's interests centred round the war, and they
could but seek distraction from anxiety in the Bacchana-
lian songs of Captain Norris, Peter Pindar's pithy epi-
grams, and Churchill's archaic, but frigidly elegant satires.
This failure sorely grieved Wordsworth, who was very
probably right in thinking that the fault lay mainly
with his friend's masterpiece. But for the past few months,
so many events in Coleridge's life had been crowding one
upon the other; he had known the gladness of surprise,
as well as a series of sorrows and disappointments of

such grievous import, that he was badly moved by the critics' lack of understanding and the public indifference, of which, indeed, he only learned after he left England for Germany.

It has been seen how, whilst he was conceiving and writing his poems, he used to go through a two-fold moral and sentimental crisis, not in sooth of a purely passionate nature, but philosophic, rather, in character. As I have already said, he felt the need of equilibrium, that kind of longing for harmony which in many of the finest minds seems to flow from the knowledge that they are inspired, or that the Spirit is upon them. His thoughts had long dwelt on the necessity for reforming his way of living, so as to fulfil his bounden duties as husband and father, and then as English citizen. He was no longer merely toying with the idea of well-doing, as he now and then did when the mood was on him, but he turned these things over in his mind until an idea crystallized into certainty. And to start with, the steps France was taking against Switzerland gave him a fresh opportunity to break with his revolutionary ideas, or a first pretext to deny them openly. He had now for some little time paid no attention to politics, and seemed to dislike all mention of them. It has been seen how, in the *Ode to the Departing Year,* at the beginning of his stay at Nether Stowey, he had drawn up, as it were, the obituary notice of the liberal ideas of his youth. A little later, when he invited Thelwall to stay, he was less desirous of rekindling his own zeal at Thelwall's democratic ardour, than seeking to convert him to his religious, and perhaps even literary opinions. To feel himself watched over by Pitt's spies when he roamed the Quantocks with Thelwall and the Wordsworths was peculiarly irksome. He feared lest the group he had brought together in all innocence might awaken that Minister's lively suspicions, and wondered whether "even riots and dangerous riots" might not break out as a consequence in his own hamlet. . . . There is no doubt he suffered keenly from knowing himself an object of reprobation to the majority of his compatriots, and that he desired to be taken once more into the bosom of that social order whence his extravagant principles had expelled him.

In the *Ode to France* which he published on the 16th April, 1798, he disowned the enthusiastic dreams of his youth, and his belief in the sacredness of the cause of the Republic. The sight of the armies of the Directoire violating the frontier of the Juras, and victoriously trampling the earth trodden by William Tell and Jean Jacques Rousseau, gave him cause to apostrophize liberty, who never "didst breathe thy soul in forms of human power." The fact must not be overlooked, that in spite of, or perhaps on account of, his philosophic attainments, he always remained rather weak as a political theorist, and never had a very clear idea as to what aspect liberty should assume in public government—liberty for which God Himself has instilled in us a feeling, and which is re-

vealed to each individual soul. . . . Therefore he ever
subordinated the beginning of the reign of independence
to the personal perfecting of mankind, and seemed logical in his own conceit, when he declared any revolution
to be immoral which was carried out by the *sensual* and
the *blind,* "slaves by their own compulsion." Here he,
at any rate, agreed with the majority of English citizens
in refusing to the French the title of freemen which
they had claimed. As soon as England as well as Switzerland was threatened with invasion, he took the last step
which still separated him from his compatriots to rally
to her flag, and in *Fears in Solitude* he went so far as to
curse France and even to speak slander of her, though he
had formerly bidden his own country to take example by
her. When his complete ignorance of the French genius
is realized, there is nothing surprising in the fact that
he adopted the hereditary prejudices of his own race
against that genius, and made the French out to be "im-
pious and false, a light yet cruel race who laugh away
all virtue, mingling mirth with deeds of murder." I do
not for a moment suspect that when he accused the
French as a whole of the crimes committed by the rab-
ble, so soon as they became a peril to the existence of his
own country, he was doing any violence to his critical
judgment. The proof of his good faith is, I take it,
to be seen in the poem called *Fire, Famine and Slaughter,* in which the miseries of the war were laid at the
door of the man whose name, formed of *letters four,* was

too horrible for the witches out of *Macbeth* to utter, namely, his old enemy, Pitt.

In turning away from humanitarianism to patriotism, he neither trod his sentimental convictions under foot, nor betrayed his conscience. But how lofty the tone of his praises of his native land! There is something religious about these accents, as it were an echo of the sacred emotion of a Christian, returning to the fold whence his sins have banished him. Though his brother might frown when he made his appeal, seeking to convince him of the saneness of his political views, he no longer felt alone, since he was sharing a sacramental communion of ten million men in the love of England. This love confirmed him in the convictions we have already seen him arrive at when he determined to fashion his life anew.

"O native Britain! O my Mother Isle,"

he cries in *Fears in Solitude,*

> Needs must thou prove a name most dear and holy
> To me, a son, a brother, and a friend,
> A husband, and a father! Who revere
> All bonds of natural love, and find them all
> Within the limits of thy rocky shores.
> O native Britain! O my Mother Isle!
> How shouldst thou prove aught else but dear and holy
> To me, who from thy lakes, and mountain-hills,
> Thy clouds, thy quiet dales, thy rocks and seas,
> Have drunk in all my intellectual life,

All sweet sensations, all ennobling thoughts,
All adoration of the God in nature,
All lovely and all honourable things,
Whatever makes this mortal spirit feel
The joy and greatness of its future being?"

And these feelings of gratitude breathed with such flaming fervour for his country were closely allied to his
virtuous intentions, or, more exactly, formed their ground-
work. What, indeed, could be a sounder basis than patriotism—which to all Englishmen implies civic pride
as well as loyalty to the existing order—for the regular
and sensible existence Coleridge meant henceforward to
lead? No good son, good brother, good husband, good
father, and good Christian can help being a good citizen
in being all the rest. One might be tempted to shrug
ironically indulgent shoulders at hearing such an ideal
of life put forward, for it does indeed smack of all the
homespun virtues, were it not that it is easy to divine
the protection Coleridge sought in it from the vicissi-
tudes he felt the future still held for him, and above all
from his own weaknesses. A wholly material necessity
for security made him long for a humdrum existence,
for he knew how ready his fanciful spirit was to spurn it.
He had to be sheltered from the storm ere he could
exploit the full resources of that spirit, and above all, he
had no hopes of succeeding in the sphere of politics. He
had proved up to the hilt that, far from his being able
to turn circumstances to his own account and to lead

others, he did but bruise himself against reality. As he wrote to his brother George he had "withdrawn himself totally from the consideration of immediate causes, which are infinitely complex and uncertain, to muse on fundamental and general causes." He meant, henceforth, to devote himself to speculative musings such as had ever attracted him, and he had always thought speculative poetry as he understood it, to be poetry in its most seductive form. Thus, when the choice of earning a living for himself and his family lay between writing for the *Morning Post,* which paper had offered him regular employment, or becoming a preacher in the Unitarian Church, he decided upon leaving Nether Stowey for Shrewsbury, because the congregation had promised him to elect him as minister at the first vacancy in that town. There could be no doubt, moreover, that he had the orator's temperament, and a recent experience in the chapel at Taunton had proved to him that he had lost nothing of his eloquence. Public speaking exactly suited the extempore genius of Coleridge who, on account of his indolence, or rather his aversion to making the effort required to carry out a piece of work in solitude, preferred the excitement of working in public, and was thrown into a state of intoxication bordering on the delirum of the soothsayer when supported by an audience.

The first time he heard him, William Hazlitt, then aged twenty, thought himself caught up into Heaven; and though that vindictive spirit later pursued him with hatred, it was because he had on first contact with him become charged as by an electric shock, with the highest intellectual ambitions, and he never forgave him for having survived their failure.

"When I got there" (i. e., to the Unitarian Chapel at Shrewsbury,) he wrote in 1823 in the *Liberal,* "Mr. Coleridge rose and gave out his text 'And he went up into the mountain to pray HIMSELF, ALONE.' As he gave out this text his voice 'rose like a stream of rich distilled perfumes' and when he came to the last two words, which he pronounced loud, deep, and distinct, it seemed to me, who was then young, as if the sounds had echoed from the bottom of the human heart, and as if that prayer might have floated in solemn silence through the universe. . . . The preacher then launched into his subject, like an eagle dallying with the wind." Young Hazlitt, whose plastic sense was nearly as much developed as his critical sense, (he studied painting under his brother John, and tried his hand at portrait-painting), was struck by the expression on Coleridge's face, no longer now the liberal apostle he had imagined, but with genius shining out from every feature, and he noted, in contrast to the magnificent breadth of his brow and the sublimity of his look, the irresolution and voluptuous flabbiness revealed by the lower part of his face. The poet's reputation had prepared him for the enthusiasm he felt. But Hazlitt's opinionated self, which kept a lifelong fidelity to

its youthful system of thought, for lack of sufficient
originality to hack a way out of it, found that Coleridge's
words illuminated truths that lay outside its scope. Trembling with the desire to know the secrets which he felt
Coleridge was able to reveal to him, he dogged his every
step. Never was lover more impatient to hear from his
lady's lips the secret of her thought of him, than William to be initiated into the knowledge of this spell-
working stranger, and have his meed bestowed upon
him. His eagerness called forth the indulgence of Coleridge, who allowed him to accompany him part of the
way, holding a positive consultation upon spiritual
themes. For, as always happens on like occasions, the
pupil puts questions to his master, less with a view to
plucking the fruits of his wisdom, than finding out what
are the hopes of harvest for the flowers his own pride
finds so heady. Hazlitt not only harried Coleridge with
questions upon the subjects that preoccupied his mind,
but he also told him of the work he was making ready
to do. He tried to explain, in particular, a metaphysical
discovery he thought to have made, and Coleridge encouraged him to pursue the inquiries which were later
on to issue in the *Principles of Human Action*. Coleridge,
however, was not the man to play a merely passive part
in conversation. Even while he was but seeking to satisfy
his admirer's curiosity, he was bound to impose his personal views upon him. The slightest suggestion gave him

the chance to glance at far horizons, or at considerations branching out on all sides until their convolutions stifled the principle which first gave them rise.

Whilst he was speaking, establishing haphazard relationships between this and that, or branching from idea to idea, "the very milestones had ears," said Hazlitt, and "Harmer Hill stooped to listen to a poet." He noticed a peculiarity that others noted later in their turn; Coleridge, he said, took a zigzag course as he walked, that is to say, he could not stay in the middle of the path, and slanted continually across it from one side to the other, as if he were trying to mark out upon the soil the summary diagram of his thought. But that thought more than satisfied Hazlitt, and after he had spent three weeks at Nether Stowey, nothing would content him but that his host should go to stay at Wem with his father. There Coleridge preached for the last time. It was, indeed, while he was staying with the Hazlitts that he received from Thomas Wedgwood, one of the three sons of the celebrated potter who had made his fortune by his imitations of antique ware, the offer of an annuity of one hundred and fifty pounds "in order to prevent the necessity of his going into the ministry," and enabling him to pursue his studies in literature and philosophy.

Though the Wedgwood brothers had been careful enough to make it clear that their gift was a wholly disinterested one, and was in no wise to infringe his liberty, Coleridge hesitated to accept the unexpected windfall he had received, though Hazlitt, who considered his leaving the Unitarian Church a woeful backsliding, pretended that he made up his mind in no more time than he might take "in tying on one of his shoes." In point of fact, his scruples were dissolved by the idea that he was now able, thanks to his generous benefactors, to carry out one of his dearest plans: "of going into Germany, where we propose to pass the two ensuing years in order to acquire the German language, and to furnish ourselves with a tolerable stock of information in natural science."

He won the Wordsworths over to his scheme, and they were to accompany him; thus, as luck would have it, his preparations for departure took his mind off the sorrow he had lately been occasioned, through Lloyd's fault, by his quarrel with Lamb. It will be remembered that he had been obliged to part with the unhappy epileptic youth, whom he had undertaken to educate. He had often seen him since, and had introduced him to his former schoolfellow at Christ's Hospital. Lloyd's prompt enthusiasm and the passionate nature of his affections were in themselves unhealthy signs, but he soon became Lamb's intimate friend. Lamb, whose mother was insane when she died by her daughter's hand, and who was himself obliged to pass six months in an asylum, during the winter of 1795–1796, in order to recover from mental derangement, was himself inclined to a certain bizarre unaccountableness, at any rate at this time of his life. It did not, indeed, exclude good sense of the rarest kind, but was sufficient to enable Lloyd to lead him astray. He agreed to collaborate with that young man in a volume to be called *Blank Verse,* due to appear in 1798, and he soon allowed himself to be persuaded into thinking that Coleridge was two-faced. In one of those boastful fits not uncommon with him, Coleridge had set up to be the type of the man of genius, in contrast to Lamb, whom he specified as the type of the man of talent. Lloyd had shown his new friend the letter in which this imprudent distinction was drawn, arrogant indeed no doubt, but truth to tell harmless enough, and this first officious action on his part had been the beginning of a regular campaign of slander against his former tutor. By dint of reiterating to Lamb that Coleridge was belittling him, while overwhelming him with protestations of affection, Lloyd ended by turning Lamb against him. Lamb, it appears, was especially hurt on hearing that Coleridge had said, speaking of some researches he was engaged upon: "Poor Lamb, if he wants any knowledge let him apply to me." But it may be seen from the importance of this, the greatest grievance he could trump up against Coleridge, that Lamb was perhaps rather off his balance at the time. Even had he managed to regain it, Lloyd would have hindered him by the continuous harrying of his own over-wrought imagination. It was with a rancour bordering on frenzy that this irresponsible creature set himself to abase the man he had lately made his idol, and to ruin his reputation not only in the eyes of Lamb, but of the literary world, if not of the world at large. He wrote a novel in which, under the name of Edmund Oliver, he described Coleridge, and divulged the secrets of his love for Mary Evans, his Reading escapade and his fatal taste for opium. He dedicated this novel to Lamb, and had it published by Cottle. He could have happened on no more appropriate publisher! Coleridge, in a letter of much dignity and great moderation, wrote to Lamb, assuring him that Lloyd had deceived him. He did not seek to deny that he had some minor faults to reproach himself with. He was but a man, and not the exceptional being which Lamb and Lloyd himself had been pleased to imagine him, at a time when their exaltation of soul had led them to deck him with every merit and every virtue. "You are restored to *comparative saneness*," (italics are mine), "and are merely wondering what is become of the Coleridge with whom you were so passionately in love; Charles Lloyd's mind has only changed his disease, and he is now arraying his ci-devant Angel in a flaming San Benito—the whole ground of the garment a dark brimstone and plenty of little angels flourished out in black. Oh me! Lamb, even in laughter the heart is sad!" Lamb did not accept an invitation from Coleridge, who knew that an hour's conversation between their two selves would have put an end to all heartburning. He answered his letter by an ironical note in which, know-

ing him to be on the eve of departure to Germany, he
sent him the following "Theological Propositions, to be
by you defended or oppugned, or both, in the Schools of
Germany.

1. Whether God loves a lying Angel better than a true
Man?

2. Whether the Archangel Uriel *could* affirm an untruth? and if he *could* whether he *would?*

3. Whether Honesty be an angelic virtue? or not rather
to be reckoned among those qualities which the School-
men term *'Virtutes minus splendidae?'* "

Luckily for Coleridge the *Anti-Jacobin Magazine,* one
of the publications which treated him most cavalierly,
reviewed Lloyd's *Edmund Oliver,* without realizing that
he had sat as model for the hero of the novel. It may
be imagined to what use his enemies might have turned
his ex-pupil's revelations just at a time when a set of
verses called *New Morality* had recently appeared, accusing him of being a theophilanthropist, and the carica-
turist Gillray had drawn him with an ass's-head holding
"dactyllic verses" in his hand.

All this was in July and August, 1798. On the 16th
September following, Coleridge set sail with William and
Dorothy Wordsworth at Yarmouth for Hamburg, where
the Wedgwoods had opened a credit sufficient to meet
all the expenses of himself and his companions. He left
his wife and two children in England, and, as he was
parting from the beings he loved best in the world, in

order to devote himself wholly to the speculations which haunted him he forbore, out of philosophic detachment, to make up his quarrel with Lamb before he left, though loving him as tenderly as ever. . . .

A certain man named John Chester had begged to be allowed to join the trio; nothing is known of him, however, save that he accompanied Coleridge everywhere in Germany, and that he had fallen head over ears into one of those admiring and sympathetic friendships which are past all reckoning in the life of this extraordinary man, though they perhaps make up its most characteristic element.

It would be a mistake to assume that Coleridge knew nothing, or next to nothing about Germany when he landed there. Indeed, some of his critics and biographers have made out too strong a case in asserting that the visit he paid to the country of Goethe had a decisive influence on his mind, and turned him from a poet into a metaphysician. Not only was his philosophic education very far advanced when he came into contact with German thinkers, but that contact itself is only a further step upon the road he had been travelling for four years at the least. Ever since 1794 he had been full of enthusiasm for Schiller, and his sonnet to the Author of the *Robbers* dates from that year. In April, 1796 he read Lessing's *Fragments,* and on the 5th May following, he wrote to Poole, in a letter in which he told him of his future plans: "I am studying German and in about six weeks shall be able to read that language with tolerable fluency. Now I have some thoughts of making a proposal to Robinson, the great London bookseller, of translating all the works of Schiller which would make a portly quarto, on condition that he should pay my journey and my wife's to and from Jena, a cheap German university where Schiller resides, and allow me two guineas each quarter sheet, which would maintain me. If I could realize this scheme, I should there study chemistry and anatomy, and bring over with me all the works of Semler and Michaelis, the German theologians, and of Kant, the great German metaphysician. On my return I would commence a school, etc. . . ."

Alongside Hartley, the disciple of Hume, he read "the noble Mendelssohn who teaches that the divine one was never crucified," and that He is Joseph's real son, and in his notebooks may be found, cheek by jowl with cookery recipes, extracts from Jacob Boehme, in which the ideas of Fichte, Schelling and Hegel are to be found in germ. He had from the beginning shown as great, if not greater, interest in lofty speculations, as in poetry, and it was because he found German ontology so closely related to his own mystical naturalism that he assimilated it so deeply and so rapidly. His heart was with Paul and John, but his head with Spinoza and Leibnitz, as he said himself. It must be remembered that while no more than a child, he felt a kind of intoxication on being initiated into the theories of the Eleati, who may be considered as the distant fore-runners of the German philosophers, and that on meeting one of the illuminati on emerging from Reading he plunged into transcendental considerations on the soul of things. His curiosity about "all strange phantasms" and the writings of all "dreamers" naturally led him to take an interest in the intellectual emancipation which Germany has sought since Luther, and which sometimes degenerated into an anarchic effervescence of mind, though it may have roused fruitful controversy. He was as far removed as possible from the French genius,—that genius which later allowed Poe to exploit his wonderful intuition by means, for example, of the methods he had borrowed from Laplace—and it is easy to feel that what he chiefly lacked was the support, or prop, of a positive knowledge of modern science, though, indeed, he looked upon "every experiment that Priestley made in chemistry as giving wings to his more sublime theological works." His impulsive temperament, and his habits of shunning reality, made him incapable of making any co-ordinated effort. Though he welcomed every idea that seemed to him capable of fitting into the vast framework of spiritual, and before long, religious philosophy, which obsessed him, he never succeeded in throwing his ideas into any precise shape, and never seriously set about making a systematic classification. If he had been content to use in poetry the admirable faculty he possessed of finding out the relations, and discovering the analogies between things as remote and as different as possible from each other, he might have given shape in visions of rare mystic beauty to his complex conception of the world. His mistake was in wanting to abstract his thought from the emotive elements, at once plastic and musical, from which it obtained the better part of its power of suggestion. Shorn of its lyricism, that is to say, above all, of the power of rhythmic life, far less illusory than one might be inclined to think it, his thought showed insufficient coherence or steadfastness in its gait to enable it to complete the circle, and verify itself by returning to its starting point. This is not to say, however, that Coleridge's pursuit of a universal system was sterile, nor that, in particular, he wasted his time in Germany. But to return to what has already been said, he was to learn less in that country from first-hand knowledge than merely to continue the bookish studies he had begun in England. He proceeded, at any rate, with no kind of order upon the inquiry he was setting on foot in this land of metaphysicians. His enthusiasm bore him along, and he let himself be led by chance, or by the whim of the moment. He asked no more of men and things, than that they should confirm the character of the longings he felt stirring within him, and each time he formed a new friendship, or became engrossed in a new doctrine, whether literary, social, or political, he only took one step further towards the discovery of his own personality.

In *Le Rêve Eveillé,* M. Leon Daudet speaks of the

aura which keeps our souls in insolation during times of meditation. It was because of that kind of mist in which he abode continually, and which was so favourable to the creation of his finest poems, that Coleridge gained little or nothing from Germany, which might not equally have enriched his mind had he stayed at home. He remained almost wholly indifferent to the varied circles he frequented, and never discovered any points of correspondence, much less of comparison, between the conclusions of his intelligence, and the reality which lay outside it.

Hearing the call of Göttingen, where, under the influence of the doctrine of *Sturm und Drang,* a literary school that had formerly been very active, and after having succeeded in sowing its works broadcast over Europe, especially in France and Great Britain, was nearing the end of its career, Coleridge was beguiled into hoping that he might discover beyond the Rhine a country peopled by superior beings. But he was soon to recover from that illusion. . . .

We possess in his *Satyrane's Letters,* later incorporated in the *Biographia Literaria,* the full story of his tour. These letters are for the most part written to his wife, but there seems to me no doubt that he wrote them less for her edification than for himself, or for posterity. Though Mrs. Coleridge's interest and curiosity may have been catered for by the details that Coleridge noted down as to his health, his doings, and behaviour in material ways in a foreign country, these details were after all only of secondary importance in the poet's eyes. He hoped by keeping up a kind of diary, to pin down various impressions that might serve him as material later on, and it is not a conversation which he invites and continues, but a monologue unrolled in his familiar fashion in these letters which he had, moreover, urged his wife to keep carefully by her.

It was characteristic of Coleridge, and of his congenital incapacity to proceed with the prudent circumspection of the experimentalist when he came into contact with reality, that, almost as soon as he landed, he summed up the French nation in general in the person of an old *emigré,* "an intimate friend of the celebrated Abbé de Lisle" (sic) whose acquaintance he had made. "His demeanour," he says, "exhibited the minute philanthropy of a polished Frenchman, tempered by the sobriety of the English character disunited from its reserve," and from this simple remark, which was all he required on which to construct a whole theory of good breeding, he deduced the conclusion that the gentleman is a type frequent in England, but rare in France, (he never went there), almost unknown in Germany, (he was as yet only upon his way thither), and that its very opposite must be sought amongst the democrats of the New World. (The ax raised against Pantisocracy had indeed gone to the root of the tree!) Coleridge's youthful verve which became a turn for caricature when circumstances allowed, was at this point drawing from the spring of one of the national prejudices that lie closest to the English heart. But our poet was not of those men who change as they learn, and for whom learning any new thing at all implies the abandonment of preconceived opinions, or the denial of former errors. They add to their heritage of knowledge without casting off old mistakes, and their development proceeds in the same way as the earth's crust was formed, by overlaying one layer with another, or to put it geologically, by stratification.

Coleridge was indeed disappointed, with his guileless ideas as to what a great man should, or should not look like, when he stood face to face with Klopstock, whose *Messiah,* at that time very popular in England, he much admired. He went to see him at Hamburg with Wordsworth, almost as soon as they set foot upon the continent, and the famous old man in whom he *recognized no likeness to the bust* he knew of him, seemed to him utterly lacking in distinction. "There was no comprehension in the forehead, no weight over the eyebrows, no expression of peculiarity, moral or intellectual, in the eyes." He saw before him a courteous but slightly ridiculous old man in a wig, with swollen, gouty legs, toothless upper jaw; and the disappontment he felt on hearing him speak was yet stronger than on catching sight of him. Wordsworth, who made himself understood of Klopstock in French, acted as interpreter, and nothing that "the Father of German poetry" said, and which was immediately translated for Coleridge's benefit, served to rouse his enthusiasm. To begin with, Klopstock was far from being a learned man, in itself a deplorable, almost unpardonable thing. He was almost totally ignorant of English literature, and had barely made acquaintance with Milton— or would admit that he had made it, for with all due deference to Coleridge, nothing would be less surprising than that he should have wished people to believe that the *Messiah* owed nothing to *Paradise Lost.* . . . But he was not very familiar with the history of poetry in his own country, and upon that subject, which, so he said, had not "particularly excited his curiosity," did no more than refer his young inquirer to a German professor. He only emerged from his reserve, and abandoned his calm, in order to complain of the English translation of his religious epic. All the translations that had been made of the *Messiah* were bad, very bad—but the English was no translation—there were pages on pages not in the original: and half the original was not to be found in the translation at all.

"Klubstick" Coleridge called him henceforth, revenging himself by this piece of mischief for having been mistaken in the Christian patriarch, who, to make matters worse, had no love for Schiller; and that he might fall into no fresh errors, he steeled himself into indifference for everything save science and philosophy in Germany, a nation of thinkers but "an unlovely race."

Before taking leave of the Wordsworths, who had de-

cided not to follow him in his wanderings, and had be-
taken themselves to Goslar in Brunswick, he spent a few
gay days in Hamburg. The town amused him, and, in
high feather, he gave a thumbnail picture of it, sketching
in against a background of bright colours a crowd whose
oddities above all caught his eyes: buxom lasses with fair
pigtails flapping over their shoulders, sturdy young fellows in jack boots solemnly holding long pipes with col-
oured china bowls. From the middle of November
onwards he lodged with a worthy pastor at Ratzeburg
near Lübeck, intending to learn German thoroughly, and
he remained four months in that village, rejoicing in the
midst of the woody lakeside scenery in a fruitful time of
rest. He admitted it himself: his habits were becoming
less irregular, and he had more control over himself. He
had from his window a view out over the lake, and no
doubt it was there, in the autumnal atmosphere which
lapped him round, and made harmony of the varying
shades in sky and water, that he first became aware of
the charm which later on was to wake once more and
root him to Keswick.

His host's children, whom he had won over by his
graciousness and simplicity, corrected his pronunciation,
and, in order to teach him words in everyday use, by
pointing out the objects to which they belong, dragged
him about with them one at a time, or all five together,
into the remotest corners of the house from cellar to
attic. It is easy to imagine this swarm of young folk

tumbling up and down stairs, bursting out into noisy peals of laughter and many a joyous *"hoch!"* Coleridge was grateful for the cordial German hospitality, and the pleasant family life in this lower middle class society— much like that in *Hermann und Dorothea*—into which he had been lucky enough to find his way, met a need sharpened in him by his orphaned state, and by making him yearn for his own country, set him dreaming about his wife and children. It made him long for news of home where he felt he would like to spend his wedding-day. . . .

He mingled in Ratzeburg society, scouring the streets, and making out advertisements pasted upon the walls, and dipping into every kind of book, including collections of jokes, in order to perfect his knowledge of German. But the population seemed to him heavy and loutish, that is to say, with none of the *buoyancy of spirits* which is the charm of people of Celtic origin, and of an almost repulsive sensuality beneath their grave exterior, or else full of a gloomy or grossly jovial good-nature. Having been born in a part of England which corresponds to the Midi in France, he had always been fairly indifferent to the pleasures of the table, and his abstemious habits detached him still farther from these lymphatic folk, who passed their time gorging themselves with victuals, for he had discovered all that digestion counts for in their *Gemüthlichkeit*. Though he was given the heartiest of welcomes, he felt he was not liked. He himself, more-

over, owned that he found it impossible to give his heart
to anyone he met. "Love," he writes, "is the vital air of
my genius, and I have not seen one human being in
Germany whom I can conceive it *possible* for me to love,
no, not *one*." He had no need to use his powers of observation in the matter. His sensitive heart itself put him
on guard. It also put him in the mood to keep up a tone
of bravado, if not indeed of bluster, in his discussions
with his foreign opponents, and he seemed to take a
malicious vanity in harassing them with paradoxes. At
Göttingen, where he went in January, able to read old
German and even old Low German "better than most of
even the educated natives," and ready to tackle metaphysical subjects,—though he made but a poor show in
the kind of talk that lies on the border line between
everyday conversation and that of a more exalted kind
—he exaggerated the independence of his intellectual attitude. He took an especial delight in startling Professor
Eichhorn, who was, however, a theologian of the Luth-
eran school, by the diabolical subtlety of his reasoning.
Three of his fellow-countrymen, the Parry brothers from
Cambridge, and Dr. Clement Carlyon have left us,—
the former in some letters, the latter in a volume of reminiscences—some exceedingly curious impressions of
Coleridge's demeanour at Göttingen. The solemn or sullen pedantry of the German philosophers urged him into
showing twice as much good-tempered excitement when
he engaged them in lofty speculations. Whatever argu-

ment was put forward against him, no one, observed the younger Parry, could succeed in flooring him, or in making him angry, and it was a joy, he adds, to hear and see him force his opponents to abandon their positions one by one. Never had he been more eclectic, than in this clash with the dogmatic German thinkers, who, in spite of the boldness of their views, showed a strong tendency to become doctrinaire, and at once put up a bristling defensive barricade around their most trifling spiritual conquests. He even found occasion to laugh at his own claims to encyclopædic knowledge, when he saw these dry-as-dusts in swarm around him, and he wrote, "I find being learned is a mighty easy thing, compared with any study else. My God! a miserable poet must he be, and a despicable metaphysician, whose acquirements have not cost him more trouble and reflection than all the learning of Toole, Porson, and Parr united. With the advantage of a great library, learning is nothing—methinks merely a sad excuse for being idle. . . . Therefore at the end of two or three years, if God grant me life, expect to see me come out with some horribly learned book, full of manuscript quotations from Laplandish and Patagonian authors, possibly, on the striking resemblance of the Sweogothian and Sanscrit languages, and so on!"

Once again he had met with the antithesis or foil to his own nature which sent him off in the farthest direction on the other side, and he felt himself fantastic in the society of intellectuals as unsprightly as well might

be. Poetry was forever on his lips, and according to Dr.
Carlyon, he was much given to reciting his verses, inter-
larding them with reflections or commentaries which
might well disguise an intent to mystify. (We might cite
in proof what he says to excuse the onomatopœia in the
first verse of *Christabel* "Tu-whit, Tu-whoo!" which was
already to be found in Shakspere, and which therefore he was not bound to defend as an eccentric originality.) Speaking was his constant pastime, and he never
showed the slightest fatigue in turning the most difficult
intellectual somersaults, observes another of the witnesses
already mentioned. He was Ariel, but an Ariel swathed
in metaphysical veils, with the gaiety of Puck, and something of the enigmatic and crazily boastful imagination
of Malvolio in *Twelfth Night*.

He preferred to criticize his own works rather than
that nothing should be said of them, and in spite of the
beauty he admitted they contained, assured everyone that
his best work had not as yet appeared in print. . . . It is
difficult not to be surprised, however, and impossible,
indeed, to avoid a certain qualm on discovering that he
in no way altered his demeanour, and continued to amuse
himself, (twice, for instance, taking a trip along the
Haase, and climbing the Brocken with his friends) after
he had learnt of his little Berkeley's death, which took
place on the 19th February, 1799. The child was no doubt
only nine months old, of which Coleridge had passed but
three with him, and it often happens that a father's

love for his son is realized only as the years go by. But in the letters he wrote to his wife, Coleridge revealed a deep, though somewhat strangely expressed emotion. I should not, on reflection, be inclined to think that his sorrow was any less sincere because he consented to mingle it with the distractions he had not the strength to forgo, and which gave him pleasure, almost unwittingly it seems, owing to his natural inclination to be moulded by circumstance. There was, besides, a kind of unreality about all Coleridge's feelings, and his manner of living wholly in ideas prevented him from conceiving the events which befell him as they befell other men with the same forceful precision as they did. He wept over the dear departed babe, and, in spite of the gaiety and high spirits he showed with his companions, he left at every inn whither he accompanied them, melancholy verses which go to prove his heart was bleeding sorely. But the essential drama was for him played out in an illusory or abstract realm. The religious dissertations he sent his wife, as though he thought them capable of consoling her, show quite well that he looked on his loss above all as a moral or spiritual problem. Berkeley had never been baptized. Coleridge wrote for him the epitaph on a child dead before it had received the first of the sacraments, and it was because Priestley denied "the future existence of infants," or doubted it, that he finally severed himself from Unitarianism. . . .

For four months longer, however, which space of time

included a short visit to Wordsworth, Coleridge assiduously continued his study of science and German philosophy. He attended Tychsen's lessons, and Blumenbach's classes on natural history and physiology, and read "with sedulous accuracy the *Minnesinger* (or singers of love, the Provençal poets of the Swabian court) and the metrical romances; and then laboured through sufficient specimens of the Master singers, their degenerate successors," not without pleasure now and then in the rugged but arresting speech of Hans Sachs, the cobbler of Nürnberg. On the other hand, his letters make no mention of any work he may have been doing in philosophy, and, despite his admiration for Kant, whose writings, he said, fortified and disciplined his understanding, there is no proof that he profited by Bouterwek's lectures to familiarize himself with the author of the *Critique of Pure Reason*. No doubt he was looking forward to delving deeper into German metaphysics when he returned home. . . . What he was busy at, for the moment, was making himself master of the language, that he might read and re-read the volumes he declared he had bought, but which he does not enumerate, and to get under way the work to which he intended to devote the best part of his life. Meanwhile, with a view to publication on his return to England, he had been making translations or adaptations of minor poets such as Stolberg, and was at the same time considering whether to turn *Faust* into English, and to write a life of Lessing. All of this, together with his learned, but to say the least, un-profitable studies of Teutonic dialects, bears witness to the desultoriness of his work, and his lack of method in setting about it. But a material proof of the instability or inconstancy of his spirit may be adduced. Though Schiller had been the first German poet he had loved, and the notion of going to see him at Jena had originally lain at the bottom of the idea of his tour in Germany, he now stated that he would not go twenty yards out of his way to meet him. . . . When, however, the English publisher, Longman, approached him later to translate *Wallenstein,* he did not refuse his services. And it was the translation of the work he liked least, of the poet from whom he felt most remote,—since he had ceased to feel any regard for him,—which gave him his solitary chance to make use of his knowledge of German!

On 24th June, 1799, Coleridge gave a farewell dinner to his friends in Göttingen, and replied to their good wishes in their own language, in a speech that was highly correct, but delivered in the most execrable accent. I wager that he was not sorry to leave them. He had not received at their hands the revelation he had expected, and it is fair to say he had done almost nothing to de-serve it. . . . He had never got beyond Leibnitz and Less-ing, who were already outworn glories at a time when the new stars rising behind Kant and Fichte were Schlegel, Schelling and Hegel. But in the very town where militant youth was rallying round Voss's *Muses'*

Almanach, he seemed never to have caught an echo of the revolution taking place in men's minds. What kind of German society, indeed, can he have mixed with in Göttingen, since he remained ignorant of the existence of Jean Paul Richter, Ludwig Tieck, and Novalis, whose names, even, he never mentioned in his letters, and since he neglected to go to Jena itself, where a school so close to his own in thought had been founded, with the *Atheneum* as its mouthpiece? There is irony in the fact that Coleridge, whose subjective conception of the universe is notorious, should have sojourned in Germany at the moment when the foundations of transcendental idealism were being laid, without knowing anything of the theorists who were enunciating that the first characteristic of all poetry is to suppress the logical reason.

KESWICK AND MALTA

KNOWING Coleridge as we now do, it is without surprise that we find him hardly home again before he again deserts it, although he had been so utterly homesick while away. . . . Landing in England in the early part of July, 1799, he was, indeed, off to London by the beginning of the following November. Meanwhile he had, through Poole's kind offices, made up his difference with Southey, who had finally left Portugal, and he went upon a kind of pilgrimage to Ottery St. Mary. I imagine that he founded many sentimental hopes upon this visit to his native heath, and it is certain that his brothers' attitude dashed them to the ground. He found they had no longer "tastes nor feelings in common." They listened to him as strangers, rather mistrustfully, only coming out of their shell to belabour him with contradictions. His old mother, who had lost her hearing, and saw her sons wrangling without understanding a single word of what it was all about, was certain, nevertheless, always to take sides against Samuel, saying, "If your poor father had been alive, he'd soon have convinced you!" Did they indeed kill any fatted calf for this prodigal son? Possibly they did, but there are ways and ways of eating it, and so chilled was Coleridge's heart by his cold reception, that he bade adieu to his family, his hunger all unappeased.

In London he had Charles Lamb, if no one else, and the tie which bound him to this dear companion of his youth, severed for a moment by the ridiculous tiff already mentioned, was now immediately knit up again, all explanation being found unnecessary.

"I live in a continual feast," wrote the author of the *Essays of Elia* about this time. "Coleridge has been with me now for nigh three weeks, and the more I see of him in the quotidian undress and relaxation of his mind, the more cause I see to love him, and believe him a *very good man.*"

"All those foolish impressions to the contrary," he added, alluding to the slanders he had once thought him guilty of, "fly off like morning slumbers. He is engaged in translations, which I hope will keep him this month to come."

The translation was that of *Wallenstein,* which had been in a measure forced upon him from without, and it went against the grain. He thought it tedious, and made no secret of the "deep unutterable disgust" inspired in him by Schiller's ideological drama, of the metre of which "he spoke slightingly and said according to his taste it dragged like a fly through a glue pot," and which he enriched with lyrical beauties, though often, it is true, falling wide of the mark in translation.

He lodged at Buckingham street, Strand, at first accepting an offer of regular work upon the newspaper staff, which had previously been made him two years before by Daniel Stuart, editor of the *Morning Post*. He took up the position of an Anti-Jacobin and a patriot, but also as an opponent of the "war to a standstill" policy of the government. His articles, packed close with reasoned logic and showing, moreover, a very real debating talent, were welcomed most warmly by the public, which was longing for peace, or, in other words, for the resumption of commercial relations with France, and Stuart was so delighted with his contributor that he proposed making him joint editor of the paper which was continually increasing its circulation. It is a fact that the *Morning Post* grew from 350 copies a day in 1795 to 4,500 in 1803, an imposing figure for the times, but still far from the 7,000 to which Coleridge was to boast of raising it from 1800 on. Unhappily, although the easy tone of his articles do not suggest that Coleridge had to burn any midnight oil to fulfil his duties as a journalist, the necessity for producing two or three articles a week soon made them intolerable to him. He answered Stuart: "I would not give up the country and the lazy reading of old folios for two thousand times two thousand pounds—in short, that beyond £350 a year I considered money as a real evil."

After the crisis he had just been through, in which he had tried to pledge himself to some rule of honourable conduct, nothing could be more fraught with significance, and that, as we shall see, a tragic one, than such an answer, playfully though it is turned. Coleridge had no lack of talent, nor even like some men of genius, of fluency, and finding his opinions harmonizing for once with the feelings of the world in general he should have felt emboldened by the happy conjuncture. But it was from something very different from any lack of material that he suffered. If he were put under any obligation, he lost his nerve, and then his head. This sublimely irresponsible creature could have no worse torture thrust upon him than the feeling of being bound by an undertaking. The thought of a duty to be fulfilled, or a task recurring regularly, cast a gloom over him, and was enough to throw him into the clutch of a torment as paralysing as remorse. There is a certain race of cats, Siamese cats I believe, which can never bear to stay in a room with the doors shut. Coleridge was like these animals. He became a prey to unendurable anguish as soon as foreseen circumstances blocked out his future, or he became responsible for what was to happen tomorrow. By giving up work on the *Morning Post,* he did, moreover, give up a comparatively easy task, in order to take up a far more galling yoke, the translation of *Wallenstein* which as he said himself had "stricken him with barrenness." But he had at any rate changed one treadmill for another. . . .

I said at the beginning of this chapter that he barely remained four months at Nether Stowey, though for the

space of a year in Germany he had never ceased longing
for the sweetness of seeing his little cottage again. His
friends were now begging him on all sides to leave London, Poole, on the one hand, and on the other, Wordsworth, who had recently settled at Grasmere in the Lake
District; and, as may well be imagined, he paid no heed
to the voice summoning him back to the countryside, so
full of dear memories which he had left, but listened instead to the one that vaunted the charms of untrodden
country. On the 24th July, 1800, he went to live at Greta
Hall at Keswick in Cumberland.

The scenery is magnificent, and the view Coleridge
could see from his window one of the most picturesque
in the world. There he wrote his last verses, and it seemed
as though nature *in all its blaze of beauty* wished to offer
the poet a setting worthy of his end. This setting is not
unlike some of Turner's canvases, a painter who, moreover, was somewhat akin to Coleridge in the quality of
his vision. Here indeed, all is defined or dissolved in
the same misty light as in the pictures of the greatest
musician whose palette has ever sung the opal tints of
light as they are diffused or refracted in water. On foggy
days, seen through the mist, whose colour hesitates between grey-blue and mauve, the red of the houses heightened by the greenery ranges the whole gamut of tones:
and when the veil of vapour lifts, the pallid sun, shining
out from behind tiny cloudlets, round and light as thistle-

down, like sheep scattered over the meadows, gleams fit-
fully for a moment, and fades into a silver sky.

Between the hills round Borrowdale to the south, and
the bulk of Skiddaw to the north, its outline jagged by
two deep clefts, the lakes of Derwentwater and Bassenthwaite which lay spread out at Coleridge's feet are more
steeply sunk than any other in the district. A line of over-
shadowing heights clad in oaks and pines sometimes wav-
ers like a gauze curtain, and sometimes mounts skyward
like "the tents of a giant camp," beyond the little wooded
islands which lie scattered over the changing face of
Derwentwater, and there is no more delicate and delightful sight than the interweaving of these lines of hills,
abrupt or curving with something perpetually elusive in
their windings. Bassenthwaite, which bends away to the
west towards the sea twelve miles away from its farthest
point, reflects a horizon of more ponderous but also
more variable cloud, and Coleridge wrote to Godwin that
he was almost become a god, so sublime were his impressions as they came and went in this "wilderness of
mountains catching and streaming lights and shadows
at all times." The river Greta, which caught the last rays
of the setting sun, almost girdled his house, and near it
the high winds sent flying like smoke the powdery foam
of the waterfall close at hand at Lodore, its roar reminding him of the Cocytus of the Greeks.

Here and there where the rocks overshadowed the waters, a bare hillside would soften into rose under a spate of thickset heather. Keswick stands huddled together in a far wilder situation than Grasmere, which is only surrounded by a girdle of gently swelling hills; and unlike Wordsworth, who was, besides, born in this part of the country, Coleridge could never get used to the harsh climate, one of the coldest and dampest in the whole of England. No sooner had autumn's magic faded than rheumatism, from which Coleridge had formerly suffered so cruelly, returned to the attack with redoubled vigour. From the beginning of the winter of 1800 he described himself as "trembling on through sands and swamps of evil and bodily grievance," and pain that was evidently of an arthritic tendency, for it knotted his joints and inflamed his eyes, thus making reading an impossibility. "The act of metre composition, as I lay in bed," he wrote, "affected them, and my voluntary ideas were every minute passing, more or less transformed into vivid spectra." A mental torture aggravated his physical suffering and was his final undoing. He wished to return to *Christabel,* of which he had only finished the first part before leaving for Germany, but he was forced into owning himself incapable of doing more than add a second canto, without being able to complete it. And he was also obliged to have recourse to a stimulant in order to achieve so much. He wandered vainly, for hours at a stretch, among the mountains, but the sought-for inspiration would not come at his beck and call, until one day, when dining with a clergyman, he let his host lead him to the very brink of drunkenness. The next day the power to write returned, but it fled incontinently. Alcohol, by putting him in some mysterious way once more into touch with the invisible world, restored for a time the power of conjuring up the terror of nameless fear which is the very essence of his power. He only felt the more heartbroken afterwards, in his despair at having survived the death of his creative imagination. For some time he tried to persuade himself that the intellectual sterility he thought had come upon him was caused by fatigue, and even more by his dislike of translating *Wallenstein*. Owing to this illusion, and then under the influence of the anxiety he felt at seeing his dear Hartley stricken with a sharp attack of illness, he himself being obliged to take to his bed, he passed alternately from a state of joy to one of sorrow. The despairing fits which prostrated him were succeeded by renewed bursts of confidence, during which he wrote two poems for Mrs. Robinson, an actress who had formerly been well known under the name of Perdita on account of her liaison with the Prince of Wales, and had now come to die in a house over-grown with ivy and roses not far from Greta Hall. But the example of diligence shown by Southey, who had come to live for a short while at Keswick, after a second stay in Portugal, soon made him see the full extent of his inability to make any sustained effort. He thought, however, that it was rather brain power than spiritual force which enabled his brother-in-law to heap book upon book or turn from writing plays to poetry, from poetry to compiling an anthology or an historical work. And Wordsworth's serene lyrical energy did more than the methodical plodding of Southey, the complete man of letters, to propel him down the slope which was to end for him in complete surrender, that is to say, in his bidding farewell to poetry. He often went over on foot to Windermere, a matter of twenty miles or so, for he was a good walker, in order to see Wordsworth. He had vaguely hoped, by taking up his abode in the Lake District, to find that close contact with the peasant poet would enable him to recreate the atmosphere in which his masterpieces had come to their miraculous flowering. Wordsworth used to read over to him his latest verses, and he listened with a feeling of deep distress, abasing himself with a kind of bitter delight, to this poetry which rolled on indeed in mighty flood, though he was aware that its meditative simplicity, overlaid with an austere and at the same time rather childish optimism, was not the last word in art; secretly comparing it with his own, in which he had succeeded in capturing the haunting mystery in all things, and in expressing the inexpressible.

Imagine him marching alongside his sturdy companion, down one of those roads which wind along the hillside, hanging between the purplish black foliage of the pines on one side, and the pale waters of the lake, just ruffled by a westerly breeze on the other. He would keep ever in his shadow. Nothing stirred him more deeply than the grave placidity of this tall, gaunt rather loosely-knit fellow, clothed like a peasant, his face seamed with long wrinkles that matched his short side-whiskers, his clogs beating out a rustic accompaniment to calm, un-emphatic words. He admired him sadly but unenviously, untouched by any such grudging feeling as a poor man may bear towards a rich one, or a weakling towards a fellow-creature in full health and strength, but almost unmanned, it may be, by the perception that comes at times to all of a happiness greater than this world may know. This static and Olympian state of Wordsworth's, and its happily fruitful results, could, Coleridge knew, never have been his at any time, unless his nature had been radically different, and he had ceased to be himself. He considered it the poet's secular privilege,—the fa-voured poet at all events, who brings forth poetry as a tree bears cherries or apples,—to reflect universal har-monies in a moral mirror in the same manner as his friend, and he marvelled with thoughts unmixed with self, at seeing him fulfil his mission, while remaining convinced of the folly of his own efforts were he to at-tempt to imitate them.

He wrote to Godwin that Wordsworth, by showing him what true poetry is, had revealed to him the fact that he was no poet. Even though such a statement may sound excessive, and though we may know it did not echo Coleridge's inmost conviction, no doubts should be thrown on his sincerity. It sums up in an absolute form a relative sense for which I have been trying to provide an explanation, and which may better be understood on opening Dorothy Wordsworth's journal at some page on which she made a note of one of the days which she and her brother spent at Windermere. . . . "As we were going along we were stopped at once, at the distance perhaps of fifty yards from our favourite birchtree. It was yielding to the gusty wind with all its tender twigs. The sun shone upon it, and it glanced in the wind like a flying sunshiny shower. It was a tree in shape, with stem and branches, but it was like a spirit of water. . . . William read Spenser a little aloud to us." The whole of Wordsworth's wisdom lies in these pages which have been chosen out from a thousand others like themselves, in all of which his sister has caught in a flying sketch his almost passive submission to the spectacle of nature. He let this "mother-heart," to make use of an expression of the poet of the *Contemplations,* lead a life akin in its essence to his own, whilst

> a deep
> And solemn harmony pervades
> The hollow vale from steep to steep,

and the "sounding cataract" haunted them "like a passion." A passion, however, which moved to its own appointed and legitimate end, creating order in virtue of the fact that it obeyed a law from on high. What full-

ness of conviction! What joyful peace in creation! What
restful knowledge of a helpful presence close at hand!
But Coleridge was not one of those people who can realize their soul by turning it effortlessly outwards upon
things, that is to say, in the conditions in which it is manifest at any particular moment, or as it reacts beneath
the influence of an emotion, with its compound of elements that properly belong to it, and of accretions from
without. He only revealed his mind when he possessed
it in an unadulterated state, and when he found it possible to create a world in the image of his own inward
kingdom. Inspiration only visited him intermittently,
and being persuaded as he now was, that he would never
again know this state of grace, he took the heroic resolution, drawn from his knowledge of the duty incumbent
upon him, never again, in the face of all unlikelihood, to
venture to become a *poet's poet*. He would do no more
than try, by rising superior to himself, to attain to an
understanding of the mechanism of lyric creation, to
study the history of events which make up the life of
thought, when thought is stirring outside appearance
known to the senses, and if not to make affirmations and
to create a philosophic system, at any rate to put forward fruitful subjects for review or to draw up a for-
mula for dreams. The *Ode to Dejection,* which is one of
the most admirable poems he ever wrote, notes down
in terms of beauty expressive in resignation, his intention to seek forgetfulness of his sorrows by means of

abstruse metaphysical researches, and may be considered as his swan song. But for a few unimportant pieces, he wrote no more poetry, excepting always that poem wherein he described the *Pains of Sleep,* and which he enclosed in a letter to Southey in September, 1803.

These lines which were not meant for the public eye belong, moreover, by their analytical character to the body of speculative work which he tried to carry out. And there is nothing paradoxical in supposing that, in gliding into rhythm in order to make the observations upon his pathological state which make up their main substance, he was only aiming at transcribing them with greater fidelity.

The date of the 4th of April, 1802, which is that of *Dejection,* marks therefore a profound change in Coleridge's life. All his letters at that time reveal the moral crisis of which this change was the result, or allude to his hopes of extracting from the sacrifice to which he had made up his mind some consolation, that is as much as to say, reasons for not thinking he had fallen short of himself or that he was less worthy of his friends' respect and of men's gratitude. He wrote in February, 1801: "I have been thinking vigourously during my illness so that I cannot say my long, long wakeful nights have been all lost to me. The subject of my meditations has been the relations of thought to things—in the language of Hume, of ideas to impressions."

Wedgwood, on the other hand, whom he accompanied

on a tour in Wales at the end of 1802, about the time his daughter Clara was born, and who noted his efforts to make himself agreeable in spite of almost continuous pain, did not describe him as idle, but rather, as full of activity; and, though he would go out for long solitary walks, he also wrote a great deal. Not that he was composing anything, for he was planning to bring out, with Southey's collaboration, a bibliographical, biographical, and critical history of English literature. But he was taking notes, and writing down impressions he had gathered in the course of his reading, and the train of thought it had started. He was above all endeavouring to keep his intuition wakeful, and to dive down deeper and deeper into his consciousness, where he was sure to find Immanent Being, that is to say, to seek to find the centre of his own nature, and there to remain in order to unravel the universal enigma by questioning his own heart. His attitude was less that of a philosopher than of a psychologist, and it owed more to the sensibility of the lyric poet than to the observation of the scientist—for he was to remain above all a poet, even when he had lost all poetic energy. His metaphysical system was now taking shape, though it did not allow him to describe either for himself or for us things as a whole, save when they appeared in his dream.

The opium to which he had once more taken, (he mentioned incidentally in January, 1800, the agreeable sensations a few drops of laudanum had given him), helped

to keep him in this particular frame of mind in which
the intellect does not string reasons together round clear
hypotheses, but in which the soul is enraptured before the
infinite horizons opening out before it, with the mirage of
an understanding of the Absolute, having ceased to distinguish itself from the shapes standing round it, par-
takers of the same symbol. However he did more than
share in the ordinary opium-eater's blissful state when
the effects of the drug first begin to intoxicate him, the
sterile excitement born of his illusory feeling of having
become a god. His faculties, exceptionally subtle as they
were, acquired a power of perception or of divination that
became freer than ever under the influence of the drug
which, as De Quincey affirms, only strengthens a man
in his natural bent. He charmed all those who drew
near him at this time by the keenness of his insight, for if
there were parts that were hard to understand in the
flourishes he scrawled upon the air, there were also some
that were resplendent with light, and his swift flashing
humour roused the admiration of his friends. Lamb, who
paid him a visit in 1802 could never have enough of
hearing him talk, and Wedgwood said that he enjoyed
general favour wherever he went. "In the midst of large
companies," notes Davy the future physicist, "he is the
image of power and activity. His eloquence is unim-
paired; perhaps it is softer and stronger. . . . Brilliant
images of greatness float upon his mind, like images of
the moving clouds upon the waters. . . . They are agi-

tated by every breeze and modified by every sunbeam."
M. Joseph Aynard, from whom I have borrowed this
quotation, remarks wisely, too, that from the year 1800
to the year 1803 Coleridge led "a life that might be called
phenomenal, by which I mean that his feeling of personality having receded to the second place of consciousness, owing to the obsession of dreams by day and by
night, he was wholly given over to the impression of the
moment with no feeling of continuity in his mental life."
He gives us the spectacle of a rarely impressionable soul
revealing more of itself to others than to itself, and, as
it were, escaping by the variety of its own throbbing re-
actions from the control of its memory, and the authority of its own judgment. That is, no doubt, why he
established a distinction—taking it over from Kant who
had used it with a merely restrictive aim—between the
understanding and the reason, allowing the latter no
more than a regulatory power.

Like the notes he made, and the reflections he scrib-
bled in the margins of books, (and those not his own
merely, but others which he had borrowed), the letters
he wrote bear witness to the curious manœuvre, perhaps the only example of the kind, by means of which,
and hoping thus to emerge into the infinite by the myriad
paths of the indefinite, he threw himself wholly upon
intuition, or let his personality surrender its divine essence until it dissolved, as it were, into shadows and
shapes of terrestrial things. He scraped together the mi-

nutest sensations, as though he might discover a synthesis in their ill-assorted union, and make up by impressionism for the lack of the rigour of speculative
method, in order to build up a philosophic system. This
passage out of a letter he sent Wedgwood on the 14th
January, 1803, in which he describes a mountain walk
gives us, too, some curious particulars as to the very peculiar mystical character of the crisis through which he
was passing, or rather as to the state of unsatisfied
receptivity in which he lived from this time forth, almost uninterruptedly until his death.

". . . I never find myself alone, within the embrace-
ment of rocks and hills, a traveller up an alpine road, but
my spirit careers, drives and eddies, like a leaf in autumn;
a wild activity of thoughts, imaginations, feelings and
impulses of motion rises up from within me; a sort of
bottom wind, that blows to no point of the compass,
comes from I know not whence, but agitates the whole
of me, my whole being is filled with waves that roll and
stumble, one this way and one that way, like things that
have no common master. I think that my soul must have
pre-existed in the body of a chamois-chaser. The simple
image of the old object has been obliterated, but the feelings and impulsive habits, and incipient actions, are
in me and the old scenery awakens them.

"The further I ascend from animated nature, from
men, and cattle, and the common birds of the woods
and fields, the greater becomes in me the intensity of the

feeling of life. Life seems to me then a spirit, that neither has nor can have an opposite. 'God is everywhere,' I have exclaimed, and works everywhere, and where is there room for death? In these moments it has been my creed, that death exists only because ideas exist; that life is limitless sensation; that death is a child of the organic senses, chiefly of the sight, that feelings die by flowing into the mould of the intellect becoming ideas, and that ideas passing forth into action, reinstate themselves again in the world of life."

Truth lies for him, as he says, in these "loose generalizations," which issue out of the sentiment of general harmony or celestial communion in which the impressions of his high sensitiveness are steeped. The thing that seems surprising, but on further reflections is seen to be so only in appearance, is that while he relegated the consciousness of his personality into the background, so as to indulge in these impressions, yet he was aware before his time of the continuity of our psychic life, that is to say, that there is no such thing in our nature as the "one nature" of Hume and that it is impossible to talk of our being as "an aggregate of separate and successive sensations." He wrote, indeed, in the admirable collection called *Anima Poetae* whose elements he began to collect together in 1803:

"Is not everyone at the same moment conscious that there co-exist a thousand others, a darker shade or less light even as when I fix my attention on a white house or a grey bare hill or rather long ridge that runs out of sight each way . . . the pretended sight-sensation is it anything more than the light point in every picture either of nature or of a good painter? and again subordinately, in every component part of the picture? And what is a moment? Succession with interspace? Absurdity! It is evidently only the *licht-punct* in the indivisible undivided duration."

Coleridge was soon to pay by terrible hallucinations for the refining of the senses given him by the use of opium. But even in his worst moments of slavery to the drug, he had ineffable moments of surcease from it, when a harmony penetrated all his sensations, which must be put down to the numbness which had overtaken his over-anxious penetration. Favoured by the dissociative power that the "dark idol" exercised over the physical and intellectual elements of his being, his mental faculties, freed, as it were, of their bonds, rejoiced in the extraordinary perspicacity of his senses. With him, however, unlike the majority of opium-eaters, it was not so much the sense of touch which was carried to its furthest pitch of susceptibility, not even the sense of hearing, but of sight, the most spiritual of the senses as Leonardo da Vinci says—as for the sense of smell, it is well known that all the derivatives of the poppy are inclined to blunt it. This musician in words was, as often happens, no auditive, and even when sounds affected him, and he did more than vaguely assemble their effects, he saw,

rather than heard them. M. Andre Coeuroy, in his very
learned and very subtle work *Music and Literature,* says
that, according to Grove, Coleridge saw in the *Funeral
March* and *Heroic Symphony* a procession in dark pur-
ple. The mild angelic strains of stringed instruments
touched him more deeply, or responded better to his
secret sympathies than wind instruments, (the violon-
cello in *The Ancient Mariner,* the harp in *Christabel,* the
dulcimer in *Kubla Khan*), and he enjoyed symphonies
less than savage chants or melodies, or those popular
Scotch songs with wistful airs which his nurse had sung
to him in his cradle. Nevertheless it was from the vibrations of light that he drew most of his pleasure, and his
interest was centred less on sounds than on the shapes
and colours of nature. "My eyes make pictures when they
are shut," he wrote in 1807 in the poem called *A Day
Dream,* which is composed of a series of pictures which
reassemble and reappear beneath the poet's closed eyelids,
first by day and then by night. But he wrote to Poole
in November, 1800, during the first days of his stay at
Keswick: "The two lakes, the vale, the river and mountains, and mists, and clouds, and sunshine, make endless
combinations, as if heaven and earth were for ever talking to each other." Thus the varied spectacle his eye
embraces from his window suggested to him the idea of
airy conversations, and no doubt can be felt that he
caught a hint as to their meaning; it was as he said in the
poem called *The Picture* which is like the twinkling soft-

ness of a landscape seen through a veil of shining rain, "in tree or wildflower . . . that this busy human heart aweary worships the spirit of unconscious life." The world was for him embodied in sight. No other sense allowed him to steal from life—by tearing himself away for an hour from his anxious self—those "dim similitudes" which "weave immortal strains," and there is hardly any other example of a soul as dreambound as his whose vague meditations were not only left all untroubled, but were on the other hand served by an attention which furnished them with a wealth of precise details. He never ceased to transfigure what he saw. "Examine Nature accurately," he says, "but write from recollection, and trust more to your imagination than your memory."

In *Dejection,* he noted the "peculiar tint of yellow green" to be seen at sunset, with such fidelity that it became a stumbling-block to Byron who proclaimed the description "absurdly false." It would be easy to multiply at leisure examples of such a strict search for the epithet, that it can be equalled nowhere save in the minute realism of the primitive Flemish painters. He drew unswervingly, for instance, the shivering bleakness of the countryside in early spring when he wrote in *Christabel:*

> Nought was green upon the oak
> But moss and rarest mistletoe.

He saw the "new moon winter bright" with

. . . the old moon in her lap foretelling
The coming of rain and squally blast.

And on the topmost branch of the tree, he discerned

The one red leaf, the last of its clan
That dances as often as dance it can
Hanging so light and hanging so high
On the topmost twig that looks up at the sky.

Baudelaire has remarked on the influence of water on
the dreams of the opium-eater. It is because the liquid
surface makes all pictures manifold, because it spreads
them out or breaks them up or transfigures them through
the prismglass of innumerable rainbow lights, disturbing
and clearing the atmosphere by turns, that Coleridge
loved lake and seaside scenery so much. He did more,
however, than merely enjoy them with the fine eye of the
connoisseur. He was able to strike chords to bind together the vibrations they set up in the air, and thus compose harmonies, for the deep mystical inclination of his
mind forbade him to be satisfied with pure sensation,
and far better than any commentary, the following page
in its exceptional beauty enables one to understand the
quality of the philosophical echoes which he could obtain from his impressions:

"A brisk gale and the foam that peopled the *alive* sea,
most interestingly combined with the number of white
sea-gulls, that, repeatedly, it seemed as if the foam-spirit
had taken life and wing and had flown up—the white

precisely same colour birds rose up so close by the ever-
perishing white-water wavehead, that the eye was unable to detect the illusion which the mind delighted to
indulge in. O that sky, that soft, blue, mighty arch resting on the mountain or solid sea-like plain—what an
awful omneity in unity! I know no other peaceful union
of the sublime with the beautiful, so that they should be
felt, that is, at the same minute, though by different
faculties, and yet, each faculty be predisposed, by itself
to receive the specific modifactions from the other. To
the eye it is an inverted goblet, the inside of a sapphire
basin, perfect beauty in shape and colour. To the mind
it is immensity, but even the eye feels as if it were (able)
to look through (but) the eye feels that the limitation is
in its own power, not in the object."

Coleridge wrote this kind of meditation at Malta where
he had hoped to find the "even and dry" climate his
health required. He had at first fixed his choice on Ma-
deira, after a tour in Scotland with the Wordsworths, a
tour which his increasing disorder forced him to abandon at the end of a fortnight.

During the whole of 1803 he was a prey to a painful
moral, as well as physical agitation, which Wordsworth
defined as "eternal activity without action," which first
made him dream of going to "Biscay" to study Basque,
then led him to stay with Charles and Mary Lamb in
the capital, where he again wrote for the *Morning Post*

for a short time; and finally after having dazzled his London friends with his insight into philosophical matters, he retraced his steps northwards, with an idea in mind of padding out the *Bibliotheca Britannica* already mentioned by adding a few volumes to it, which should treat severally of metaphysics, theology, medicine, surgery, canon law and alchemy, etc.

There were moments when he would suddenly set off with no settled end in view, as though wishing to flee from himself, and walk forty miles or so until he was exhausted, upon the pretext that he thus forced his rheumatism to fly to his extremities. His eccentric manners startled all around him, and he could no longer keep from them the fact that he was taking drugs, for he was continuing to take large doses of opium, but perceiving that its effects bore ill upon his indisposition, which had taken "this asthmatic turn," he also used ether, and was trying to procure some Chang for he thought this Indian preparation of hempseed was the *Nepenthe* spoken of by Homer. Wordsworth saw him one day in a "half stupefied" condition; but he pleaded such tortures to justify his recourse to the drug, that his excuses found grace even in Southey's eyes. It is true that the horror of his state passes the bounds of the imagination. He endured it without cease and without rest, and his very sleep was haunted by such terrifying nightmares, that the unhappy man preferred to lie awake for three nights out of four, sooner than face the hell before him.

I have already said that Coleridge had written a poem about his nightmares, and that it was, perhaps, with a view to greater exactitude that he used verse, rather than prose, to describe their nature: "My heart," he said, "was aching, my head all confused." There is, however, no searching after the picturesque in this confession, to which he has given a moral or abstract sense, and which should in this respect be compared with De Quincey's. In similar circumstances the latter chiefly sought, indeed, to describe his sensations, and above all to note down the fantastic transformations which the images that peopled his dreams underwent. There is no doubt that Coleridge, whose retina we know was of an astonishing activity, saw images every whit as variegated as De Quincey's go thronging past his mind's eye. But he only attempted to extract the symbolical or spiritual meaning of his hallucinations. It was a drama of conscience that he described, not a complacent analysis of his torments, and therein he revealed the native uprightness of his soul, which, until the end of his life, was protected by the sting of religious scruples from his own weaknesses. And so, as he wrote to a friend, his "night screams seemed to carry him beyond mere body," and the sufferings he endured were like the "tortures of guilt and what we are told of the punishment of a spiritual world."

The tempestuous rain which had been beating down upon the Lake District ever since the autumn of 1803 had

sadly affected Coleridge. He lingered on for nearly another six months at Greta Hall, whither Southey, who
was destined to live out the remainder of his days there,
had returned; and after a stay at Grasmere, where he
had been kept stationary for a month by an attack which
was probably due to the intoxication of the drug, and a
further visit, first to Liverpool, then to London, he finally
set sail on 2nd April 1804. His mind was at ease as far
as his wife's affairs were concerned, (he had left behind
untouched for her use the amount Wedgwood gave him
as an annuity), and for his own part he had accepted a
loan of nearly a hundred pounds from Wordsworth,
and was counting on another hundred which his brothers had promised him. Sir George Beaumont, too, that
artist-Maecenas, had made further provision for him,
and he was armed with letters of introduction to the
Governor of Malta, Sir Alexander Ball.

He may have first intended to go to Sicily, where nature seemed more smiling than in the ancient Phœni-
cian colony; but when he landed at Valetta on the 18th
April, 1804, after a tiring sea-voyage, broken by a short
visit to Gibraltar, he decided to go no further. Another
circumstance finally decided him to stay on in Malta. Sir
Alexander Ball, who besides being Governor, was also
judge in the island, offered to take him into his office,
until his secretary, who had recently died, could be re-
placed, and to give him the same salary, eight hundred
pounds a year. The idea of not only covering his ex-

penses but of being paid as well, came at an opportune
moment to provide Coleridge with an argument of which,
in his exhausted condition, he was not slow to avail himself. He meant, no doubt, not to return to England until he should have seen Syracuse and Italy. But he felt
no curiosity at being so near Africa, at the very heart of
the world where Greco-Roman civilization had flourished. He had already told Thelwall of old, he did "not
like history." Far from his imagination being stirred, or
his soul set brooding over ancient buildings or other remains which might reveal the genius of vanished races
or peoples, he would scarcely throw them one heedless
glance.

"Dear Sir Walter Scott and myself," he wrote in *Table
Talk,* where he recorded his conversations with Tieck
and Joseph Green, "were exact but harmonious opposites
in this: that every old ruin, hill, river, or tree, called up
in his mind a host of historical or biographical associations . . . whereas for myself, notwithstanding Dr. John-
son, I believe I should walk over the plain of Marathon,
without taking more interest in it than in any other
plain of similar features." . . .

He took no interest in "things contingent and transi-
tory," and the liveliest and most picturesque sights only
sent his thoughts roving into the blue. At Gibraltar, he
turned aside from watching the mixture of races in their
"discordant complexity of associations," in order to take
refuge, far above the hurry and bustle, in the feeling of

the harmony of "the abiding things of Nature, great, calm, majestic, and one." Reality had no power to bind him. He was the exact opposite to a realist, because he everywhere sought the unity in diversity, and must needs sunder it from what the intellect can conceive of, and the senses perceive.

"I feel too intensely," he says somewhere, "the omnipresence of all in each. . . . My brain fibres or the spiritual light which abides in the brain marrow . . . is of too general an affinity with all things and though it perceives the difference of things yet is eternally pursuing the likenesses, or rather, that which is common between them."

Coleridge did not fail to make a conquest of Sir Alexander Ball, and he performed greater services for him than the Governor could have looked for in an ordinary secretary, particularly in the wording of his diplomatic correspondence. In general, however, things were not left to his own initiative in the office. All that he was left to do was to carry out purely routine duties, that is to say, sign his name, register oaths made before him, and take depositions. Although they occupied most of his day, and were tedious enough, these tasks left him complete freedom of mind. Undisturbed by worry or fatigue he could, as soon as evening came on, sit down to read philosophy, particularly Kant's, which he had begun to study thoroughly, and the variety of notes he then accumulated, on psychology, as well as morality and metaphysics, prove that intellectually he was highly alert whilst at Malta, though pathologically he was deteriorating.

The healthy island climate, hot enough in summer for the cactus to grow in the open air, as it does in Africa, had at first seemed to do him good. But the damp sirocco which blows from the south soon began to get on his nerves and made his spirits sag. His rheumaticky limbs seemed as heavy as "lifeless tools," and the pain he suffered was "gnawing his vitals," nor did the combined effects of laudanum, ether, and menthol have any effect. Lonely, far away from friends, at the very gateway to the East, on one of the highroads frequented by traffickers in the drug, it was inevitable that Coleridge should give way more than ever to his passion. Not that his ever-watchful moral sense ever ceased for one instant to point out to him the danger of this passion, nor did his sense of dignity ever resign itself to the collapse for which he felt himself heading. But he was incapable of getting on to his feet again through his own efforts, and none of those who admired and loved him were there to seize him by the hand and pull him out of the mire. Soaking in opium, and unable to stop doing so, he could see himself, with a pathetic anguish that passes all expression, draw nearer and nearer to that degree of intoxication which leads to the decay of the brain cells. He was haunted by ideas of suicide, from which the thought of his children kept him. The death of Captain John Words-

worth, the poet's brother, drowned off Portland in February, 1805, had plunged him further into the struggle
with sombre ideas. He felt a lively affection for that
officer, and when Lady Ball broke to him the news of his
death in the great drawing-room in the Governor's palace, the blow was so fierce that, staggering as though he
had been felled to the ground, he was obliged to take
to his bed, and do no more work for a fortnight.

When the secretary who was to replace him arrived
at Valetta, he set forth for Sicily like a man walking
in his sleep, perhaps charged with some mission to fulfil,
or some political report to draw up on the revenues and
resources of the island, and after living some time at
Syracuse, he reached Naples on the 15th December, 1805.
He left, so he said, all his papers in the latter town when
he hurriedly left it for Rome. But he stayed over five
months in the Eternal City, and had he really forgotten
them, had ample time to have them sent on to his new
address. In truth, nothing seems more problematical than
the existence of the documents he alleged he had collected
relating to statues, pictures, buildings, and the fine arts
in general, both in Naples and Rome. Without imputing
to him any lack of straightforwardness, we may, from
this time on, throw doubts on most of the events he mentions, or suspect him of altering their character. He began to confuse dreams and reality, intention and fulfilment, and had but to imagine anything, to think it had

come to pass, or at the lowest, to deduce from a fact the possible consequences it held, and to believe in these more strongly than in the fact itself. . . .

He came into contact at Rome, in the house belonging to Wilhelm von Humboldt the Prussian Ambassador, with distinguished and even eminent characters: Angelica Kauffman, the American painter Washington Allston—who moreover painted his portrait—perhaps Thorwaldsen the Dane, and he had but to talk to them—brilliantly as was his wont—about the works to be seen in the museums, and he would then think he had written about them. I do not imagine, however, that he held forth with any originality on æsthetic subjects in the company of these neo-classicists, and I should rather incline to think that he did no more than indulge in ingenious digressions on the commonplaces of academic art, quite in the style of the time, which had advanced less as far as painting and sculpture were concerned than in poetry. But what more curious testimony could we have to his restlessness and his diseased tendency to fabricate myths than his story of his headlong flight from Rome! Being advised that Napoleon had sent out a warrant for his arrest, on the score of certain articles of his which, however, were published anonymously in the *Morning Post,* and thus contributed to the breaking off of the Peace of Amiens, he hastily, so the story goes, made for Leghorn with a passport from "the good old Pope," Pius VII, and embarked in the first ship to raise anchor—an American sailing vessel. This ship having been captured by a French man-of-war, he had cast all his manuscripts overboard by the captain's orders, as though meaning by this action to relieve his Yankee of all responsibility, though how implicated one might be hard put to it to say. . . . Let us make no mistake in the matter: the manuscripts thrown into the Mediterranean went straight, no doubt, to the land of dreams, there to join the papers left behind at Naples. A kind of shyness, an instinct to take cover spiritually, lay at the root of all these inventions of Coleridge's, the excuses he trumped up, and the pretexts he made out for himself, so as continually to defer the fulfilment of the work expected of him. His soul in its weakness, ashamed of failing in its duty through frittering away its genius for want of resolution, was seeking to defend itself not only from his friends' reproaches, but from his own blame by swathing itself in legends, and telling itself lies just as it told them to others.

After an absence of two-and-a-half years, Coleridge returned to England in August, 1806; but he stayed on in London, instead of at once going to see his family, his wife and children, the thought of whom, however, had saved him from suicide. He was exhausted by the fatigue of the voyage, which had lasted fifty-five days, during which time he had twice thought to have lost his life. That is, at any rate, what he wrote to Josiah Wedgwood, in a letter in which he excused himself at length for not

having expressed sooner his sorrow at the death of
Thomas Wedgwood, which had taken place on the 10th
July, 1805. His wife, it is true, had not informed him of
his death, fearing lest he should be as deeply affected as
by that of Wordsworth's brother. But when he heard it,
either from Lamb or from Daniel Stuart, both of whom
he met in London, he refrained for a week from sending
Josiah his condolences. In order that Coleridge might
continue to receive the full pension of £150 which he
had undertaken to provide in company with his brother,
Josiah had now, however, assumed the dead man's obligation as well, and such generosity was deserving of
something better than silence. But Coleridge who, like
all opium-eaters, can hardly be said to have had much
sense of time, had also come to the pitch of moral collapse which makes a man dread taking on the slightest
responsibility, and be almost staggered at the idea of
wielding a pen. Coleridge owned, too, to Josiah Wedgwood, that he was obliged to grant himself an interval
whatever the matter in hand, and that too, not so much
out of idleness, as on account of a strange cowardice
which made him put letters aside for weeks unopened,
even from those he loved the best. He dared not ask for
news of his friends, and was so strongly convinced that
he could not live with his wife, that he was thinking of
getting a separation. Wordsworth, who was informed
of his intentions, and was perhaps longing for him to
hear the great poem he had just finished, *The Prelude,*

tried to induce him to return to Keswick, but he could only resume his friendship with the Wordsworths again on neutral ground, at Coleorton, on a farm belonging to Sir George Beaumont.

In the letter he wrote to Josiah Wedgwood, Coleridge complained of being "worse than homeless"; now however he seemed to delight in being a vagabond, and to find that being a parasite on others suited his state of unproductive weakness better than anything else. In London he accepted the offer of a lodging in the offices of the *Morning Post,* which Stuart now owned, and he only called in at Keswick in order to fetch his son thence, and to take him along with him to Coleorton. He adored Hartley, whom he had formerly called a "limber elf," on account of the fairy sprightliness of his mind, and the sight of him, so he said, "filled his father's eye with light." He wrote to Poole in 1803: "Hartley is a strange, strange boy, exquisitely wild, an utter visionary; like the moon among thin clouds, he moves in a circle of light of his own making." But the precocious, morbidly sensitive child, so like himself in his irresolution and impatience of all control, his dreamy tendencies and disconcertingly subtle analytical genius, did not induce him to consent to return to family life. He told Wordsworth, in the verses he wrote for him after hearing *The Prelude,* which are as it were a postscript to *Dejection,* that fate was now insisting that he should "pluck the poisons of self-harm." He guessed that, as indeed events were soon to prove, now she had Southey's example before her eyes, his wife, who had many and many a time complained of his maladjustment to life, would ceaselessly bemoan the fate which had given her as a husband, instead of that most methodical and hardworking of men, a man given over to the whim of the moment, incapable of doing any settled, remunerative work. Whatever it might cost him, he preferred to deny himself his son's society, rather than be laden with recriminations by this embittered woman, who had not only never sympathized with him, but never even understood him. He admitted her virtues better than she realized his qualities, and liked and respected her more than she admired or loved him. But he found nothing more painful than to see how low she assessed the drama of conscience which was rending him. When, with the utmost reluctance, he let himself be persuaded into going down to Ottery St. Mary with her, and then, after the reconciliation brought about in his little native town by his brother the Rev. George Coleridge, on to Bridgewater in Somerset, he suffered so much from enduring the poor woman's daily presence, that he felt the need of pouring out his soul in letters to a young man of twenty-two, whose acquaintance he had but lately made. An exceptional young man indeed, and one particularly fitted to receive his confidence, as we shall see later on. . . . But let it be imagined for a moment what comparisons Sara was likely to make between her own condition and that of her sister Edith who had married Southey, and it will then be found easy to guess what must have been Coleridge's state of mind when he saw how, a prey as she was to malice and envy, his wife felt no pity for his despair, and only considered the material aspects of the frightful situation with which he was wrestling. His little son Berkeley's death a few years earlier had finally severed his connexion with Unitarianism. Sentimental reasons led him this time also, to turn his metaphysical researches in a religious direction, and to attempt to arrive at a kind of synthesis of all philosophical systems, which were to be reconciled together under the ægis of faith. The arguments of a practical kind which Mrs. Coleridge opposed to his spiritual torment, spurred him to entrench himself in the position to which his dreamy nature had brought him, which was that of a mystical spiritualism. He felt the need of comfort and consolation, of efficacious help against the tyranny of his vice to which he was determined not to give in, and in the isolation in which he found himself his meditations rose like a prayer that he might enter into the succour of the divine presence.

CHAPTER III

THE DAMAGED ARCHANGEL

It was at Bridgewater in Somerset in July, 1807, at the house of a Mr. Chubb, that Thomas De Quincey first met Coleridge, whose acquaintance he had dreamed of making since his return from Malta, and whom he had at first missed seeing by a couple of days at Nether Stowey. The young man of whom mention has just been made in the last chapter, had sung the praises of the authors of the *Lyrical Ballads*—soon to be known as the Lake School of Poets—at a time when, as he boasted later, the public knew nothing of them, and the critics spoke slightingly of their work. He had a restless, ardent, enthusiastic mind, and although his constitutional heritage was an exceptionally burdensome one (he and his sister were the sole survivors out of a family of eight, none of whom had reached maturity) Thomas De Quincey had early given signs of being what the world has agreed to call a prodigy. At fifteen, he was so well versed in the Greek language, that one of his masters said of him that he could better have harangued an Athenian multitude, than any orator of his own country could address an English one. Being of the opinion that the teaching and staff were ridiculously beneath his intellectual level at a certain school in Manchester where his guardian had seen fit to send him, bearing in mind the fact that the best pupils were sent on to Oxford with a bursary, he ran away from it five years too soon almost to a day, with a volume of Euripides in one pocket, and one of English poetry in the other. In vain did he try to explain away his flight to his mother, pointing out how incapable he was of stooping to his schoolfellows' childish studies, and still more, perhaps, to the foolishness of their chatter. The conclusion was forced upon him that even between the closest of kin, there is something *incommunicable,* which can never be got over, try as one may. He had means, and stood in no need of his uncle's pettifogging manœuvring to have him go up to Oxford at reduced fees. But the arguments he had mustered to win Mrs. De Quincey over to his way of thinking froze upon his lips as soon as he caught sight of the stony face she had put on to welcome him. He wandered through Wales, keeping himself alive on sloes and blackberries by day, and camping out by night in a tent "not larger than an ordinary umbrella"; never venturing into an inn save when it came on to rain, but luring the whole company whenever he did so, into discussions in which he so perfected his gift of natural eloquence that he became one of the most brilliant talkers that have ever existed. With the small sum of money that had been given or lent him as he went along, for the sake of his bonny face he came to London, but was soon driven by hunger into the clutches of a money-lender.

Nothing can have seemed at the time more extraordinarily novel in its appeal, than the tale he published in 1821 of the events during this part of his life, and which no doubt gave rise to the whole body of literature of social compassion. The story of the wretched little waif, with pinched looks, and stunted mind, with whom he used to spend the night, in the money-lender's house, sleeping on the floor, with a bundle of papers for all his pillow; and the other story about Ann, the prostitute who gave him a "glass of port-wine and spices" when he was on the verge of dying of starvation, and for whom he felt the same chaste love as for a favourite sister he had lost at the age of six, are both, moreover, justly celebrated, at any rate in England.

Prepared as he was by his sensitive heart to feel for the misery surrounding him as though it were his own, and becoming acquainted with the horrors of the lowest depths of a great city at an age when the soul can least shake off the impressions made upon it, De Quincey never afterwards lost the look of fear that would sometimes flicker across his face, or light up caverns of gloom behind his blue eyes.

He had at length been discovered in London, and sent to Oxford, where he threw himself passionately into his studies again, but without making friends with any of his fellow-students, nor speaking to them more than he could help, laying upon himself the rule "to associate with none," in order, as he said, "that I might like all men"; so over-sensitive had he become after his stultifying experience of the powers of evil.

With his slight shoulders, too slight for the size of his head with its overhanging forehead, his gentle, and ever so slightly effeminate manners, and his musical voice, he made a lively impression on all who came into contact with him, and rarely failed to charm when he so wished. Ready to be grave with thinking folk, or to wax merry when people were gay, he could pass from one mood to the other with surprising rapidity, and would take a perverse pleasure in altering or disguising the truth to suit his purposes, in spite of his fundamental sincerity.

Since he had read the *Rime of the Ancient Mariner*— a poem to which he attributed a decisive role in the development of his mind—Coleridge had always had a fascination for him, made quite irresistible by the legend surrounding him. When he learnt that the "bard of Quantock" was turning his whole attention to metaphysics—his own favourite study—his enthusiasm became greater still. He almost reached the point of sailing for Malta, so as to hear from the very lips of the inspired great man, what might be the answer to the riddle of the universe. But there was something more which had, from the beginning, given De Quincey a fellow-feeling for Coleridge. Just at the very time when Coleridge first bound himself by the chains of slavery to the "dark idol," De Quincey was being initiated into its delights. In order to rid himself of a very painful fit of toothache, he had, indeed, acting under a friend's advice, bought some opium at a London chemist's and thus turned into a drug fiend overnight.

People in Coleridge's circle had their suspicions as to his vice, though they might not know precisely what that was. Cottle, in particular, the Bristol publisher with whom De Quincey had soon begun to do business—his mother having now gone to Weston Lea, near Bath—must have had many a tale to tell of the sad habits growing upon the man whose first benefactor he had been. He did not fail to pass on to De Quincey all the more or less authenticated information he had received, either from Coleridge, or else from that unhappy creature, Charles Lloyd, whose scandalous novel about his former tutor had, it will be remembered, been published by him.

De Quincey, who was still at the rapturous stage of opium-eating—he only allowed himself doses in moderation about once in every three weeks—had listened to the revelations of Coleridge's moral distress with an avidity which may well be imagined. Perhaps he was reminded of himself by more than one trait in his hero's character, and may have felt a shiver of intellectual heroism run down his spine at the thought that he, too, was heading in the same dangerous direction. But hearing people talk to him about Coleridge was no longer enough to satisfy him. He must know him, and would have paid any price, run anywhither, or done any mortal piece of mischief whatever, if only he might see and hear him. Hearing of his presence at Bridgewater, he instantly left Bath, and this is how he described later on his first interview with him.

"I had received directions for finding out the house where Coleridge was visiting, and in riding down a main street of Bridgewater, I noticed a gateway corresponding to the description given me. Under this was standing, and gazing about him, a man whom I will describe. In height he might seem to be about five feet eight (he was, in reality about an inch and a half taller, but his figure was of an order which drowns the height); his person was broad and full and tended even to his complexion which was fair, though not what painters technically style fair, because it was associated with black hair; his eyes were large, and soft in their expression; and it was from the peculiar appearance of haze or dreaminess which mixed with their light that I recognized my object. It was Coleridge. I examined him steadfastly for a minute or more; and it struck me that he saw neither myself nor any other object in the street. He was in a deep reverie; for I had dismounted, made two or three trifling arrangements at an inn-door, and advanced close to him, before he had apparently become conscious of my presence. The sound of my voice, announcing my own name, first awoke him; he started and for a moment seemed at a loss to understand my purpose or his own situation; for he repeated rapidly a number of words which had no relation to either of us. There was no *mauvaise honte* in his manner, but simple perplexity, and an apparent difficulty in recovering his position among daylight realities. This little scene over, he received me with a kindness of manner so marked that it might be called gracious."

There is nothing less surprising than that Coleridge should have confessed his weakness to De Quincey, if not, perhaps, as the latter pretended, in the course of their first interview, at any rate very shortly afterwards, when it is borne in mind how easily one initiate into the delights of "just, subtle and all-conquering opium" confides in another. Amongst people who are addicted to the same pernicious practices a kind of complicity springs up, which makes them pour into each other's ears with a satisfaction which might almost seem indecent, the slightest details of their passion, as well as its effects; how much the more, then, does this become true when such people are psychologists, whose main curiosity centres round analysis of the feelings. It is certain, on the other hand, that De Quincey was cunningly falsifying the truth when he stated that Coleridge let him read his mind as an open book, whilst he, for his part, confessed nothing to him in return. I should rather be inclined to believe that, in order to lead Coleridge on—his age at that time being thirty-five—to tell him all there was to tell, De Quincey, who had just entered his twenty-second year, made the most he could of his own failings. . . .

Whatever may have been his influence, however, on this man so much older than himself, he only used it with a laudable object in view, since he dissuaded him from finally breaking off relations with Mrs. Coleridge. He offered to accompany the poor woman and her two children to Keswick, so that whilst accepting the proposal made to him by the Royal Institution to give a set of sixteen lectures in London, his friend might reflect at leisure upon a step as to the gravity of which he must not blind himself. . . . De Quincy knew, too, both from what Coleridge had told him, and from the nature of the dissatisfaction at which Mrs. Coleridge had hinted in his presence, that a small sum in cash would help to smooth matters down between the two. Coleridge's qualities as a conversationalist, which, as Cottle remarked, were just then more marvellous than ever, as much on account of his lofty views as of his extensive knowledge, allowed De Quincey to hope that the best possible results might ensue from this public appearance at the Royal Institution. Meanwhile, he enjoined upon Cottle to send the poet the sum of three hundred pounds, in the form of an unlimited loan from "a young man of fortune who admired his talents," but who desired to remain anonymous. His first suggestion had been to offer five hundred pounds; but Cottle, who considered he had a right to interfere in anything concerning Coleridge, took it upon himself, because of what he called his knowledge of his friend's unmethodical character, to persuade De Quincey into being less generous than he had first intended.

His mission over, that is to say, Sara and her two children having gone back to live near Wordsworth, De Quincey hurried to rejoin Coleridge in London, in the uncomfortable rooms Stuart allowed him to use in the offices belonging to the *Morning Post*. Coleridge was to speak on poetry and the fine arts. De Quincey was seething with impatience to hear him, and the pick of London's brains or breeding were making ready to assemble together at the doors of the Royal Institution in Albemarle Street, all agog to listen to a lecturer with a reputation for genius, about whom certain indiscreet hints had been thrown out as to his eccentric habits.

But at the bare thought of what was expected of him, and of the seething excitement caused by his name, Coleridge was suddenly seized with panic. The arguments he had done his best to muster had been thrown into disarray, and like a general looking helplessly on at the rout of his army, he had, before a single shot was fired, seen his dialectics scatter to the winds. Stuart having, however, advanced him the hundred pounds to be paid for the lectures, he insisted upon going on to the platform, like a condemned man to the scaffold, with Lamb, Poole and De Quincey encouraging, supporting, almost lifting him by bodily force. But alas! hardly had he appeared twice, when courage failed him to face the public again, as Lamb wrote to Manning on the 20th February,

1808. And De Quincey wrote that he dismissed "audience after audience, with pleas of illness." The author of the *Confessions of an Opium Eater* further reported that he had "seen all Albemarle Street closed by a lock of carriages filled with women of distinction, until . . . their own footmen advanced to the carriage-doors with the intelligence that Mr. Coleridge had been suddenly taken ill"; whereupon they turned and sped homewards in a high state of dudgeon. People soon weary of everything, even of catching their deaths of cold, in pure snobbery, to listen to a fashionable lecturer, and it happened that when the time came that Coleridge made up his mind to speak again, he did so to well-nigh empty rows of benches. It might have been better for his fame, had those ladies who most staunchly admired him followed the example of those who had given up all wish of hearing him, for they were disappointed in him. And at the same time, he baulked the hopes of his most faithful friends. For indeed, though he had, in his lack of self-confidence, told Campbell "this is my solemn determination not to give a single lecture till I have in fair writing at least one half of the whole course," yet he improvised from notes alone, or rather, floundered through a mass of untidy papers. . . .

"His lips," wrote De Quincey, "were baked with feverish heat, and often black in colour; and in spite of the water which he continued drinking during the whole course of the lecture, he often seemed to labour under an almost paralytic inability to raise the upper jaw from the lower. In such a state it is clear that nothing could save the lecture itself from reflecting his own feebleness and exhaustion except the advantage of having been re-composed in some happier mood. But that never happened: most unfortunately, he relied on his extempore ability to carry him through. Now, had he been in spirits, or had he gathered animation and kindled by his own emotion, no written lecture could have been more efficient than one of his unpremeditated colloquial harangues. But either he was depressed originally below the point from which reascent was possible, or else this reaction was intercepted by continual disgust from looking back upon his ill-success, for assuredly he never once recovered that free and eloquent movement of thought which he could command at any time in a private company. The passages he read, moreover, to illustrate his doctrines, were generally unhappily chosen, because chosen at haphazard, from the difficulty of finding at a moment's summons these passages which his purpose required. Nor do I remember any that produced much effect except two or three which I myself put ready marked into his hands among the *Metrical Romances,* edited by Ritson. Generally speaking, the selections were as injudicious and as inappropriate as they were ill-delivered, for among Coleridge's accomplishments good reading was not one. He had neither voice (so at least I thought) nor management of voice. This defect is unfortunate in a public lecturer, for it is inconceivable how much weight and effectual pathos can be communicated by sonorous depth and melodious cadence of the human voice to sentiments the most trivial; nor on the other hand, how the grandest are emasculated by a style of reading which fails in distributing the lights and shadows of a musical intonation. However, this defect chiefly concerned the immediate impression; the most afflicting to a friend of Coleridge's was the entire absence of his own peculiar and majestic intellect; no heart, no soul, was in anything he said; no strength of feeling in recalling universal truths, no power of originality or compass of moral relations in his novelties—all was a poor faint reflection from pearls once scattered on the highway by himself in the prodigality of his early opulence —a mendicant dependence on the alms dropped from his own overflowing treasury of happier times."

Coleridge's first lectures are only known to us through the notes taken down at the time by Crabb Robinson. In the guise—a fragmentary one it is true—in which he tells of them in his diary, they show signs of a certain confusion or incoherence, and give the impression of having been composed with no previous plan in mind. Coleridge, who had given up the idea of discussing art, for lack of the energy needed to set about looking for the papers he would require, talked, so to say, by fits, about Greek polytheism, the origins of tragedy, the principles and essence of poetry—which was, so he said, universality

—and the character of Hamlet, who of all characters in Shakspere was the one he was most familiar with, for he had made a long and deep study of him during his visit to Malta.

Though he did not come up to the hopes of his friends, who had been expecting wonders, he produced a fairly strong impression on most of the audience, to whom psychological and moral criticism was quite new, and who were not aware of attempts already made in Germany, at the philosophical interpretation of literary works. But he was in the mood to make his failure out as more important than it really was. He insisted that it was the evidence of a complete collapse. On the 10th February, a short while before he had undertaken these lectures, he had written to Lamb, in one of the volumes he had borrowed from the library of rare books which the humble India House clerk had succeeded in collecting, by denying himself tobacco, and even by going short of food. "Oh Charles, I am very ill. Vixi." The sarcasm of his enemies, and a caricature which came out, depicting him standing and declaiming at one end of a table, all the occupants of which were fast asleep and snoring over bottles and glasses with their mouths wide open, made him determined to leave London, after a further few months of uncertainty as to what he was to do, going to and fro between the offices of the *Morning Post* and the house belonging to his old friend of Christ's Hospital in Chancery Lane. Here the "damaged archangel" as his friend had called him on his return from Malta, would forget his miseries for awhile, as he discussed the qualities of the Elizabethan poets, or launched out into magnificent plans for the future, only to relapse suddenly into despondency, lamenting his fate with a variety of expressions, which his morbid imagination made inexhaustible. "Each one of us, too, dies many times before his death," wrote Lamb one day. The thought had no doubt struck him on one of these occasions when he saw his friend sink into the nethermost pit of despair. He made every effort to revive him, and in order to give him a chance so to shine as no longer to doubt his own genius, he used to invite people in to listen who had only to hear him to become his most enthusiastic admirers. Lamb succeeded in persuading him that, although he was unable to speak in public at stated intervals, he was perfectly capable of expressing himself magnificently in his own good time, and was possessed of a natural eloquence which allowed him to strike home to the soul, even though his powers of elocution might fail him when he expected them to come at his beck and call. Coleridge, who, as we have seen, did not belong to that particular brand of orator whose thoughts never flow unless their tongues be first set wagging, and who could equally well work himself up into a state of excitement when seated pen in hand in front of his table, as when faced with a select audience, made up his mind to return to his old idea of a review, into which he could tumble all the ideas jostling together in his mind, and thus scatter them before the public at large.

He was aware what a treasure store he had been amassing during twenty years of reading and thinking, and the thousands of notes he had taken on all subjects showed that it was not in his mind only that it existed. He wrote to his friends to inform them of his wish to make some use of these materials, and the program he laid before them was so vast and grand, that the acutest minds among them could not but fear lest he should not be able to carry it through. He intended nothing less, in fact, than to deal in this review, which was to be known as *The Friend,* with the true and only principles of morality, their origin and development, the influence of moral habits upon taste, and the nature of literary taste, for example, the taste of great authors. He meant to explain the affinities of the fine arts among themselves, such as the affinity between architecture and gardening, between the art of dress and music, poetry, and painting. Finally, he meant to study history and the present state of all literatures, providing "sources of consolation to the afflicted in misfortune or disease, or dejection of mind;" would recall persons and anecdotes he had come across "in the course of his own life and travels," and would describe a "theory of education in the widest sense."

Prompted thereto by De Quincey, who adored dancing, and had even planned out a philosophy of the subject (he called it "the very grandest form of passionate

sadness" ever devised by man) Coleridge even thought
of talking about this art. But a Quaker of his acquaintance, who had perhaps suggested the title of his periodical, protested most vehemently against such a scandalous
proceeding. Coleridge vowed in vain that he would con-
fine himself to "the scientific dancing of the Ancient
Greeks;" he was obliged to submit to the reproof administered by this austere follower of George Fox. This
time, however, unlike the time when he had edited *The
Watchman,* he made no mention of current politics, and
went so far as to cut out passing events altogether, although these are what "the general reader deems himself entitled to expect" in a review, as he quite candidly
admitted himself. Truth to tell, apart from all pecuniary
considerations, and the need he felt of ridding his brain
of the speculations with which it was overflowing, he
was mainly guided by the desire to issue a series of mes-
sages to his fellow countrymen, and to help to fortify
their souls against *"Jacobinism,"* that is to say, the dema-
gogic tendency and frivolity of the accursed French mind.

Filled with apostolic intention, an apostolate which,
parson's son as he was, more and more took on a religious tinge, he thus determined, at the beginning of
1809, to set off for Allan Bank, Wordsworth's new house
in the Lake District, and there to publish a weekly paper. He did not come to his friend's house as a guest, but
rather as a regular member of his household, and it was
far enough from the place where De Quincey had taken

his wife to enable him to feel certain of being able to have all the quiet he needed; for, on the material side alone, his task seemed to be bristling with difficulties. It is true that the part of the world where he proposed to publish *The Friend* is remote and wild enough. But when he wanted a printer, what induced him to think of sending to Penrith, a small town some twenty-eight miles or so away from Allan Bank, when he had one ready to his hand at Kendal? This little place, which was nearer to him by about ten miles, had the further advantage of a daily post, whilst the steep mountain-side above Penrith forced the few vehicles that used to go there to take a longer way round. So, too, having only been able to secure type and paper at great trouble and expense, he met with a series of difficulties in sending out the terms of subscription, which caused a delay of several months in the appearance of the paper. When the first number was at length issued, he did not, still thanks to the precarious means of communication between Penrith and the rest of England, receive some of the subscriptions until twenty-one weeks later. It is unnecessary to add that the subscribers themselves did not receive *The Friend* without a similar delay.

It would have been difficult, in these conditions, not to make his readers feel dissatisfied, even had they found the rather stodgy material he served up to them to their taste. . . . Ninety out of the six hundred and thirty-two subscribers whom *The Friend* started out with, fell away after the fourth number. In January, 1810, two-thirds of the remaining number had also deserted. . . . The first number had, it is true, come out with an immense delay behind the published time, and though the second duly appeared on the right day, it took no less than eight weeks for the third to put in an appearance.

On the 15th March, 1810, Coleridge found himself forced—without, however, informing the subscribers of the fact—to stop publishing his periodical, which had only appeared twenty-seven times in over nine and a half months. . . . He attributed this lamentable result, partly to his state of health, which was still bad, partly to the dryness of the questions he had proposed to discuss, partly, too, to his bad luck, and, in particular, to his delusion as to the help De Quincey might afford him. He had had no difficulty in persuading that young man to accompany him to the Lake District, and as he thought he saw signs in him of "a great turn for manual operations, for he is, even to something of old bachelor preciseness, accurate and regular in all he does," had congratulated himself on having acquired a recruit so happily endowed with the qualities in which he knew himself by experience to be chiefly lacking. Put to the test, however, De Quincey showed himself to be quite as unpractical, and more irresolute and fanciful even than himself. "I . . . saw too much of his turn of mind anxious yet dilatory, confused from over-accuracy, and at once systematic and labyrinthine, not fully to understand how great a plague he might easily be," he wrote, a few weeks after his arrival at Allan Bank.

Suffering nearly as much already from opium-poisoning as Coleridge, De Quincey, who had lost his grip of his moral sense, seemed to take a wicked delight in yielding to all the suggestions made him by the demon within. He might almost seem to have been seeking to avenge his own eccentricities by amusing himself at the expense of the poet's addled wits, and by thinking out new means to add to the causes of the impotence which had fallen on the head of this genius, who, however, he declared, would outlast Goethe. He made him his scapegoat, in the sense that he loaded his own perverted tastes upon him by way of experiment. He played upon the unresisting instrument which echoed the same tones as his own, and, "laughing horribly," accused him to posterity of many follies, which probably germinated, for the most part, nowhere else than in his own brain. For he was incapable of making any distinction between what he heard from reliable sources, and what he imagined. Even in the most unimportant matters, he treated reality as though it were a work of art, in order to give it the haunting quality in which it is usually lacking.

But there is no intention of systematic disparagement, nor of malice aforethought, in the confidence he made upon the subject of Coleridge. De Quincey had no thought of bringing his idol low by thus laughing him to scorn. On the contrary, he looked upon his oddities as so many signs of grace. Such is the effect of the distortion wrought by the influence of opium upon even the soundest of minds. De Quincey intended, by thus painting him in a grotesque light, and declaring him to be worthy of admiration despite his foibles, to act as the "bard of Quantock's" humourous apologist. It in nowise detracted from his worth that he would rise of an evening, and make his appearance with a curious erection of kerchiefs over his nightcap, in order to hold forth upon metaphysics, when he was incapable of putting pen to paper, and used to dictate articles for *The Friend* to Wordsworth's sister and sister-in-law, Sarah Hutchinson, whose reverence for his thought almost vied with Dorothy's own. And could anything seem more pathetic than the story of how he had attached to his person a "salaried assistant" to stop him from going into the opium-vendor's booth, but had pushed the poor man down and marched over his body, overmastered by the violence of the desire which urged him towards the fatal drug?

Though De Quincey, when he went to the Lake District, seems to have taken upon himself the part of a mischievous and malicious sprite dancing attendance on Coleridge in his dealings with Wordsworth, whom he could never forgive for having cut the pages of one of his books with the butter-knife, with the young and pleasant-spoken but rather "stiff little lady" whom Wordsworth had married in 1802, with Dorothy, so retiring but yet so fervent and fresh, with Southey, upright but longwinded, he was not able to pretend that the effort represented by *The Friend's* publication was of no value, that it had no originality. The passionate taste for abstract thought which animates Coleridge's articles is, in fact, combined in almost unique fashion with an ardour of proselytism which was in its essence democratic, even when the end which it aimed at was a conservative one, and rather national than universal in its bearing, practical rather than speculative.

The politico-social theories professed by Coleridge, who claimed to be Burke's successor, do not proceed from experience, but from certain principles which must be sound because they are innate,—for he had a horror of "idealess facts misnamed proofs from history." It was because he saw the French Revolution as the very expression of that scientific or mechanist philosophy, which is criminal in that it warps the mind of the people by giving them a materialistic idea of life, that he attacked both that and also the *Contrat Social* with a violence of invective which already foreshadows Carlyle. In order to be able to communicate his certainty of the spiritual nature of the world, a certainty which was wholly intuitive with him, or animist if that word be preferred, or transcendental, the most urgent need, as Coleridge saw it, lay in the assertion that motives are more important than results, and that the right way of thinking,—that is to say, according to revelation or understanding, which, as we know, he distinguished from reason in the same manner as Kant, but attributing special virtues to it,—is better, if not more effective, than action dictated by logic and simple prudence.

We only know the collection called *The Friend* in the form of a systematic treatise in three parts, each corresponding to the volume in which it was published. It is probable that Coleridge touched it up considerably, at a time when the religious tendencies of his mind were still more strongly accentuated. But the essential things are to be found, and the order in which the author has tried to dispose it only half makes up for the disorder of thought which gathered its massive elements together. As it stands, it is striking enough in the almost desperate desire it shows on Coleridge's part to fit every doctrine he could lay his hands on—even though he might spoil it by overtaxing it—within the framework of his proof. He brought to this task all the stubbornness, we may almost say the unscrupulousness shown by a man, who, in order to persuade a woman or a child to behave as he knows to be right, uses every argument which comes into his head, even though it may be mere sophistry.

It has been seen how, at the blackest moment of his yielding to vice, he never ceased to cling with all the strength of will left to him—to the thought of an ideal, not only civic but religious, to which he might conform in life and deed. Now he wished to make this ideal known and felt by all. When he went to Coleorton to meet Wordsworth, who there read him *The Prelude,* the poem he composed in his turn under the influence of that work which harrowed his heart with its serenity is already a proof, coupled with his faith in resorting to prayer, of the hope, or longing, he felt, as already indicated, to regroup his thoughts, and reconstitute his ego, in the light of a mystical system. If, curiously enough, what helped to turn his mind away from Catholicism, as he noted at Malta, was the external and picturesque character of religion, with its pomps and ceremonies, towards which he felt an insurmountable repugnance, his Christianity was continually being refined away, mainly indeed under the influence of a theologian he had discovered, Archbishop Leighton of Glasgow, and he had already begun to give the lie to his own ideas by refusing to believe that Jesus was more than a "Platonic philosopher" as he said to Crabb Robinson. On the other hand, he joined forces with Pascal (a mind which he was surprised that France could ever have produced), when he said that the mysteries of the Church can never be explained beyond question, and that the dogma of the Trinity cannot be grasped by the reason alone. Only a moral proof can be adduced, for, if they ceased to be objects of faith, they would, by reason of their own evidence, make idle the necessary intervention of our free will or make the testimony of grace of none effect,—the grace in which he saw the intuition of the essential unity between the divine mind and our own. There was, to him, no possible confusion between his own idea of this unity, and that of

the pantheists—whom he henceforth classed with atheists
—since it was in himself and his own consciousness that
he could discover God, and not in things known to the
senses. He had no doubt on the thesis, "*mind* is distinct
from *matter*." And alongside this wholly subjective certainty he laid down another, similar to it in character, and
essential to his need of moral security, by proclaiming
the truth of Christianity, and seeking after a kind of
apologetic of the subject. Sentiment played such an important part in Coleridge's mind, that it was bound to
influence his endeavours as a thinker. Although he spoke
of his interest in religion as an "intellectual passion," and
found it impossible to conceive of it in other than abstract terms, yet it was because its coherence gave his heart
the body of doctrine which most fully satisfied it, that
he sought to find rest in it. He was to enrich it by his
musing thoughts, and by the new-found charm which he
gave it, was to bring back to it many restless souls, "in-
stilling" into these, to use the words of Newman who
owes much to him, a philosophy of a rarer and more
subtle kind.

"I have found more in the Bible," he was soon to go
as far to say, "than in all other books together." Like many
other speculative intellects, who yet are incapable of separating the true from the good, he could not indulge in
wholly detached researches, which were not directed to
the discovery of any ethical system. "My system," he
writes, "if I may give it so fine a name, is the only attempt

I know ever made to reduce all knowledge into harmony. It opposes no other system, but shows what was true in each." This true thing seemed in his eyes to be found in the Christian religion, and he meant to make every effort to fasten on to it all forms of thought known at the time, under the pretext that he wished to hold up to it "a perfect mirror."

The Friend is no more than the foundation of the building, or the peristyle of the temple he was eager to consecrate to God's service, and I shall have occasion to return to the essentially religious character of his philosophy or his metaphysics, which finally turned into a kind of Christian socialism. His attacks upon the Rights of Man, the contrast he drew between Reform and Revolution, his parallel between Rousseau and Luther, or Voltaire and Erasmus, his search for Kant in the pages of St. Paul, were undertaken with a view to clearing the ground. The further he went, the more steadily did he turn his face in the direction of theology, although the active curiosity as much as independence of his mind prevented him from assuming a purely orthodox attitude towards it. But nothing positive is to be found in the polemical pages of *The Friend,* which, moreover, reveal the indecision of his mind, rather than its preferences.

Four or five months after the death of that periodical, Coleridge was still sunk in a kind of torpor, to the great despair of his wife whom he had now rejoined, and who, seeing him thus prostrated, did not know "what to think

or to do." The wretched man felt a hostile atmosphere
growing up around him. Sara's sighs, Southey's silence,
and Wordsworth's headshakings expressed only too
clearly the disapproval people felt for his sterile, inactive
life. "Begin to count my life, as a friend of yours from
1st January, 1809; judge me from the 1st January, 1809,"
he had written to a friend on the eve of founding his
weekly. He could never console himself for its failure,
and decided in his distress to turn to Lamb, less, no doubt,
for help, than for the sympathy of which he stood in
need. If, then, he agreed to go to London to stay with Ba-
sil Montagu, Godwin's philanthropic friend, from whom
Wordsworth had succeeded in getting him an invitation,
it was because he could thus have an excuse to keep away
from a circle where he felt himself no longer welcome,
and a chance to live near the only person whose affection
was neither protective nor condescending. Southey's la-
borious austerity of life called down too great blame upon
his own disorder and lack of will power, and the moral
superiority Wordsworth could not help rather heavily
displaying, inflicted on him the worst humiliation in the
world. Poor Lamb, on the other hand, who kept his life,
which a tragedy had stained with blood, almost shame-
facedly in the background, and passed for an amateur
writer since he earned his living in business, inspired in
him no painful feeling. He could make a brother of a
man thus living outside the pale, in whom irony was
toned down by loving-kindness, and who declared, "I

can never hate anyone that I have once seen," for his love for humanity made him take it as it was, with all its vices which, as he well knew, go hand in hand with virtue. Did he not, indeed, once exclaim one day when Holcroft and Coleridge were discussing in his presence about man as he should be, "Give me man as he ought not to be!"

The cause of the moral discomfort which had determined Coleridge to leave the Lake District, and which was partly due to his intuition, was soon to be revealed. Hardly had he gone to stay with Montagu than his host repeated to him, perhaps with some exaggeration, the words which Wordsworth had used to recommend him less to his sympathy than his charity. But Montagu had not altered the meaning. Wordsworth had indeed gone the length of expressing the negation of the faith he had hitherto felt in his friend's future, declaring that he had no more hope for him, and had ceased to believe in the possibility of his improvement. Coleridge saw that what he had vaguely feared, and had tried to avoid by fleeing to London, had now come upon him: he had been disowned by the superior mortal, the demi-god whose cult he had kept up for fourteen years. The idea of being put to shame by the man to whom he thought the growth of his poetical genius was due, threw him into deep desolation. There can be no comparison between this complete overthrow, and the thousand and one disappointments he had hitherto experienced, owing to the ingratitude, injustice or misunderstanding of his other friends. He said himself all these were no more than "flea-bites," and the poem he wrote under the still lively impression of his sorrow is one of the most moving he ever wrote:

> I have beheld the whole of all, wherein
> My heart had any interest in this life
> To be disrent and torn from off my Hopes
> That nothing now is left. Why then live on?

He thought, and went on thinking for a long time after, that when Wordsworth cast him off he dealt him his death-blow, and he longed to die. All the affection his old Christ's Hospital school-fellow could show him was needed to soothe his despair. Lamb, who had the sincerest admiration for him (he was more exciting to be with, he said, than fifty ordinary people), lavished upon him without stint the admiration he felt. He almost exaggerated it, in fact. He refrained, at any rate, from diminishing its effect by any of those blandly mischievous remarks to which his critical sense prompted him, and contrived things so that his friend might meet at his house that chosen band whose flattering attention had already so happily contributed to revive him after the failure of his lectures. Gradually, in the society of Crabb Robinson, who had returned from Spain, and was to be the prime mover in his apparent, though incomplete reconciliation with Wordsworth, of Manning the tongue-tied lover of China, of that enigmatic man, Thomas Griffith Wainewright, a sort of Beau Brummel, whose fingers were laden with handsome rings, and who in the end turned out to have a mania for poisoning people, Coleridge recovered enough self-confidence to undertake once again to do some public speaking. This revival of energy was especially helped on by Crabb Robinson, who had visited Germany and pursued his studies there, and was enabled by his knowledge of philosophy to switch the conversation, or rather Coleridge's own monologues, on to the subjects of which he was fondest. A breach soon parted the Montagus and their guest, who no doubt bore them some ill-will for the part they had agreed to play towards him, by rescuing him at Wordsworth's request as so much flotsam. He left them to go to stay with John Morgan, one of the old friends of his happy time at Bristol, who offered him the most open-hearted hospitality at his house at 7, Portland Place, Hammersmith, and whose wife and sister-in-law displayed towards him that solicitous affection, and interest delicately tinged with curiosity which touched him most nearly.

He had taken a new lease of life. Henceforth he carried out, no doubt not without a backsliding or two, and with ups and downs which prevented him from ever finally attaining his object, one of the bravest attempts at recovery ever made by a man who has fallen into the clutches of opium. Dr. Beddoes having died, who had endeavoured to cure him of the poison at Clifton, he put himself into the hands of Dr. Abernethy, to whom De Quincey maintained that he owed his cure. . . . During his stay at Hammersmith, he even went so far as to leave the Morgans' roof-tree occasionally and go into lodgings, in order to follow as faithfully as possible a cure prescribed by some other physician. Alas, in 1814 again, far away from his family, which he had been obliged to hand over to his brother-in-law's care, he was again taking not less than two quarts of the drug every week, and even upon occasion one pint in twenty-four hours.

"Conceive a poor miserable wretch," he wrote, "who for many years has been attempting to beat off pain, by a constant recurrence to the vice that reproduces it. Conceive a spirit in hell, employed in tracing out for others the road to that heaven, from which his crimes exclude him! In short, conceive whatever is most wretched, helpless, and hopeless, and you will form as tolerable a notion of my state, as it is possible for a good man to have. . . . In the one crime of opium what crime have I not made myself guilty of!—Ingratitude to my Maker! and to my benefactors—injustice! and unnatural *cruelty to my poor children!*—self-contempt for my repeated promise —breach, nay, too often actual falsehood!"

No matter. He was to continue to struggle on with the Morgans' help, and then with Dr. Gillman's—and

to succeed in spite of everything in putting into his unfinished body of work the essential part of his genius,
that is to say, enough magnetic charm to set flame to the
ardour of a new generation.

PART V

THE SEER OF HIGHGATE

CHAPTER I

CREATIVE CRITICISM

ON the 18th November, 1810, a prospectus of the London
Philosophical Society, established at Crane Court in Fleet
Street, announced the beginning of a new set of lectures
to be given by Coleridge "on Shakspere and Milton in
illustration of the Principles of Poetry and their Application, as Grounds of Criticism, to the most popular Works
of Later English Poets, those of the Living included."

This time the audience which came to hear him, consisting of no less than five hundred persons, mostly from
among the choicest intellectual spirits of the time, met
with no disappointment. The lecturer had the greatest
success of his life, and was hailed with delight even upon
snobbish grounds, as witness Byron's letter to Harness:
"Coleridge is a kind of rage at present." He still, no
doubt, on more than one occasion kept his hearers waiting outside in the cold, either because he had forgotten
the day on which he was supposed to speak, or had been
unable at the last moment to drag himself out of the
lethargy by which he was overcome, or even because,
having conquered his drowsiness, he had then ended by
sinking in a heap to the ground, as related by De Quincey. . . . On the other hand, as Crabb Robinson re-

marked, on this very occasion of the Crane Court lectures, he had some habits he either would, or could not overcome, "the vices of apologizing, anticipating and repeating," and of flowing on and on, in long digressions. If a new pathway opened up along his road, he was obliged to go down it, and lo! and behold, he would find himself straying a hundred miles or so away from his subject. The program made it clear that he meant to talk about *Romeo and Juliet* and the character of the women in Shakspere: "He began with a defence of school flogging, in preference at least to Lancaster's mode of punishing," without even trying to trace the slightest connexion between that question and the one with which he was supposed to be dealing. Finally, as he said himself, comparing himself to people who have a greater command of words than of ideas, his examples "swamped his thesis." He was one of those who "use five hundred more ideas, images, reasons, etc., than there is any need of to arrive at their object, and only leave their dazzled listeners one vague impression that there has been a great blaze of colours all about something."

This was, as a matter of fact, his greatest failing. His too great riches were his downfall, or at any rate, his lack of conciseness, the result of his intellectual instability, forbade him to follow up any rigorous chain of reasoning, or to work out any set of thoughts by logic until they fused into one. His thoughts were "music" as he very justly said himself. He suggested, rather than affirmed, in a state bordering on dreaming, which might almost be called half unconscious or super-lucid rather than extra-lucid. Though, as Crabb Robinson again suggested, "an enchanter's spell seems to be upon him, which takes from him the power of treating upon the only subject his hearers are anxious he should consider, while it leaves him infinite ability to riot and run wild on a variety of moral and religious themes," yet his lectures gave his audience spiritual pleasure above and beyond all comparison, whenever he was in his best vein, as often happened during the three sets of lectures which he gave at three different times in 1810–12, 1813–14, and in 1818. On these occasions he was wonderful, and "for the greater part intelligible tho' profound." "As evidences of splendid talent, original thought and rare powers of expression," Crabb Robinson goes on to say of these lectures, "they are all his *admirers* can wish." Characteristically enough, as giving evidence of the kind of subconscious work that went on in his mind whenever his genius was upon him, he was, according to Dr. Gillman, never so eloquent as when, putting his notes aside, he "spoke extempore" or let his mind glide serenely as a swan over the glassy depths of a flowing stream of ideas.

The combination of his poetic intuition, psychological sensitiveness, and familiarity with every kind of philosophy, was to give birth to the most stimulating criticism which has ever existed, the most highly fertile in discovery for minds set free of prejudice, and curious in matters of artistic creation. But criticism such as this cannot be understood without reference to Coleridge's poetical works, and the methods or spadework which led up to the miracle of its unfolding. Working with other means, but under the same impulsion, it also was able to fill and possess the universal mind, beyond the shams and shows of outward seeming. It was the result of activity on the part of a mind superior to most, which was able to think as it felt, and could draw no arbitrary distinction between thought and the sentiment, or at any rate sensation, which gives it life.

Assuming that a man does not create, that he only discovers relationships which had escaped other men until he saw them, or that he only finds out once more what has always existed, when he thinks that he has come upon some new thing, there is no essential difference between speculations such as those of Coleridge, and the novels or plays of imaginative writers. It is an illusion which induces us to distinguish between a critic and a writer of fiction, upon the plea that the latter infuses life into people, whilst the former restricts himself to studying books or analysing authors. Each in his several way only expresses his meaning through the medium that serves him best, and thus reflects one aspect of eternal truth. If it be put forward that the novelist and dramatist are higher in artistic quality, it must yet be admitted that the lyric poet is perhaps superior to both, though he does no more nor less than transcribe to paper the ferment of his soul, or reveal how sweet life tastes to his lips, while all the genius he shows is a mere matter of arranging words thus and only thus.

So Coleridge's teaching aims at proving, at the outset, that the laws of imagination are "the laws by which our feelings form affinities with each other and with words." He thus rejects, and we can reject with him—relegating them to the background with romantic writers and dramatic authors to whom their art means nothing beyond a trade, or a game with rules—those dogmatic critics who think that all that is necessary in examining works of art is to classify them according to an unchanging standard. His literary judgments—and this is what constitutes their exceptional merit—do not rest upon generally applicable moral principles, like those of his predecessors. They consider the creations of genius as an organic whole, and there is no foreign element in their appreciation of intrinsic value.

Coleridge never took the trouble to collect these judgments into any handy form. They are scattered like islands through his writings (*Biographia Literaria,* Volumes I and II of the *Literary Remains, Miscellanies, Table Talk*) and as far as a large portion of them are concerned, have only come down to us in the form of personal or shorthand notes taken during his lectures by his admirers, Crabb Robinson and Collier especially. They can, therefore, not be studied in detail, or one after the other, but as one whole, stretching over the whole decade, in order to gain some general idea as to what they were.

No doubt other people—Goethe in *Wilhelm Meister* being first among them—had made an attempt at showing what is the structure of Shakspere's plays and characters. As early as 1759 Lessing, who, calling him "the mirror to nature," had insisted on pointing out the tragic greatness of his plays by comparing them with Corneille's, and it cannot be denied that Coleridge found in German criticism—which for lack of national masterpieces to study, as I have said elsewhere, had had to fall back on English poetry and drama—the confirmation of a certain number of the discoveries to which his own researches had been leading him, if, indeed, he had not borrowed some of his reasoning from Herder, Schlegel, and Jean Paul. Owing to his never having mentioned these loans and similarities, he has been accused of plagiarism, though this accusation might with better reason have been put forward in connexion with his philosophic speculations. Though no credence can be given with regard to these latter to the excuse he made in *Anima Poetae,* it seems irrefutable with regard to his literary work.

"In the preface of my metaphysical works I should say —'Once for all, read Kant, Fichte, etc., and then you will trace, or if you are on the hunt, track me.' Why, then, not acknowledge your obligations step by step? Because I could not do so in a multitude of glaring resemblances without a lie, for they had been mine, formed and full-formed, before I had ever read of those writers, because to have fixed on the particular instances in which I have really been indebted to these writers would have been hard, if possible, to me who read for truth and self satisfaction, and not to make a book, and who always rejoiced and was jubilant when I found my own ideas well expressed by others,—and lastly, let me say, because (I am proud, perhaps, but) I seem to know that much of the matter remains as my own and that the soul is mine. I fear not him for a critic who can confound a fellow-thinker with a compiler."

There is no doubt, at any rate, in regard to his understanding of genius and his estimation of æsthetic values, that what he says here is exactly true, and that he merely forgot to mention the arguments in support of his thesis, and the comparisons worthy to illustrate it, which he took from the pages of German essayists. Besides the fact that it is built up upon quite a different plan from Lessing's *Hamburgische Dramaturgie,* which harks back to the principles of Aristotle, his discussion reveals a closely knit unity of thought of a profoundly and unmistakably personal character. It were niggardly indeed to take him to task for a few similarities between his conception and Schlegel's, more particularly on the subject of Shaksperian drama, when it is manifestly the result of long psychological meditation, and attentive observation of the creative activity of his own mind. For, in fact, Coleridge's criticism does proceed from introspective labours, which, even when they wear an objective air, as, for instance, whenever he quotes examples, can yet only be compared to that phenomenon of adaptation known as mimetism, which was true of no other criticism before his.

In considering, as I have said further back, the creations of genius as organic wholes and products *of the nature of man,* Coleridge did not behave towards them as a theorist, but as though he were once a poet, whom intuition persuades of the profound unity of a work of art, by helping him to discover it for himself. Truth to tell, Coleridge's critical self did not entirely hide his metaphysical bent, which is revealed by the way in which he gathers together and sets out his private impressions under the influence of his doctrinal thought, in order to bestow upon them the authority of general laws. Nevertheless, the principles he deduces in his interpretation of various masterpieces are suggestions merely, and are not laid down as binding. He elucidates them, as it were, or makes us discover and point them out for ourselves at the same time as he does. He carries out an experiment under our very eyes, by probing these masterpieces until he comes upon the souls of the authors, but it is easy to feel that the analysis of his own individuality serves him as a guide.

It is, besides, most likely that he became attached to Shakspere through reading *Hamlet,* which he made his constant study in Malta, owing to the likeness which was, he admitted, to be seen between the hero's character and his own; and Shakspere, by offering to him the picture of this perfect agreement between the material and spiritual, or the sensuous and intellectual planes, stirred up in him the longing to renew the miracle in the ideal world, and then to find out for himself in what measure, or with what variety, that miracle is reproduced in the choicer minds. It is because the passionate interest which drew him to Shakspere—which landed him at one bound straight at the heart of the most complex work of art that has ever been known—let him grasp the secret of its unfolding, that he discovered the method by which he might follow the gleams which shine out from the hearth of artistic thought into its remotest projections of form, like the ramifications of a tree.

So those people who heard Coleridge talk about Shakspere's plays felt less as though they were listening to an explanation of the plays, however ingenious, than as though they were present at their inception, or watching them burst into new life before their eyes. Not only is there nothing artificial about Coleridge's criticism, it is neither merely logical nor merely rational. He does not take the characters of Hamlet, Macbeth, Othello, Iago, Falstaff, Richard III or Lear to pieces like so many parts of machinery, nor dissect them like so many corpses. He approaches them as living beings, "intensely individualized," and studies them as they quiver into life beneath the forms of sense, with perspicacity which yet fully respects their contradictions, discovering the sign-manual of truth in these very contradictions. He shows us Shak-spere, "the myriad minded" as he calls him, manifesting one aspect of his astonishing power in each one of his plays, and revealing the fundamental differences of the types he brings together, the variety of the elements which goes to make up their indestructible unity, just as it makes up the whole work which flows into the great harmony of nature. For, be it noted, Coleridge, who took over—while he lent it a yet deeper significance—the above-mentioned definition of Lessing, and said of the author of *The Tempest* that he was "a nature human-ized," pointed out before Emerson did, the universality or impersonality of Shakspere's characters as the very consequence of their breadth and diversity; comparing them in this respect to Spenser's, who merely embody the spirit of chivalry, and even going so far as to spurn Swift altogether for his arbitrary misanthropy, so limited in its range.

One might be tempted, at times, to reproach Coleridge with a certain tendency to seek an abstract meaning in Shakspere's plays. He does not, however, read into them any moral, psychological, or philosophical element in-compatible with their character; no other dramatist's work contains such a host of reflective characters, who can, in spite of the violence of their passions, examine their conscience so minutely. Coleridge always remained, besides, attached to his one object, I mean, that no metaphysical or merely æsthetic consideration turned him aside, as it did the German commentators, to follow Shakspere's "omnipresent creative power" in all his many-sidedness, nor induced him to forget that the important thing with this poet of all poets is the miracle of the continual transformation of the chimerical adventures of a soul through the facts of reality, reality transposed on to the plane of Beauty.

The analysis of the characters of Shakspere's plays by Coleridge is a model of suggestive subtlety, and it is necessary to take into consideration the date at which it appeared, for it gave rise to a host of imitators. The works of William Hazlitt, of Hartley Coleridge, our Coleridge's own son, not to speak of more recent studies, have made us so familiar with this type of exegesis, that we almost forget who originated it. The independence of his mind, and his deliberate frankness in regard to Shakspere's characters, is to be seen in the unexpectedness of the almost paradoxical opinions which he expresses, thereby revealing at the same time his acute powers of discrimination. What could have seemed newer, and more exact in its very novelty, than what he says of Othello who, until this time had usually been considered as the prototype of a jealous man, but in whom he saw, not a monomaniac, himself creating the phantoms which tormented him, but a man deeply in love, simple to the verge of credulity, whose sensuality when it was worked upon by an underhand influence became exasperated to the murder point. Speaking elsewhere of Polonius, he raises his voice in protest against the tradition which represented him on the stage as a sort of buffoon. He qualifies him as the personified image of wisdom, and makes it clear that we are mistaken in him because we lend too favourable an ear to Hamlet's satirical remarks. Though the Prince of Denmark with a scornful and falsely haggard glance calls him a rat, after he has run him through with a sword behind the arras, this is because he sees in him the incarnation of an order which his impetuous soul could least abide, and he suspects him of complicity in his uncle's crime. If Polonius's counsels to Laertes are remembered, however, and the panegyric with which Ophelia honours his memory, it will be recognized that the poet, far from meaning him to have a look of the grotesque, typified in him the statesman whose feelings have been blunted by affairs, but who has been able to extract from his experience of life and study of the human heart the lessons they have to teach.

But these are the opinions or judgments of a psychologist and moralist, as are also the remarks Coleridge makes upon Hamlet himself, and Lear, the majestic picture of old age and its tyranny, aggravated by the habit of enforcing prompt obedience; and though, in the historical part of his work, our critic reveals himself as inferior to Lamb, who was far better acquainted than he with the English Renaissance poets; though he refrains from talking of Ford, Webster, and Marlowe among Shakspere's contemporaries;[1] though, in conclusion, the fairy element in the plays written by this Protean genius eludes him—I shall say why later on—yet he talks of the alchemy of his art with infinitely delicate feeling, and a happy and befitting choice of expression, initiating us into the secrets of his musical incantation. For when he talks of the magic of poetical language, Coleridge does not mean technique in the strict sense of that word, nor when he lays it down as a principle that what gives a distinctive style to language is the order itself in which the poet arranges the words he selects, and their *untranslateableness* into equivalent terms. For Coleridge the excellence of a poem like *Venus and Adonis* dwells in the "perfect sweetness of the versification," its "adaptation to the subject, and the power Shakespeare therein displays, in varying the march of the words without passing into a loftier and more majestic rhythm than was demanded by the thoughts, or permitted by the propriety of preserving a sense of melody predominant."

It is hardly necessary to point out the value of such a way of looking at the creation of lyric poetry. Its complete efficacy is proved, moreover, in the test to which Coleridge applied it in Wordsworth's works—his

---

[1] I cannot here resist the pleasure of offering as a fitting subject of meditation on the part of those who would like to turn the actor Shakspere into the stalking-horse for some nobleman, this opinion of Coleridge's upon Beaumont and Fletcher: "No doubt," he declares, "they imitate the ease of gentlemanly conversation better than Shakespeare."

estrangement from the author of *The Excursion* having allowed him to recover his independence of mind, and to put the man he had raised to the rank of a god once more into the place where he belonged. Although that place is still one worth having, and he recognizes the austere purity of Wordsworth's inspiration, the freshness of his feeling, the sureness of his eye, he reproaches him with the inequality of his style, that is to say, when we know what he means by this, the inappropriateness of his language to his thought. It seems to Coleridge that there was an almost constant disproportion between the tone adopted by Wordsworth and what he had to communicate. His images are too great for his subject, or his "ornament" too rich, or too precious, or too detailed for the matter it overlays.

Nothing could be more just than what Coleridge says as to the essentially variable character of expression, wherein lies the condemnation of the dogma of the beauty of form existing in and by itself. In the same way as he distinguishes true simplicity from "sheer matter-of-factness," he refuses to be taken in by pomposity or bombast, by an elegance of diction which can be slipped into as a man may put on his best coat, or by what was known half a century later in France as "artistic writing." There exist for Coleridge not only one, but two, three, four, or five ways of writing—as many styles in fact as artists have temperaments. Hence comes his admiration for Rabelais and Cervantes, for Dante and Milton, whose exquisitely "artificial" language he considered a special merit. The pages he has left us on *Paradise Lost,* and, above all, on the character of Satan, are, moreover, among the weightiest which we owe to his inspired eloquence, and no one has shown more clearly than he how much imposing grandeur there is in this most characteristically English poem, in which all the music which was henceforth to be expelled from Puritan churches seemed to be gathered up.

No doubt Coleridge's opinion in matters of faith endeared to him the austere and almost Biblical figure of the Christian *vates* whose egotism he considered a "revelation of spirit" and who had achieved in his own existence the unity for which he never ceased to sigh. But though he declared him superior to Dante for having better succeeded in combining his doctrines with poetry, he did not fail to recognize that the author of the *Inferno* ("the living link between religion and philosophy") bore away the palm for power and for the picturesqueness of his turn of phrase, or rather, for the quality of *style.*

A further proof is here to be found of Coleridge's supple and open mind, in the way he pays such just homage—contrary to his secret preference—to the genius of the old Ghibelline poet, and in the admiration which I have just said he proclaimed for Rabelais and Cervantes, in talking of whom he laid down a luminous distinction between wit and humour. This distinction proceeds from the theory whereby, in a manner that to some folks has never seemed quite clear, he separates imagination—primary and secondary—from fancy. He lays stress, however, on the creative activity of the spirit, to prevent its being confounded with the passive association of images in the mind. "The Imagination then, I consider either as primary, or secondary. The primary *Imagination* I hold to be the living Power and prime agent of all human Perception, and as a repetition in the finite mind of the eternal act of creation in the infinite *I am*. The secondary *Imagination* I consider as an echo of the former, co-existing with the conscious will, yet still as identical with the primary in the *kind* of its agency, and differing only in *degree,* and in the *mode* of its operation. It dissolves, diffuses, dissipates, in order to re-create; or where this process is rendered impossible, yet still, at all events, it struggles to idealize and to unify. It is essentially *vital,* even as all objects (*as* objects) are essentially fixed and dead.

"*Fancy,* on the contrary, has no other counters to play with, but fixities and definites. The Fancy is indeed no other than a mode of memory emancipated from the order of time and space; while it is blended with, and modified by that empirical phenomenon of the *Will,* which we express by the word *Choice.* But equally with the ordinary memory the Fancy must receive all its materials ready made from the law of association."

Is it perhaps easier to grasp the difference Coleridge was striving to point out by means of an example? Three

French seventeenth-century writers will provide me with one. Racine, who gave his tragedies their driving force from within, and ever distilled poetical power out of them by the simplest and most harmonious means, uses primary imagination. La Fontaine uses secondary (or detailed) imagination when he reverts to subjects treated by Æsop and Phædrus, or old French fabliaux, in order to "make his honey." On the other hand Scarron's *Virgile Travesti* which is a mere burlesque parody, obtaining effects which quickly pall, from contrast or unexpected comparisons, only depends upon Fancy. There is no doubt that the inspiration of Memory was here chiefly concerned, and that freed from "the order of time and space" it presided over the tricks of the jesting versemonger, as he put into the mouths of gods and goddesses the talk of the folk of the suburbs and of market-women. No creative activity, or in other words, poetic energy, lies behind this game, in which choice alone selects from the profusion of images opened up to the mind by the field of mnemonics. The fact that Coleridge did not see that one kind of fancy—Shakspere's for example in *A Midsummer Night's Dream*—possesses the very qualities of imagination by its power of depicting a world of things which are not present to the senses, does not in the least invalidate what he has to say about the kind more usually met with. That only proves that he had a greater bent for dreaming than day-dreaming, as we have said before, and that in spite of his predilection for the marvellous, in spite, too, of the ease with which he lived and moved in what it is commonly agreed to call the supernatural, he was not of a romantic turn. His seriousness made him impervious, even rebellious, to the charm of the fanciful mind, or a certain airy grace, even maybe, a certain lightness of touch. . . . But, as he was careful to make clear, "distinction is not division," and the differentiation of fancy in order to establish a hierarchy amongst intellectual faculties does not involve opposing it to the imagination, nor even separating it off from it. The definition given by Coleridge of the Beautiful, the reduction "of multitude to unity" does, besides, implicitly mean collaboration or reconciliation between the most diverse forms of the mind's activity, with the object of jointly striving for superior harmony. Such a harmony can only be realized by genius, for its works, in contrast to those of mere talent, are not determined by "accident," and consequently imply an alliance between *reason* and *understanding,* or to speak another language than this pseudo-Kantian jargon, nearly constant obedience paid by inspiration to the rigorous discipline of judgment. To Coleridge's mind, the poet has no other object—and this is the essential point, too, in Baudelaire's and Poe's theory of æsthetic—than to seek after a higher form of pleasure "through the medium of beauty," a purely imaginative pleasure, bearing no analogy with any other, and its far-off aim should be to make man better in the highest or most generous sense of the word. So all ideas of teaching or of submission to some utilitarian or even moral principle are necessarily foreign to such a way of considering poetry and the arts. We must refer to Coleridge's own lyrical poetry in order to understand its subtlety, for in thus setting it forth he has done no more than comment upon his own work, and by illustrating it with examples as I have shown, define the present-day conception of *poésie pure*.

This inspiration which Coleridge places under the control of intellect and its most steadfast faculty, logic, in order that he may make of the poet in Baudelaire's words "a magnetiser and a sleepwalker" (*un magnétiseur et un somnambule*) is not, according to him, to be found in instinct, nor yet does it gush forth from the heat of passion, wherein he is at variance with Lamb and De Quincey, who consider it as a matter "of the feeling alone." He evidently attributes a mystical character to it, and would fain liken it to grace. He believes, at any rate, that it comes from above, and that the language by which it makes itself known is divine. It speaks to us of heaven and the infinite, so that we may recall our origin and remind men of it again. Like the philosopher, in fact, whom Coleridge would like him to resemble, the poet must make it his mission to transmit a message from the other world. There is no true philosophy in existence which is neither spiritualist nor religious, that is to say, which, by revealing the essential part of our soul does not make us regret the bliss of its past life, and long for that of its future. The only inspiration worthy of the name, which has no connexion with the delirium of passion or over-wrought sentiment is therefore a kind of intuition (*insight*), or of ecstatic foreboding, and nothing can be more favourable to it than the soothsaying state of dreams. Coleridge thus closes the circle with which he has hedged round his own personality. He restores the importance due to the unconscious, (*the genius in the man of genius*), which played so great a part in his own lyric creations. "You never dream," he said one day to William Hazlitt, to explain to him his indifference to the *Arabian Nights*. And when he added: "There is a class of poetry built on the foundation of dreams," he was not far from thinking that this class was the chiefest of all, if not the only one worthy of achievement. It does not result from a victory gained by our mind over resistance to secret forces, but from turning a mysterious gift which has been made us, to good account. And on the whole, however large a share Coleridge may give to the intervention of the will in the building up of the structure of lyric poetry, his best poems are those in which he gives musical expression to the visions not of this world which took his breath away. Between literary creation and the deepest state of dream-ing (which he distinguished from nightmare) in which "the waking state of the brain is recommencing" he could see no difference. "Dreams," he declared, "have nothing in them which is absurd and nonsensical." And he said again, "though most of the coincidences may be readily explained by the diseased system of the dreamer, and the great and surprising power of association, yet it is impossible to say whether an inner sense does not really exist in the mind, seldom developed, indeed, but which may have a power of presentiment." These symbols by means of which Coleridge could draw near to profoundest reality, were given him in dreams; fragments in image of his soul's inward communing with God.

CHAPTER II

VOLUNTARY PRISONING

THE ten years in the course of which Coleridge expressed his critical ideas in speech or in writing were among the most painful in all his erratic career. He was really thrown into an almost trance-like condition whenever he talked, and with such penetrating genius, about poetry, for as soon as he settled down to do any work requiring an effort of will, apart from the promptings of the familiar standing at his side, and whispering all his subtlest thoughts in his ear, all that resulted was ranting second-rate enough. The articles he composed in 1811 for the *Morning Post,* now jointly owned by Street as well as Stuart, upon what was happening in Spain, were only a bald summary of events. Since the comments he made upon these bore no sign of the political acumen he had shown when working on the staff of the *Morning Post,* the parallel he drew between the revolt of the Spaniards against Napoleon, and the Dutch against Philip II, was of little enough value, and he was never carried away by any fervour of conviction. Not only did his eloquence flag, but even his style faltered, and floundered into common-place. Whenever his thoughts became more coherent, and he tried to control his words, these turned out to be hardly worth uttering. The lecturer whom the public had acclaimed, captivated by his "large dark eyes" and "his countenance in an excited state glowing with intellect," was as poles asunder from the journalist who toiled and dozed by turns over the pages the *Post* was waiting for. A strangely dual personality indeed! In moments of inspiration he became wholly oblivious of his hearers or readers. The sentence with which he rounded off the series of articles on art which he had sent to the *Bristol Journal,* at the instance of his friend Washington Allston, the artist, bears testimony to this: he announced that he would put off discussing the subject "in a loftier mood" until later on, and for "a more appropriate audience" seeing that it is a "profanation to speak of these mysteries."

For Coleridge was two men at one and the same time: the one a wholly spiritual being who spoke of poetry as though he were poetry's very self, the other a creature always alternately down in the depths or up in the clouds, who sometimes ignored the other, and sometimes ousted him from his position, according as whether opium were losing its blissful hold, or a craving for a fresh dose were creeping on. The second was, unfortunately the one known to the world at large, the one who mingled daily with his fellows, causing even those people who felt most friendly disposed towards him to lose heart of grace, owing to that habit of his of harping on his faults, whilst lifting not a finger to reform them, as well as by his sincerity, coupled with his everlasting falsehoods. He seemed to the shrewdest a welter of contradictions, and to himself, though he came, indeed, to have a profound knowledge of his own nature, a sorry subject of bewilderment. One day when his *alter ego* was to speak to the good folk of Bristol, he was seized by a sudden whim to alight at Bath in order to escort a lady who had travelled down in the same coach as far as her brother's house. He found in her a friend, so he was wont to explain. But, I imagine, since this eccentric creature can hardly be suspected of harbouring thoughts of gallantry, that he simply discovered a good listener in his fellow-traveller, at some moment when the presence of someone to whom he could talk was the one thing that could enable him to rise superior to his fits of giddiness, and the yearning to escape from the dreams prowling around him. For shame and humility added their weight to the load of unbearable excitement and depression, and suddenly, as soon as night came on and loneliness, panic terror would have him in its clutches. At Bristol even Joseph Cottle, who had not seen him since 1807, was struck by "the wild eye! the sallow countenance! the tottering step! the trembling hand! the disordered frame!" Coleridge, who had one of his repentant fits upon him, in which he would take much the same topsy-turvy pride in making out his state as worse than it really was, as the backboneless characters of the Russian novel, drew an appalling picture of his state for the benefit of this publisher, who had helped him at the beginning of his career. This time he had no fellow-sufferer, such as De Quincey, to whom to confide his passion for opium, but without a trace of the diabolism and romancing of the Opium Eater, he secretly enjoyed detailing his exceptional case in full, for the benefit of this shocked and quickly outraged Pharisee, though to himself, no doubt, he seemed to be merely following the dictates of sincerity by making a clean breast of it. The wretched man, who had resigned from the *Morning Post* because Street had rejected an article against the Duke of York, and who had not succeeded in entering the *Times'* employ, was furthermore battling with the most involved financial embarrassments. Though his earlier drama, now re-christened *Remorse,* had, through Byron's good offices, been successfully staged at Drury Lane in 1813, he had long ago run through the hundred pounds brought in by this windfall. On the other hand, Josiah Wedgwood, having learnt with indignation that he had left his children to Southey to support, cut down his share of the annuity, and he was now nursing hopes of being able to wheedle some money out of Cottle. But Cottle, instead of opening to him his purse-strings, and "conscious of being influenced by the purest motives" plied him unmercifully with a sermon, following it up by a long missive, in which he traced out his failure step by step. True, he was shortly afterwards overcome by remorse for the cruelty of this deed, and wrote to Southey bidding him combine with his friends to provide Coleridge with a pension. But Southey, who had received no answer to the letter he had sent, pointing out that the time was now ripe for the eldest boy to go away to school, refused to take any steps whatever in favour of a man thus wanting in character, whose condition Cottle had himself called "desperate." He had no intention of doing any more than see to the present and future needs of the poor children he had taken under his wing, and informed his correspondent that he had already been promised twenty-five pounds by Lady Beaumont, and ten pounds from Poole, not to mention the help he hoped to obtain from the uncles at Ottery.

He could not refrain, however, from asking Cottle what had become of Coleridge, to which Cottle replied that he knew no more than that the unhappy man had taken refuge with his friend John Morgan in a small house at Calne in Wiltshire. Coleridge had now gone back to this friend, who had promised to give him a helping hand along the road to recovery, though he had been keeping out of his way on account of the assiduity he displayed in mounting guard over him, as he himself, indeed had begged him to do. Josiah Wade, on the other hand, to whom he had made as full a confession as to Cottle, and whose guest he had been while he was in Bristol, had not shown firmness enough to suit his taste. Coleridge thought it cruel of Mrs. Morgan to answer, when he told her he preferred death to the sufferings he went through for want of opium, that it would be better to be dead than to live as he was doing, but he had come to think it far too soft-hearted on the part of Wade to let him have the drug every time he clamoured for it.

For it must be acknowledged, although this need not be taken as running counter to what I said before as to the persistence, despite all backsliding, of his moral sense and his longing to triumph over his helpless slavery, that he had become used to the fruitless warfare he had been waging so many years; he had been wavering back and forth between resignation and hope so long that this had become his normal state. But there is worse to come. The bane seemed less precious when it could be had for the asking, and he never enjoyed it so much as when he had to employ subterfuge to obtain it. It is possible too that, although he still yearned for recovery, as in a dream, yet he may have lost all but an abstract idea of the duties conscience imposed upon him, and attained to all intents and purposes to a kind of fatalism, which made him slough off all responsibility, and expect others to fend for him. But would anyone treat him just as he would treat himself if he had the requisite power, enticing him gradually back into the right paths, neither repelling him by over-much strictness, nor spoiling him by over-indulgence? He debated the possibility of entering an asylum. But before making up his mind to live with madmen and degenerates, he wanted to make quite certain of exhausting every other means of salvation. True, he used under Dr. Daniel's treatment to carry resistance to his bodily craving for stimulant to its utmost limit, and

yet enjoyed peaceful moments, and a self mastery that
had been very nearly complete, and was it not almost as
much for the sensual pleasure of the thing, as from the
relief from pain it afforded, that he was sometimes overtaken by desire for the poison, even before the moment
when he could do without it no longer? A question such
as this could have but one answer. But he would not admit that he had truckled to failure, and he declined to
cringe as a sinner come to repentance. Even at his lowest
ebb, no one had ever heard him renouncing the glorious
calling of the writer. Nor had it ever seemed to him of
more importance not to loosen his hold upon it, for a
kind of persecution mania had come upon him, causing
him to see plagiarists, if not rivals, all round him, ready
to pounce upon his ideas for their own ends. Thus it
flashed across him when he read a sketch by William
Hazlitt on the decline of comedy, that he had held forth
in Lamb's house in the presence of the younger essayist.
Childe Harold was evidently concocted upon a recipe he
had devised six years previously, and entered into one of
his notebooks, and his very articles were a prey to penny-
a-liners and politicians, and were the mainstay of more
than half the speeches heard in the House of Commons.

If, in face of his own feebleness and incapacity, he was
now ready to retire almost completely from the social
fray, this was because he meant, so to speak, to make sure
of his half loaf, and to safeguard his intellectual independence by trying to live in conditions that suited his

miserable state. In the hopes of being able to carry out his work he might, so he informed Cottle, make up his mind to start a kind of elementary school for a limited number of pupils—a project that roused Cottle's ire, appearing to him the depth of "degradation and ignominy."

Whilst he was pondering upon the subject of the play Byron had suggested he should write—*Zapolya,* a mediocre production enough—he was collecting together his poems and preparing to issue them in a newly arranged edition, together with a few as yet unprinted pieces, under the title *Sibylline Leaves.* Thanks to instructions left by his aristocratic patron, who had forwarded a hundred pounds before he left for the Continent, Murray was about to publish *Christabel.* But he was chiefly engaged upon a great work on *Christianity Considered as Philosophy and as the Only Philosophy,* and the more he became convinced that truth is inspired, the higher value he set upon his own redemptive mission. Hence his return to the Morgans, with whom he spent the greater part of 1815, and the month of January, 1816, the first of his *Lay Sermons* being written in their house. It was doubtless at the suggestion of these kindly folk, who realized how frail was their hold over such a restive patient, that he went up to consult Dr. Adams in London, and took lodgings in a chemist's house for the process of the cure. This was surely, putting his head into the lion's mouth or, as Lamb suggested, like shutting oneself up in the Vatican Library so as to be sure to have no temptation to read. He told his story to Dr. Adams at great length, however, protesting his firm resolve to submit to any kind of treatment to eradicate his vice, and accusing his friends, and above all the Morgans, of not helping him with sufficient energy to arrive at this end. Dr. Adams, though he may have been unaware of Coleridge's reputation, was none the less struck by his brilliant mind. On the 9th April, 1818, he sent a letter to his colleague James Gillman, a surgeon at Highgate, whom he knew to be interested in psycho-pathology, telling him all about the remarkable literary man who had been to consult him, expatiating on his charm of character and communicative nature, which would make his conversation every whit as interesting as the study of his case.

Although Dr. Gillman had not been in the habit of receiving resident patients, Dr. Adams's letter was expressed in such terms that he felt unable to return a point-blank refusal. He asked his correspondent for an interview, and it was determined that he should go to his house that very day, accompanied by Coleridge in person.

At the time fixed for the meeting Coleridge alone put in an appearance. Instead of the slightly eccentric figure he expected to see, no doubt full of quaint foibles, and afflicted with occasional absence or lapses of memory, what was Dr. Gillman's astonishment upon meeting the most self-possessed person he had ever come across, and of the most affable manners. Coleridge had sallied forth for this interview, which was to decide the whole of his future life, girt in his irresistible charm. He was excited at the idea that, should Dr. Gillman take a fancy to him, he stood a good chance of making a complete recovery, without really cutting himself adrift from the world. Besides, he was delighted with everything he had seen of Highgate, in those days a pleasant village three miles or so to the north of the City, standing on a ridge overlooking the Nightingale valley; beyond it lay the green slopes and shady walks of Hampstead, Constable's favourite haunt, with houses embosomed in flowers nestling among the trees.

It seemed to Dr. Gillman's fancy as though he were doing the honours of his house to some great prince of the mind in the person of this man of forty-four, neatly attired in dark colours for the occasion, who leaned upon his stick as he walked. His hair was already turning white, his face was pallid and puffy as any Buddha's; he was obviously smitten by the double stigmata of pain and disease. But it was impossible to refrain from gazing into the magnificent eyes, that seemed to gaze beyond men and things with an expression which clutched at the heart strings. He seemed to be suing no favour at James Gillman's hands, as he narrated his misfortunes, but to be rather some victim of destiny who has at length come upon some other soul worthy to understand him. No haughtiness was here, however, nor over-emphasis: only the noblest and most engaging simplicity, and a certain whimsicality, which, like the details in the foreground of a picture, served but to throw his thoughts into truer perspective, and to give greater depths to the generalizations he flung out to his dazzled listener. He would hardly brook a single question, but conducted the conversation himself, outlining a sketch of his future life at Highgate, much as twenty-two years before this at Bristol, he had unrolled the panorama of the Pantisocratic Society he had dreamed of founding. Though he explained to the doctor what were the conditions upon which he might consider becoming his patient, he left him without coming to any definite decision, for he had no wish to appear to force his hand by pressing his advantage home. James Gillman, who had already pleaded the meagreness of the hospitality he was able to offer, was upon due deliberation to feel perfectly free to receive him or not into his house as he chose. But upon his return to London, Coleridge immediately wrote him a letter, in which he set forth precisely all the business part of their conversation, and declared himself ready to move to Highgate there and then. He added, when he came to the end: "And now of myself. My ever-wakeful reason and the keenness of my moral feelings will secure you from all unpleasant circumstances connected with me save only one, viz., the evasion of a specific madness. You will *never* hear anything but truth from me; prior habits render it out of my power to tell an untruth, but unless carefully observed I dare not promise that I should not, with regard to this detested poison, be capable of acting one. Not sixty hours have yet passed without my having taken laudanum, though, for the last week, comparatively trifling doses. I have full belief that your anxiety need not be extended beyond the first week, and for the first week, I shall not, must not, be permitted to leave your house, unless with you; delicately or undelicately, this must be done, and both the servants, and the assistant, must receive absolute commands from you. The stimulus of conversation suspends the terror that haunts my mind; but when I am alone, the terrors I have suffered from the laudanum, the degradation, the blighted utility, almost overwhelm me. If (as I feel for the *first* time a soothing confidence that it will prove) I should leave you restored to my moral and bodily health, it is not myself only that will love and honour you; every friend I have (and thank God! in spite of this wretched vice I have many and warm ones, who were friends of my youth, and have never deserted me) will thank you with reverence. I have taken no notice of your kind apologies. If I could not be comfortable in your house and with your family I should deserve to be miserable."

This is indeed a valuable document, shedding light into the innermost recesses of Coleridge's complex psychology. It would be a never-ending task to try to unravel it completely. But does it not reveal the weakness hidden beneath the feeling which made Coleridge take advantage of his friendships? In the ostentatious way, too, in which he talks of his frankness, does it not also disclose a desire to deceive himself, as he had deceived others, as to the weak spots in his make-up, which led him to take so many dream-compositions for finished works, and so many illusions for reality? How sincere he appears, on the other hand in his will to recover, and to prove himself worthy of the true-hearted man into whose hands he was committing himself. Nor does he anywhere appear more like himself than in the tone of bland courtesy which informs the last lines of his letter. His circumspection in assuming an obligation betokened a like circumspection should he have one to bestow. He arranged matters with Dr. Gillman upon a generous and lordly scale unknown to the ordinary mortal. He belonged, in fact, to another world than ours, or had travelled hitherwards from another universe altogether. Surely it was to bear witness to this that he drove up two days after his letter had been written with the proofs of *Christabel* in his portmanteau. And does not this unfinished masterpiece, lopped of its final jewel, bring to mind the broken sceptre with which the unhappy King of France rapped upon the Castle gate at Broye, after the disastrous field of Crecy, to sue for shelter from those within?

CHAPTER III

RELIGION AND PHILOSOPHY

IT was not long ere Coleridge proved how beneficial had been the effects of his stay at Highgate by a fresh spurt of activity. Although, as he himself acknowledged, *Zapolya* was a failure, composed from first to last at Dr. Gillman's house, in the room overlooking the country which served him both as study and bedroom; yet this was due to the fact that his poetical inspiration had for several years back given no sign of existence, and his creative imagination was now only exercised upon sociology, philosophy and criticism. But whilst he was engaged upon the *Biographia Literaria,* which came out in 1817, he was also composing the second of his *Lay Sermons,* and gave a last set of lectures in 1818 at Flower-de-Luce Court.

His evolution in the direction whither he was seen to be tending when he edited *The Friend* had now reached its culminating point, and he drew up a conservative program in his sermons, the first of which is called *The Statesman's Manual, or The Bible the Best Guide to Political Skill and Foresight,* the second *A Lay Sermon Addressed to the Higher and Middle Classes of Society upon the Present Distress of the Country.* Coleridge's place was now fixed. He now took up for good his position in regard to the "presumptuous and irreligious philosophy" which had led up to the French Revolution. All that was romantic in his nature, and that had blossomed out into the generous illusions of his youth, was to be seen afresh in the way he made shift to bring his intuition to bear upon moral and political issues, comparing and even confounding the values or art, life, and social life itself. His faith in the unity of our nature, and in the close and harmonious links between heart and mind, is pathetically evident in his attempts at humanizing his ideal, and applying it practically. As he went on in life, and his horror of the materialism of the age grew apace, his philosophy aspired the more to become utilitarian, whilst it was in reality growing more and more sentimental. But however eager he might be to give men his message in order to "regenerate" them, he always secretly hoped to find in metaphysics, or even in transcendentalism, some revelation of supernatural things, though what this might turn out to be he scarce could tell, and thus to be supplied with arguments in support of the Truth. To form an idea as to the state of his mind when he became an inmate of Dr. Gillman's house, it is only necessary to read the *Biographia Literaria,* which begins by setting forth his philosophy, but closes with an apology for Christianity, and a profession of faith. No more formal admission could be made of his inability to shape into a doctrinal whole his answer to the how and why of the universe, than this curious work, full of digressions from beginning to end, and as lacking in homogeneity as well may be, but rich in critical and moral insight. It might almost seem that when he subsequently broke away from rational philosophy, it was because he saw he was unfitted to make use of the resources this philosophy furnished to his hand. He was disappointed in all systems, and, short of founding one of his own, took refuge in faith, much as some women flee to the cloister because love has not given them their heart's desire.

Whilst, however, in *Lay Sermons, Aids to Reflexion and Church and State,* he was toiling to pile one stone upon another of the edifice he proposed to consecrate to God, he contrived to lay aside a stone or two with which he thought to found a temple to the Divinity of the Occult, if need should ever arise. In 1817, Tieck, who paid him a visit, revived his curiosity in German literature, and he straightway began the study of the German mystics, Steffens, Schubert, Heinroth, and Swedenborg the Swede, in order to seek illumination from them. Furthermore, the very sciences he had accused in the *Statesman's Manual* of claiming to perform miracles he now summoned to his aid in an essay on the theory of life, which remained unfinished, however, and revealed the paucity of his attainments in chemistry and biology. He was ill at ease except when standing midway between the orthodox and the visionaries, and in no other conditions could his wavering soul branch out into dreams that were limited yet infinite at one and the same time. He discovered an affinity between himself and William Blake, whom one of his friends had brought to his notice, and habitually associated with Edward Irving the apocalyptic preacher, and Julius Hare, to whom John Sterling introduced him shortly after this time. Not long before his death, although he was by then deeply imbued with Christian faith, he re-traced in Wordsworth's company the journey he had made in his prime, led on by the hope of making great discoveries, and at Bonn had interviews with Niebuhr, Decker, August Wilhelm Schlegel, and all the illuminati of the place. He was like another Dr. Faust, refusing the pact with Satan, but furtively deciphering, in dark books on witchcraft, hidden by the Bible propped open before him, all manner of magic spells. So, without in any way denying the sincerity of Coleridge's attitude towards religion, it may safely be said that he withdrew into it only for lack of any other that might come nearer to his intellectual requirements. In order to wage war upon the age, whilst he sought in vain an answer to the enigma from the critical method, he preferred, if one preconceived belief were to be pitted against the other, to hold by the divine origin of that Book "the study of which . . . is beyond any other entertaining, beyond all others tends at once to tranquillize and enliven, to keep the mind elevated and steadfast, the heart humbler and tender."

It was again in this "department of knowledge which like an ample palace contains within itself mansions for every other knowledge" that he felt the ground firmest beneath his feet, and found most subjects wherewith to illustrate his principles, and the greatest number of precepts which he might develop, interpret, or comment upon. His imagination which tended towards the marvellous, and in some respects had an almost Oriental side to it, could, moreover, expand at ease in that atmosphere, and his eloquence wreathe itself in clouds. "I am deceived," he declared in the *Statesman's Manual,* "if you will not be compelled to admit that the prophet Isaiah revealed the true philosophy of the French Revolution more than two thousand years before it became a sad irrevocable truth of history," and foretold the calamities which were threatening England itself at the time. In another verse he found the prediction two thousand years before the event, of the early winter that turned the Grande Armée in Russia back upon its disastrous retreat. But his sermons have more in them than mere soothsaying and dreamy mysticism: common sense, we might go so far as to say, horse sense, lit up by poetry and even occasional humour, whereby the evils beneath which civilization is groaning through the growth of industry, and the remedies most suited to the English temper, are pointed out. This strength of concentration, so essential in building up a system, which he had lacked at the time *The Friend* had made its appearance, Coleridge now manifested in order to justify a theory of the civil order based on government by the possessing classes, and grounded in religion, both as regards politics and sociology. Now that Napoleon, whom he had called Anti-Christ, was beaten, he insisted on the urgent need for the Three Kingdoms to parry the danger created by new economic conditions, calling the attention of every man of enlightenment to two errors, each as mischievous as the last: the first, that of allowing the people to wallow in ignorance, with no hope of improving their lot; the second, that of expecting them to require no more education, once they had learned to read. "The social question is a moral question," said Coleridge, declaring that there could be no order within the nation, whilst disorder reigned in the souls that went to make up the whole. The working class must be assured the material security it needed in order to set its steps in the path towards improvement, if it was to produce its share of the harmony without which no state can properly function. "Go and preach the Gospel to the poor," said Coleridge as early as 1795, in one of his Bristol lectures. He never altered upon this point. He wanted religion to turn into fact, through fulfilment of the Church's teaching. Coleridge, the conservative, who thought that authority was vested in the nobility as of divine right, (he noted and deplored, moreover, the tendency for the commercial spirit to usurp its place), yet laid down as a principle, that the privilege of government implies strenuous duties in return. The aristocracy could not for a moment, without failing in its mission, refrain from educating "its clients and natural dependents" by

applying the principles of Christianity. For the education of the people, which seems to lose in quality what it
gains in quantity, is a means, not an end in itself, since
such an end can only be conceived as an untrammelled development of our God-given qualities, a climb to greater
and ever greater moral heights. But if the aristocracy is
to remain worthy of the part it has to play, it behoves it to
react against that presumptuous physical and psychological empiricism which aims at overthrowing the only true
philosophy, that is to say, religious philosophy, or the
philosophy to be found in religion. It is essential that the
highest classes should purify themselves by drawing nigh
to the Church, and seek its aid in re-establishing idealism
in the souls of all, beginning with its own members.

Which Church however? The multiplication of sects
had weakened the authority of Gospel teaching, and the
best of the Nonconformists, the Quakers, were hardly
Christians at all. Their teaching was barely different from
lay morality, and they had given up the speculative side
of religion altogether. Salvation could come but from the
Church of England, that is to say from the High Church
party, if it would but shake off its inertia, train more
preachers and theologians, and revive the spiritual tradition of the seventeenth century which had been shat-
tered by the eighteenth. The crisis England was going
through, which its leaders refused to take seriously, in the
optimism in which they had enveloped themselves ever
since Waterloo, was, so Coleridge felt certain, to be im-

puted to the withering of men's minds, wholly bent as they were on utilitarian projects, and with material gains in view. This is the main point of his plea, and the one he most insisted on, and it was this, as John Stuart Mill noted, which made so deep an impression on the rising generation, especially on Carlyle and Ruskin. The intuitive philosophy of the author of *Sartor Resartus,* which set idealist metaphysics over against rationalism, the preaching on art of the apostle of Pre-Raphaelitism, as well as the Oxford Movement, the effect of which can still be felt at work today, all alike originated in Coleridge's pressing appeal to the initiative and "social interventionism" of the upper classes, fifteen years or so before the first democratic reforms were carried out in England. The "heroes" whom Carlyle saw as signposts on the road to progress, took up the gist of Coleridge's message by calling upon God's elect to devote themselves to their task as "protectors of the people." He might be dubbed a socialist, since he could see no other master of the individual fate than the state, yet he may also fairly be called a theocrat for his assertion that a paternal government was bound to keep a Christian watch and ward over the well-being of its sons. The State is guilty, and prepares its own downfall, when by "the presentation of juster views and nobler interests" it does not freely remedy defective economic and social conditions. The landlord is bound to do all necessary repairs unless he wants to see his despairing tenants, goaded to frenzy, "digging or blowing up the foundation of a house in order to employ the materials in repairing the walls." So Coleridge, whilst he pointed out the general remedies, with a view to developing the conscience of the citizens, and to make subsistence easier for them, drew up an immediate program of reforms, of which the most important—apart from the abolition of lotteries and the revision of fiscal policy—were concerned with the employment of children in factories. It is well known that English cotton manufacturers used habitually to employ children under ten; country Bumbledown supplied these captains of industry with the poor little wretches, whom foremen, standing over them whip in hand, used to hound to work like slaves. Such proceedings distressed Coleridge's tender heart; besides, he had never forgotten the ill-treatment he had met with at Christ's Hospital. Acting under cover of the Bill proposed in 1818 by Sir Robert Peel, he had circulars printed and distributed, in which he called for an amendment to labour legislation in favour of the children "bred up in cotton," as he used to say, with an irony reminiscent of Swift's. The Bill was thrown out by the House of Lords, and this failure made such a strong impression upon Coleridge, that his faith in England's moral superiority was shaken. He remained more deeply persuaded than ever of the necessity to instil a new vigour into the anæmic conservatism of his country, and to awaken its slumbering religious sense by a return to the spiritual communings and outpourings of the past. Religion that is not translated into action is no religion. In order to give vitality to religious teaching, while leaving dogma out of account altogether, he wrote *Aids to Reflexion,* which draws its inspiration from the writings on sacred subjects of old authors like Henry More, Jeremy Taylor and "a mere selection from the writings of Archbishop Leighton." He had at first meant to do no more than compose a manual of extracts from the last-named author, whom he thought "next to the inspired Scriptures and as the vibration of that once struck hour remaining on the air," but he let himself be carried further than he had intended, and, in a style so like that of his models that it might be taken for theirs, he fashioned for himself a soul in their likeness, in order to set out his conception of Christianity, under the guise of aphorisms and commentaries from the Old and New Testaments. He was making an effort to rally people of intellect round the Church of England, and it has been said, that no other of his works had as resounding an effect as this, which was decisive in its influence. If the revival in the Established Church was complete by 1850, twenty-five years after the *Aids to Reflexion,* this was owing to Coleridge, for even the Catholic reaction led by Newman, which in its turn called forth a defensive movement, emanated from him.

Coleridge, who declared to Allsop—one of his most fervent admirers—that miracles "are supererogatory" and that "the laws of God and the great principles of the Christian religion would have been the same had Christ

never assumed humanity," did not always speak in orthodox language. He took in regard to revealed religion,
just as Newman reproached him in his *History of My
Religious Opinions* "a liberty of speculation which no
Christian can tolerate," accusing him of having advocated
conclusions which were "often heathen rather than Christian." In particular his position as regards the Trinity
would appear to be suspect, and his ideas upon the
Logos are less in accordance with the Gospel of St. John
than with Platonist philosophy. We may in fact be permitted to deny the success of his attempt at the "adaptation of Kantian principles to English religious sentiment,"
to make use of the same expression as Crabb Robinson, in
his summing up of the *Aids to Reflexion*. But his way of
bringing critical methods to bear upon the discussion or
examination of theological questions, and, as he said to
Allsop, to ensure the transcendence of the moral over the
intellectual, charmed and stimulated English minds,
which have ever been fond of arming themselves with the
whole apparatus of logic, in order to broach problems
in which sentiment and reason are most closely bound
together.

The *Aids to Reflexion* invested Coleridge with sufficient authority to permit him to stand boldly forth, five
years after their publication, as the defender of the Church
of England, in a little book entitled *Church and State,* on
the subject of the proposals for Catholic Emancipation.
Though he acquiesced in these proposals, and in the ap-

pearance in Parliament of representatives of a Church which owed allegiance to a foreign power, yet it went against the grain with him, and he did so only because he could see no moral possibility of acting in any other way. But he censured the way the reform was carried out, under pressure of "fear and passions." *Church and State* which has no more than a documentary interest among Coleridge's works, makes clear the nature of his feelings in regard to religion—namely those of a patriot, if not a nationalist, of rather narrow views.

It is to be noticed, that, whilst as I have said, he continued to interest himself in metaphysics, he no longer spoke upon this subject in public, and had intercourse with his equals only upon the common ground of religious philosophy or of theology. His keenest pleasure lay in expressing his ideas on the problems that occupied his mind, in the restricted circle of admirers whose faithful adherence surrounded him at Highgate with a comforting atmosphere. He had, further, one disciple, Joseph Henry Green, of Lincoln's Inn Fields, who was introduced to him by Ludwig Tieck during his visit in 1817, and came regularly week by week to take down from his own lips the main features of the great and noteworthy book he meant to write. Green's pen would run on at the master's dictation, or he would jot down notes of his inspired utterances. But the *Spiritual Philosophy* to which he devoted himself immediately after Coleridge's death, is no more than an abortive attempt at systematizing the doctrines which Dr. Gillman's patient had preached piecemeal.

There is no Coleridgian philosophy properly speaking. Everything that the mind can most clearly grasp in the conscientious piece of work to which Joseph Henry Green gave up his life, must be ascribed almost entirely to the German transcendentalists. To combat the sensualism of the age, that of Locke, Hume, and Hobbes, among others, which was rising higher than ever, Coleridge could only avail himself of the arguments used by German thinkers, but it at any rate adds to his glory that he bore a share in their introduction into England. Try as he might, he never succeeded in ridding his idealism or intuitivism, of their influence, and they provided the materials or canvas whereon he embroidered his most dazzling verbal inspirations. It was to themes borrowed from Herder, whom he had formerly accused of "sprawling in the 6-inch deep Gutter of muddy Philosophism," or from Kant, "whose moral system he declared to be "unnatural," or again from Fichte, in whom he saw a "caricature of Kant," that his imagination would help itself when he enchanted his hearers by relating to them at length his sublime daydreams. The phantoms he sent flitting past their gaze, to which his poetic genius gave an illusory form, melted away as soon as that genius no longer lent them its life. In order to body them forth in a lasting fashion, or to give them a kind of arbitrary or conventional existence, independent of his own, he had not the patient dialectic of the Germans at his command, nor as M. Pierre Lasserre points out, the obscurity of their language to help him. . . . It was but as a liquid flows, or a current flashes, broken short when his voice fell silent, and the light in his eyes dimmed, that he communicated the conviction of the Absolute that abode within him, and which, as Schelling and Fichte themselves declared, can be verified by the Unconscious alone. If they only are philosophers who employ the methods of science, or are less anxious to view things in the round than see abstract problems in the stark positive light indispensable to the study of phenomena, then Coleridge cannot be accounted a philosopher. Nor, in spite of the logic admired by De Quincey, did he possess as a metaphysician that two-fold faculty of synthesis and analysis which comes naturally to German minds, enabling them to enter into the slightest details of a speculative problem, without losing sight of its general aspect, and over and above all this, he was too deeply engrossed with the varying phases of Truth.

I would here repeat once more what I said when speaking of the tour through Germany, as to his inability to undertake a systematic classification of his ideas, and his natural disposition to interpret mystery through rhythm. His metaphysical system, if indeed he owned to any such system, can be shown to be lyrical or, to speak more exactly, musical in its essence. It is but the reflection or the expression of his feeling for the spirituality of the world. Whenever he gives vent to it, an impression is left on the mind, sounding across the language of German philosophy, or of Berkeley himself to whom that philosophy was so deeply indebted, as of a world well worth the capture unfolding before it, but such an impression is a fleeting and purely ideal one, a mirage, a will o' the wisp. Once the deed of wizardry is done, naught can be seen but a little powder sinking to the bottom of the phial held in the hand of this magician of the mind. Listen to Crabb Robinson on the subject.

"I think I never heard Coleridge so very eloquent as today, and yet it was painful to find myself unable to recall any part of what had so delighted me—i. e., anything which seemed worthy to be noted down. So that I could not but suspect some illusion arising out of the impressive tone and metaphysical language of the orator. He talked on for several hours without intermission. His subject the ever recurring one of religion, but so blended with mythology, metaphysics and psychology, that it required great attention sometimes to find the religious element." And Robinson says again, somewhere else, "Coleridge, as usual, very eloquent, but, as usual, nothing remains now in my mind that I can venture to insert here. I never took a note of Coleridge's conversation which was not a *caput mortuum*. But still there is a spirit, and a *glorious* spirit too, in what he says at all times."

Coleridge only follows, or seems only to follow, a fortuitous association of ideas. Penetrating pen in hand into the domain of transcendental ideas, he is never truly original save when, under the visiting of inspiration, he rises above reason, or sets flitting "from their secret nests," by means of introspection, like the Hopes he speaks of in one of his poems, some of the secrets of the deep activity of his soul. Upon this point it is best to consult the first of his meditations, from which I have taken the lines of so rare a quality I append below. Nothing could arouse greater interest than the matter here recorded, when he lets his impressions have their own way with him, or when he speaks of the travail of his mind, more particularly under morbid or abnormal conditions. And in its subtlety it does, perhaps, contain the germ of experimental psychology.

"The soul within the body," writes Coleridge in *Anima Poetae*—"can I any way compare this to the reflection of fire seen through my window on the solid wall, seeming, of course, within the solid wall, as deep within as the distance of the fire from the wall. I fear I can make nothing out of it; but why do I always hurry away from any interesting thought to do something uninteresting? As, for instance, when this thought struck me, I turned off my attention suddenly, and went to look for the copy of Wolff which I had missed. Is it a cowardice of all deep feeling, even though pleasurable? or is it laziness? or is it something less obvious than either? Is it connected with my epistolary embarrassments?"

Surely Coleridge is here finding himself out in the very act of woolgathering, and forcing himself to admit the spiritual infirmity which held him back from becoming the philosopher he had all his life aimed at being. Since he lacked the power to bind his intellect down to any rule, and had not that kind of mind of which Descartes, who considered that *to guide one's reason* should stand as the one valid aim, furnishes the finest example, Coleridge waited expectantly for metaphysical grace, just as he waited to finish *Christabel* until he was in the same elect state in which he had written the first half of that poem. He waited, no doubt, in quivering impatience, and in nowise passively, as it has been alleged. But even the excitement into which he worked himself in order to induce it to light upon him proved sterile. Here again, once he had renounced poetry, and apart from criticism which gave his intuitive and plastic genius occasion to practice upon imaginative work, and psychology, whereby he studied the mechanism of the mind in his own person, he could do no more than grope about in the confusion and disorder of a workshop bearing only the faintest resemblance to a laboratory, in order to seek some clue wherewith to decipher the universe.

Although Coleridge acted as an originator in the realms of lyric poetry, and was at the same time a precursor as far as observation of the phenomenon of artistic creation was concerned, yet when it came to religious and political philosophy he did no more than breathe life into dead bones, and it may not unjustly be said that the trace he has left upon philosophy proper is almost non-existent.

The work he wished to consecrate to the Supreme Being, and for which he could do no more than gather the materials his disciple Green used to the best of his ability, had already been carried out several years before his death by Hegel. Though indeed poets and imaginative writers such as Keats, Shelley, Poe, Browning, Baudelaire and Villiers de l'Isle Adam [1] on the one hand, and essayists such as Hazlitt, Carlyle, Ruskin, William Morris and Walter Pater on the other, owe him much; though theologians such as Maurice, Sterling, Hare and Irving, and even Newman, as I must once more repeat, revised their religious opinions upon his account,[2] or stated them more strongly, yet his metaphysical ideas were behind the times even when they were current—Carlyle having popularized all that was German in them, much in the same way as, in France, Victor Cousin and Jules Lachelier attempted to popularize the "thing in itself." An analysis of Green's work would, therefore, be not only tedious but vain, since he sought to refute the mechanical interpretation of life and nature, and to re-edit nearly all the arguments to be

[1] Arthur Symons in *The Decadent Movement* sees a combination of Swift, Poe and Coleridge in the author of *Akadysséril*.

[2] Coleridge's thought may also easily be traced as the origin of American transcendentalism, whose prime instigator, Emerson, then about thirty years of age, went to see him at Highgate upon his visit to London in 1832. And none of those who know how much of this transcendentalism has been retained by M. Georges Duhamel will be surprised to find a phrase of Coleridge's reproduced almost word for word, in this remark by the author of *La Possession du Monde:* "si la civilisation n'est pas dans le coeur de l'homme elle n'est nulle part."

found in Fichte and Schelling, only leaving to Coleridge his specious way of interpreting the distinction established by Kant between Reason and Understanding.

I cannot help, however, wondering whether, short of being a philosopher, a man may not stand for a philosophic outlook upon things, and by his example, his intellectual passion itself, his curiosity and his unrest, the quality of his insight and the images called forth in him by his feeling for life, give an impression to those who see him and hear him, as of a mind striving to find words for its innermost wrestling with mystery. Can such an one not fitly be likened to some great actor, daily interpreting a fresh masterpiece, which else were lost for ever, and which, by some miracle none may know, he has committed to memory, only to forget it thereafter to all eternity? Would the effect upon his audience of his acting, and of the words his motions accompany, thus be any less profound; and even though they were to preserve a very vague idea of these, would they then have gained nothing thereby?

"Coleridge," wrote Carlyle in his *Life of Sterling,* "sat on the brow of Highgate Hill in those years looking down on London and its smoke tumult like a sage escaped from the inanity of life's battle; attracting towards him the thoughts of innumerable brave souls still engaged there. His express contributions to poetry, philosophy, or any specific province of human literature or enlightenment, had been small or sadly intermittent; but he had, especially among young inquiring men, a higher than literary, a kind of prophetic or magician character. He was thought to hold, he alone in England, the key of German and other Transcendentalisms, knew the sublime secret of believing by 'the reason' what 'the understanding' has been obliged to fling out as incredible. . . . A sublime man, who alone in those dark days had saved his crown of spiritual manhood. . . . The practical intellects of the world did not much heed him, or carelessly reckoned him a metaphysical dreamer; but to the rising spirits of the young generation he had this dusky sublime character, and sat there as a kind of Magus girt in mystery and enigma; his Dodona oak grove (Mr. Gillman's house at Highgate) whispering strange things, uncertain whether oracles or jargon."

"Nothing could be more copious than his talk," Carlyle noted also, "and furthermore, it was always, virtually or literally, of the nature of a monologue; suffering no interruption, however reverent, or hastily putting aside all foreign additions, annotations, or most ingenious desires for elucidation as well-meant superfluities which would never do. Besides it was talk not flowing any whither like a river, but everywhither in inextricable currents and regurgitations like a lake or sea; terribly deficient in definite goal or aim, nay often in logical intelligibility; what you were to believe or do, on any earthly or heavenly thing, obstinately refusing to appear from it. So that, most times, you felt logically lost, swamped near to drowning in this tide of ingenious vocables, spreading out boundless as if to submerge the world.

"He began anywhere: you put some question to him, made some suggestive observation: instead of answering this, or decidedly setting out towards answer of it, he would accumulate formidable apparatus, logical swim-bladders, transcendental life-preservers and other precautionary and vehiculatory gear, for setting out; perhaps did at last get under way,—but was swiftly solicited, turned aside by the glance of some radiant new game on this hand or that, into new courses; and ever into new; and before long into all the universe where it was uncertain what game you would catch or whether any.

"His talk, alas, was distinguished like himself by irresolution; it disliked to be troubled with conditions, abstinences, definite fulfilments;—loved to wander at its own sweet will, and make its auditor and his claims and humble wishes a mere passive bucket for itself!

"Glorious islets, too, have I seen rise out of the haze; but they were few and soon swallowed in the general element again. Balmy, sunny islets, islets of the blest and intelligible."

It is scarcely necessary to point out the spite in these lines, which reveal Carlyle's dislike of Coleridge, as well, perhaps, as his irritation at having to play second fiddle during their talks. He had been taken to Highgate by his friend Irving, and was so much disappointed in Mr. Gillman's guest, that he never spoke of him unless to poke fun at him, except in the preface to his *Essay on Novalis,* in which he acknowledged him to be the precursor of his own German studies. Indifferent to the charms of this visionary genius, the sole impression that remained with him was that he had struck him as being morally impotent. But when his verdict is compared with the passage from Crabb Robinson which I quoted above, it can be seen to be an attested fact that Coleridge, although he may have professed no regular philosophic system, yet summed up in his own person, that yearning for the unattainable which some few souls know. For those who were vexed with heart-searchings as deep-felt as his, he movingly interpreted the still, small voices they dimly heard within. He created for them the illusion that with him as their mouthpiece, these voices were making essential truths plainer to understand, and gave them grounds for strengthening their faith in the very existence of these truths.

But I am tempted to go further, and to say that what Mallarmé did as regards poetry, for frequenters of his Tuesday receptions in the Rue de Rome, Coleridge succeeded in accomplishing on behalf of something profounder and subtler still, for the benefit of his visitors to Highgate. He was gifted with the magic power to fling open at certain moments, through the medium of words, a window upon his soul, and those who then were drawn near him could gaze upon that flame of divine certainty which else dawns only in moments of contemplative conviction upon the inward eye of the greatest mystics alone.

CHAPTER IV

SPIRITUAL HEIGHTS

THE beginning of his stay at Highgate proved particularly painful to Coleridge, who was now obliged for the first time to follow a rigorous course of treatment. At that time, no doubt, the cure for drug-taking was more empirical or less scientific than today, and however careful Dr. Gillman may have been to regulate the doses he administered to his patient, he was unable to prevent him suffering during the fasting time in between. For a whole year and more Coleridge endured such fierce and unremitting pain, that it kept him walking almost incessantly up and down his room like a caged tiger, for seventeen hours at a stretch. In order to remedy the state of depression he fell into, Dr. Gillman advised the seaside, and he went to spend a few months at Muddiford in Hampshire. But as soon as he returned to Highgate, he bravely went back to his prescribed fast, only taking opium when so prescribed by his host, whose wife, Anne, watched over him with the most wideawake and delicate care. Coleridge was particularly touched by the pains this intelligent woman took to make his life as pleasant as might be, and he many a time performed further feats of endurance simply to earn her sympathy, though he had already thought himself come to the end of his tether.

In the even flow of his new existence, amid the security and rather monotonous quiet it procured him, the
comforts of which he enjoyed to the full whenever his
physical torments were lulled for awhile, he seems, moreover, to have reaped a moral benefit. His will was
strengthened and restored, and he was lapped in a kind
of lofty resignation. His conscience was finally purged of
dross. It had been with a view to putting the coping-
stone to his work that he had made up his mind to submit to a treatment so painful in its immediate effects, that
courage to do so had hitherto failed him. No sooner, however, did he begin to write, than he was attacked on all
sides, though mainly by William Hazlitt, who did not
even wait for his *Lay Sermons* to appear ere he tore them
to shreds in *The Examiner*. Coleridge had been rash
enough to say of these sermons, that they were rather the
overflow of an impassioned mind than an ordered and
premeditated work. This admission, made all in good
faith by a critical intellect untouched by the blindness of
pride, was turned as a weapon against him, and all seemed
in league to prevent his return to the literary life from
which he had seemed to have withdrawn himself for
ever. Byron's quip upon the *Biographia Literaria* is not,
however, really malicious and does, in a manner, seem
justified. "Coleridge," he says in the dedication to Don
Juan [1]

---

[1] Further attacks upon Coleridge are to be found in Byron's *Don Juan*
(cantos I, III, IX), and it should here be pointed out that the former had
brought them down upon his own head by giving vent in his *Biographia*

has lately taken wing
But like a hawk encumbered with his hood
Explaining metaphysics to the nation—
I wish he would explain his Explanation.

But though the anonymous critics in the reviews joined issue in making fun both of Coleridge's work and of the poet himself, for whose exile they were partly responsible, their idea was not to show up its weak points, (these they were unable, out of sheer ignorance, to detect), but to jibe at its strong ones. All that went to make up the charm and originality of that work, great as in so many respects it was, they took as target for their mockery: it is, indeed, dumbfounding to discover that it was just those pages in which Coleridge speaks so pungently yet delicately of his childhood and youth and of his travels in Germany, or in which he studies so penetratingly the art of Wordsworth, that they singled out for their hottest abuse. *Christabel* fared equally badly at their hands, although it had aroused, not only the enthusiasm of fellow craftsmen, but the admiration of amateurs devoid of prejudice on the score of true poetry, and three editions had followed fast upon each other's heels in the course of a year. The *Edinburgh Review* characterized the masterpiece as "absurd" and the *Monthly Magazine*

Literaria to the vexation he felt upon seeing the Rev. Mr. Mathurin's *Bertram* put on the stage at Drury Lane instead of his own *Zapolya*. Byron's malice flowed freely at the expense of this display of ill-temper which, moreover offered an easy target for ridicule owing to the slightly pedantic rigmarole in which it was concealed.

declared it "only fit for the inmates of Bedlam." Nothing that Coleridge wrote was spared. The *Edinburgh Review* especially excelled in this task of destruction, in which, moreover it had earned a reputation as of Tarquin mowing down the tallest poppies before Gabii, for nearly all the glories of the England of that day, from Keats to Shelley, were served by it in much the same fashion as *that bookworm,* the hermit of Highgate. His *Pains of Sleep* were "mere raving without anything more affecting than a number of incoherent words," and the *Statesman's Manual* was the work of a sleepwalker who "mutters all unintelligible and all impertinent things," and his admiration of Kant was due to that philosopher's system being the "most wilful and monstruous absurdity that ever was invented." If by some chance this spiteful review happened to include one sensible criticism in the farrago of abuse it broadcast, it naturally took no account of the fact that the defect at which it was railing was the reverse of some quality so miraculous as to escape its attention. Thus, while reproaching Coleridge with the ease with which he could let his imagination play round every kind of object, so that it "prevents him from weighing the force of any one or retaining the most important in mind," it wrote that "his ideas are as finely shaded as the moon upon the clouds."

Coleridge was at first indignant over the animosity shown in these attacks. They became so violent that Murray, his publisher, rid himself of his works in a great state of alarm, passing them on to Curtis, another publisher, who promptly went bankrupt, thus causing the greatest hardship to the unfortunate poet, who was already very short of funds, having been led by a generous impulse to hand over the twenty-four pounds he had made by *Christabel* to his old friends the Morgans, who were in difficulties. He wanted to protest, for no one took up the cudgels on his behalf, and even Southey, in particular, remained silent, though he had great influence with the *Quarterly Review,* and Coleridge had himself defended him in *Biographia Literaria.* But Jeffery, his former admirer, to whose good faith he now appealed, answered him, through the agency of Hazlitt, by calling down scorn upon his head. He then abandoned the idea of prosecuting *Blackwood's Magazine,* which had accused him of living at his family's expense, when the truth was he had made over his pension to them, and from the time of his stay in Malta had never stopped payment of an insurance premium in his wife's favour. . . .

His friends no doubt prevailed upon him not to start a lawsuit they thought he must lose from the outset: he proposed to prove nothing more nor less than that he "worked like a slave from morn to night and received less than a mechanic's wages." They had not, however, as much difficulty in dissuading him as they might have feared upon seeing his despair. He soon, indeed overcame the instinctive revolt he had been unable to stifle, at finding all these scribblers upon his back, who had not even the excuse of hatred when they levelled at his reputation, and who wantonly ruined his final efforts to garner the corn that was still, as he wrote a little later, *on the ground.*

Since the help and encouragement he had looked for from his contemporaries to realize his undertaking were denied him, thanks to the stupidity and concerted malice of the critics, he decided to withdraw definitely from the world, and thus to devote himself to his task, supported by a handful of faithful friends. He had ceased to expect anything whatever from the world, and had made up his mind to work for posterity alone, and for those steadfast few, by whom posterity was pre-figured to him, for he appealed to them on behalf of his work alone, judging himself impartially, as though in pleading for himself, he pled on behalf of a child of grace, all unworthy though it might be of the gifts God had given it.

His *Great Work* was in his mind's eye whenever he spoke of what still remained for him to do, and in comparison with that, all he had hitherto done, though good in itself, seemed to him of minor importance. He had not much to say on anything besides the philosophical questions that filled his thoughts when people paid him visits at Dr. Gillman's house, chief among them being Charles Lamb, of course, as well as De Quincey, Crabb Robinson, the surgeon, Joseph Henry Green, who wrote at his dictation, and made an attempt at arranging his speculations into some coherent scheme, Leigh Hunt, John Sterling, Hare, Irving, his own nephew Henry Nelson Coleridge, and Thomas Allsop, a young City man, who had made his acquaintance during the 1818 Lectures. He kept up a regular correspondence with the last-named, in which, like a lover who can never be done conning over the words his mistress has but lately uttered, though now she is gone from his sight, Coleridge noted down his slightest thought, in spite of the fact that they were constantly meeting. It was to this spiritual confidant he disclosed his intention of asking his friends for the help they alone could give him, begging him to tell him frankly whether he would be demeaning himself in their eyes by so doing.

"Gifted with powers confessedly above mediocrity, aided by an education, of which, no less from almost unexampled hardships and sufferings than from manifold and peculiar advantages, I have never yet found a parallel, I have devoted myself to a life of unintermitted reading, thinking, meditating and observing. I have not only sacrificed all worldly prospects of wealth and advancement, but have in my inmost soul stood aloof from temporary reputation."

Such was now his actual state of mind, that he could trick himself into believing that fame and fortune might have been his. He resigned himself as he said "to the abandonment of the greatest hopes of his life," thanking God the while for granting him strength. But this abandonment was far removed from renunciation, and was no sign of humility. It should be viewed rather in the light of deathless arrogance, or that lofty form of pride which is alone compatible with wisdom. Coleridge expected nothing more from men, but on his own score he had no doubt at all. He acquiesced in putting himself in debt to a few exceptional individuals, who did him the honour of having faith in him, believing that they would be repaid an hundred fold by the work their generosity permitted him to accomplish. So it was the fear of being misunderstood alone, which made him ask Allsop if he would not be lowering himself by acting in the light of principles which those only who can rise above the morality of the vulgar are capable of entertaining. His question contains no more than the faintest suspicion as to his idea of its value, and the dignity of the part he meant to play. And when he wrote "Am I qualified? Have I the right to act thus?" he anticipated no denial. Aloof as he was to the pomps and vanities of the world, he was in nowise detached from the interests and pleasures it dangled before the imagination, its sensuality, if I may use the word in its widest sense, as witness his *Garden of Boccaccio,* which he wrote in 1828, as though through the wicket of the Italian Renaissance he would breathe in the intoxicating charm of youth and love.

All this went to make up a life which burned away in the sublimest and most enthralling speculations possible to a man of sedentary habits, prematurely failing in bodily powers, but changelessly young in his ringing tones, and the shining look in his eyes as, like Plato in the groves of Academe, he greeted and entertained visitors, taking them into the Gillman's garden when the weather allowed, or else for walks along the road from Highgate to Hampstead. Stooping forward, with shaggy head sunk on his breast, zigzagging along with short and rather uncertain steps, spindle-shanked and knock-kneed, thus he progressed between the houses gay with flowering trees, that met one another in a canopy of leafy branches far above his head.

In summertime all was a riot of fragrance and bird-song in the flooding light, and Coleridge would take this as the text for endless variations on the theme of the variety, ingenuity and beauty of God's handiwork. It is pleasant to picture him meeting John Keats along the road, and haranguing him upon a hundred subjects each as unlike as possible to the last. "Of nightingales, of poetry, of poetic sensations, of metaphysics, of the different sorts of dreams, of nightmares, of dreams accompanied by the sense of feeling, of the primary and secondary consciousness, of monsters, of kraken, and of sirens." "Death is in that hand," said Coleridge to the friend he was with when Keats, who had turned back in order to ask leave to shake him by the hand, had finally gone on his way. Consumption had not yet set its mark upon the poet of *St. Agnes' Eve,* but Coleridge had a foreboding, or foreknowledge even, of his approaching end. . . .

Sometimes Dr. Gillman, who watched tirelessly over

him, forebade his admirers to see him, for fear of the excitability which set in as soon as he began to talk, or else he would allow no more than a short visit to his bedroom. This room, to which he was more and more confined, especially after 1822, his host having had its ceiling raised to allow of his keeping his library there, became the scene of some of the most wonderful of his extempore talks as he lay propped up in bed. To his hearers there was something almost uncanny about that weak voice, further enfeebled by suffering, which rose muffled from among the pillows, as it planned and shaped these mansions of the mind. For sorrow that never more might he thus hear Coleridge speak as though his genius, triumphing over the stricken body, already gave earnest of his immortality, Lamb lamented after his friend had vanished: "His great and dear Spirit haunts me; never saw I his likeness, nor probably can the world see it again. I seem to love the house he died at, more passionately than when he lived. What was his mansion, is consecrated to me as a Chapel."

He had his good days, however, when his lifelong taste for walking would return, and he would set out on foot as far as Highgate, or go to London upon occasion to see his friends, more especially Lamb, in whose house he felt himself peculiarly at home. In 1824 Crabb Robinson found him at a *dance and rout* in the house of his disciple Green, and heard him philosophizing in evening dress, knee breeches, lace ruffles and all, in the centre of a group of attentive admirers in the ball-room, with all the subtlety and convincing fire of his best days.

His greatest sorrow was that, although Wordsworth had now become reconciled, Southey who had never forgiven his lapses and mistakes, still clung to the reproachful silence, in which, in the name of puritanical morality, he had so long enshrouded himself. An idea verging on remorse obsessed him that his brother-in-law, the man who had undertaken to bring up his children, held him so strictly to account, and his peace of mind was broken. Moreover, a misfortune betokening God's wrath, as he thought, smote him in 1826 through his dearest affection. His eldest son, Hartley, so like him in his fanciful dreaminess, and sensitive delicacy, but who also inherited his weakness of character, had antagonized his teachers at Oxford by the boldness of his religious opinions, and been sent down from the University upon a charge of habitual drunkenness. Coleridge appealed in vain to the authorities, but they refused to reverse their decision, and the young man was obliged to leave Oxford with nothing further in hand than a "compensation" of three hundred pounds to wipe out his debts. He was to suffer all his life, from the harshness of the sentence "severe, no doubt, but not unjust" as his own brother admitted it to be, and it prevented him from occupying that place in the world to which his rare intellectual qualities might have led him to aspire.

The news shook Coleridge "like thunder out of a clear

sky." In his despair, he accused himself of having fostered his dear Hartley's evil bent by over-indulgence, or at any rate by neglect, and he even took to opium once more, hoping that the fumes of the drug would call a truce to the thoughts which rent him. His faith, at any rate, revived under this trial, which lent wings to his mysticism, and his sorrow was somewhat comforted when the dignity of the headmastership of Helston Grammar School in Cornwall was conferred upon his son Derwent, who had been ordained in 1825 by Bishop Carey of Exeter. His daughter Sara's marriage in 1829 to his nephew Henry Nelson Coleridge, was also a solace to his feelings. This lovely girl, of whom it was said that "her father looked down into her eyes and left in them the light of his own," was of exceptional beauty as well as talent. She had published a few years previously a translation of the *History of the Abiponians* by the Jesuit Martin Dobrizhoffer, which Coleridge declared to be a masterpiece, and she was unfailing in the constancy of her visits to Highgate, in order to warm by her love and cheer by her wit the heart and mind of the aged recluse.

"He is a good soul, full of religion and affection, of poetry and animal magnetism," Carlyle said of him after a visit he paid him. "He gave you the idea of a life that had been full of sufferings, a life heavy-laden, half vanquished, still swimming painfully in seas of manifold physical troubles and other bewilderment. Brow and head were round and of massive weight, but the face was flabby and irresolute. The deep eyes of a light hazel, were as full of sorrow as of inspiration; confused pain looked mildly from them as in a kind of mild astonishment." He was indeed unlike the hero, or rather superman whom Carlyle went out for to see. But it was so much the worse for the famous Scotchman if he thought him "profitless." His rugged, if not brutal, intellectual virility made him nearly incapable of understanding that subtle genius, so feminine seeming in certain respects, in which he could see no *profit*. Even his detachment, his serenity, in the calm place whither he had fled for refuge after a life full of turmoil, Carlyle looked at askance; far from attracting him, they horrified him, as further proof of his weakness. He would have expected something more from a thinker than this "musical energy," which he nevertheless noted so aptly, which made beads of moisture stand out on Coleridge's radiant face after a monologue which had lasted two hours, broken only by Dr. Gillman's recurring plea, "Oh your tea's cold, Mr. Coleridge!"

"Better than I deserve," would murmur the incorrigible soliloquizer, in a courtly tone, deeply fraught with piety, as he took from his host's hands the cup of tea he was deferentially proferring, but marking by his protective attitude as he did so, how jealous he was of the responsibility resting upon him.

Carlyle understood him, no doubt, less than the good Highgate doctor, who noted, "I do assure you that through all the years he lived with us I do not remember once to have seen him fretful or out of humour; he was the same kindly affectionate being from morning till evening, and from January till December. He delighted to reconcile little differences, and to make all things go smoothly and happily. He was always teaching the Beautiful and Good, while his own daily life was the best illustration of the good and beautiful which he taught." And Sara too, for her part, spoke of the light which shone forth from him which "made heaven in some sort more visible to our apprehension." The day after his death she wrote: "You know how long and how severely he suffered in his health, yet, to the last, he appeared to have such high intellectual gratifications, that we felt little impulse to pray for his immediate release, and though his infirmities had been grievously increasing of late years, the life and vigour of his mind were so great that they hardly led those around him to think of his dissolution. His frail house of clay was so illumined, that its decaying condition was the less perceptible."

Untinged it is true by asceticism, smiling and mild-spoken, a curiosity which one might call profane for ever awake, in no way anxious to cut short the time of his trial, in spite of the growing frequency of his attacks, thus did Coleridge linger out his remaining days, reading, dreaming, laying down the law, amusing himself by growing flowers and feeding birds in Dr. Gillman's garden. Prospero in his island, rather than a saint in his cell is nearer the truth, if one would form an image of him in his last days.

"I am dying," he said on the 11th July, 1834, "but without expectation of a speedy release. It is not strange that very recently bygone images and scenes of early life have stolen into my mind, like breezes blown from the spice-islands of Youth and Hope—those twin realities of the phantom world. I do not add love, for what is Love but Youth and Hope embracing and so seen as *one*. . . . Hooker wished to live to finish his *Ecclesiastical Polity;* so I wish that life and strength had been spared to me to complete my *Philosophy*. For, as God hears me, the originating, continuing and sustaining wish and design in my heart were to exalt the glory of His name; and, which is the same thing in other words, to promote the improvement of mankind. But *visum aliter Deo,* and "His Will be done!" Fourteen days after he had uttered these words, in which all of Coleridge is summed again, he died peacefully at the age of sixty-two.

Shortly beforehand he had fixed upon his own epitaph fashioning it and re-fashioning it until it took its final form:

Stop, Christian Passer-by! Stop Child of God!
And read with gentle heart. Beneath this sod
A poet lies: or that, which once seem'd He.
O lift one thought in prayer for S. T. C.
That He, who many a year with toilsome breath

Found Death in Life, may here find Life in Death.
Mercy for Praise—*to be forgiven* for Fame
He asked and hoped through Christ. DO THOU THE
   SAME.

"Coleridge is dead! Coleridge is dead!" Lamb went on saying over and over again, struck to the heart by the death of his friend, whom he survived by no more than a few months.

They buried the author of the *Rime of the Ancient Mariner* quite close to Dr. Gillman's house. He lies in the crypt in Highgate Grammar School Chapel, near his wife, who died in 1845, his daughter Sara, his nephew Henry Nelson Coleridge, and his grandson Herbert Coleridge. The post-mortem failed to reveal why he had suffered so long. His manuscripts and all his books he bequeathed to his disciple Green.

BIBLIOGRAPHY

Poetical Works. ed. J. D. Campbell. London. 1893.

Complete Poetical Works. ed. E. H. Coleridge. 2 vols. Oxford. 1912.

Biographia Literaria. ed. H. N. Coleridge and Sara Coleridge. 2 vols. 1st. ed. 1817. 2nd. ed. 1847.

Anima Poetae. ed. E. H. Coleridge. 1895.

Critical Annotations. ed. W. F. Taylor. 1889.

Essays and Lectures on Shakespeare and Other Old Poets and Dramatists. Everyman's Library. 1907.

Coleridge's Literary Criticism. With introduction by J. W. Mackail. Oxford. 1908.

Conciones ad populum or Addresses to the People. Bristol. 1795.

The Watchman. 10 numbers. Bristol. 1796.

The Friend. 28 numbers. Penrith. 1809–10.

The Statesman's Manual. 1816.

Aids to Reflection. ed. H. N. Coleridge. 2 vols. 1843. New edition with the *Confessions of an Inquiring Spirit.* 1884. Reprinted in 1904.

Lectures and Notes on Shakespeare and Other English Poets. ed. T. Ashe. Bohn. 1883.

Miscellanies, esthetic and literary. ed. T. Ashe. Bohn. 1892. with *Theory of Life.*

Table Talk. ed. T. Ashe. Bohn. 1896.

Church and State. 3rd. ed., 1839. With Lay Sermons. 2nd. ed. Letters. 1785–1834. ed. E. H. Coleridge. 2 vols. 1895.

BIOGRAPHY AND CRITICISM

Allsop. Thomas. *Letters, Conversations and Recollections of S. T. C.* 1836. 2nd. ed. 1864.

Aynard. J. *La Vie d'un Poète. Coleridge.* Paris. 1907.

Brandl. A. *S. T. C. und die Englische Romantik.* Berlin. 1886.

Caine. T. Hall. *Life of Samuel Taylor Coleridge.* (Great Writers series.) 1887.

Campbell. J. D. *Samuel Taylor Coleridge. A Narrative of the Events of His Life.* 1894. 2nd. ed. 1896.

Carlyle. T. *Life of John Sterling.* 1851.

Cestre. Charles. *Les poètes anglais et la Révolution française.* Paris. 1906.

Coleridge. E. H. *Life of Coleridge.* Chambers Cyclopædia of English Literature. Vol. III. 1903.

——— *Letters from the Lake Ports to Daniel Stuart.* 1889.

Cottle. J. *Reminiscences of S. T. C. and Robert Southey.* 2nd. ed. 1847.

Estlin Letters. *Letters of S. T. C. to the Rev. J. P. Estlin.* ed. H. A. Bright. 1884.

Fausset. Hugh L'Anson. *Samuel Taylor Coleridge.* 1926.

Gillman. A. W. *The Gillmans of Highgate. With Letters from S. T. Coleridge.* 1895.

Gillman. J. *The Life of Coleridge.* 1 vol. only published. London. 1838.

Green. J. H. *Spiritual Philosophy Founded on the Teaching of the Late S. T. Coleridge.* 2 vols. 1865.

Greever. Garland. *A Wiltshire Parson and His Friends, the Correspondence of William Lisle Bowles.* 1926.

Hazlitt. W. *My First Acquaintance with Poets.* 1823.

———— *The Lambs, Their Lives, Their Friends and Correspondents.* 1897.

Herford. Prof. C. H. *The Age of Wordsworth.* 1897.

Knight. W. A. *Life of Wordsworth.* 1889.

———— *Wordsworthiana.* 1889.

Lamb. Charles. *Christ's Hospital Five and Thirty Years Ago. The Two Races of Men. Essays of Elia. Works.* ed. E. V. Lucas. vol. II. 1903.

———— *Letters.* ed. Lucas. 2 vols. 1912.

Lucas. E. V. *Charles Lamb and the Lloyds.* 1898.

Quincey. De. *S. T. Coleridge. Collected Writings.* Vol. II. 1889.

———— *Coleridge and Opium Eating. Collected Writings.* vol. V. 1890.

Robinson. H. C. *Diary.* ed. Thomas Sadler. 1872.

Stephen. Sir. L. *Coleridge. Hours in a Library.* Vol. III. 1892.

Trail. H. D. *Coleridge.* (English men of letters Series) 1884.

Watson. Lucy; née Gillman. *Coleridge at Highgate.* 1926.

Wise. T. J. *Biography of Coleridge.* 1913.

Wordsworth. Christopher. *Memoirs of William Wordsworth.* 1851.